A Call to Action

Studies in the
Postmodern Theory of Education

Joe L. Kincheloe and Shirley R. Steinberg
General Editors

Vol. 324

PETER LANG
New York • Washington, D.C./Baltimore • Bern
Frankfurt am Main • Berlin • Brussels • Vienna • Oxford

Curry Stephenson Malott

A Call to Action

An Introduction to Education, Philosophy, and Native North America

PETER LANG
New York • Washington, D.C./Baltimore • Bern
Frankfurt am Main • Berlin • Brussels • Vienna • Oxford

Library of Congress Cataloging-in-Publication Data
Malott, Curry.
A call to action: an introduction to education, philosophy, and native North America /
Curry Stephenson Malott.
p. cm. — (Counterpoints: studies in the postmodern theory of education; v. 324)
Includes bibliographical references.
1. Indians of North America—Education. 2. Indian philosophy—United States.
3. Multicultural education—United States. 4. United States—Ethnic relations.
5. United States—Race relations. I. Title.
E97.M34 191.089'97—dc22 2007027323
ISBN 978-1-4331-0173-1 (hardcover)
ISBN 978-1-4331-0172-4 (paperback)
ISSN 1058-1634

Bibliographic information published by **Die Deutsche Bibliothek**.
Die Deutsche Bibliothek lists this publication in the "Deutsche
Nationalbibliografie"; detailed bibliographic data is available
on the Internet at http://dnb.ddb.de/.

Cover design by Clear Point Designs

The paper in this book meets the guidelines for permanence and durability
of the Committee on Production Guidelines for Book Longevity
of the Council of Library Resources.

© 2008 Peter Lang Publishing, Inc., New York
29 Broadway, 18th floor, New York, NY 10006
www.peterlang.com

Printed in the United States of America

Contents

Preface: Outlining a Call to Action

Revolution is not a *word* but an *application*; it is not *war* but *peace*; it does not *weaken*, but *strengthens*. Revolution does not cause *separation*, it generates *togetherness*. (John Africa, Quoted in Abu-Jamal, 1997, p. 65)

The purpose of this preface is only *secondarily* concerned with providing an outline of the present volume, *A Call to Action*, which has been completed at the end of this essay. The primary concern here, in this preface, and what therefore lies ahead of you, is the manifestation of *me* setting out to introduce and outline the concept of *calling to action*/advocating for change/supporting revolutionary transformation. The idea of calling one to action is defined here as a critical engagement with solidarity/unity/togetherness because in this day and age, in this dark hour (see Chapter One), there are no other options—it is simply just *that* time (Trudell, 1995). It is taking an active role in collectively solving our own problems—a task that requires solidarity. However, when engaged in such transformative work, we have to be cautious against trickery and not allow ourselves to be led to confuse the problem with the solution.

For example, it is true that government assistance (i.e., welfare) for those "in need" is conducive to the driving down of wages by maintaining the existence of a large reserve pool of labor passively waiting for the clarion call of capital. And yes, when not actively selling our labor for a wage, we are therefore dependent on the government for sustenance, which puts those relegated to the status of *worker*, the vast majority of humanity, collectively the working class, in a disempowered state of dependency serving the interests of the rich/the ruling class or the ruling elite. It is also true that when welfare programs are "reformed," that is, reduced and/or eliminated, and "people in need" therefore have fewer "legitimate" avenues for satisfying their basic needs (food, clothing, and shelter, for example), working class *crime,* as well as other forms of self-destruction, increases, such as child, spousal, alcohol, and drug abuse.

It might come as a surprise, but I am ready to concede here to the pro-capitalists in their assertion that *poor people need to figure out how to empower themselves and pull themselves up by the bootstraps out of poverty and suffering* because nobody will do it for them. However, the "pulling" *I* am referring to here, unlike the pro-capitalists or those who coddle the aggressor in other ways, does not mean to suggest being a better, more hard-working, responsible, law-abiding slave in the system that exists, thereby referring to the problem, capitalism, as if it were the solution and thus the source of our salvation—salvation from our own inherent weakness from the devil (see Chapter Two).

Rather, by "pulling" I mean uniting and fighting the bosses and *pulling* ourselves up by the bootstraps out of capitalism and thus out of manufactured scarcity and therefore poverty; out of white supremacy; out of patriarchy; out of trickery and exploitation and *into* freedom and utopia—to use our creative capacities to freely humanize the world in a loving and responsible way with clarity and coherence. In other words, we need to take control of our own labor power and create the conditions for a truly democratic, environmentally sustainable society, that is, one that respects the sacredness of the land and all that is—*by the bootstraps.*

The implication of "pulling" ourselves out of misery, globally, will require complete systemic change and total global revolution (nothing short will suffice), and this complex and contradictory process of humanization is a process we have been engaged in for a long time—for countless generations. We therefore have many teachers represented throughout this book generously giving life to this project with rich substance and vitality.

What I have gone to some length to demonstrate, both quantitatively and qualitatively, throughout this volume, is the case for what it is within the world that demands such fundamental transformation. What this research points to is a massive system of indoctrination designed to lead the vast majority of humanity away from our natural vocation, that is, humanization, and toward the normalization of having one's creative capacities externally controlled (dehumanization). As a result of these insights, we learn that the solution to dehumanization resides in the development of critical consciousness within all of us, which requires discipline, clarity, and coherence, first and foremost. This is the task of critical pedagogues/cultural workers, and is a philosophical issue. The following points begin to roughly outline this *call to action* for solidarity, which, again, requires critical consciousness:

o From this realization we critically realize that freedom requires the unity of common interests against an equally common oppressor. Chapter Two makes no mistake about this concrete reality, despite discursive attempts to distort our perceptions and thus severely degrade our actions and choices, as teachers and otherwise, and the practice it demands no matter what we are doing or how we are participating in the capitalist system of oppression.

o Because Eurocentrism has been one of the main tools employed in the service of indoctrination, we have to fight it at every turn. Eurocentrism, or white supremacy, has most destructively given way to genocidal oppression, also documented in Chapter Two. White supremacy, perhaps first and foremost, is designed to divide people who, at different levels of severity, are all victims *and* servants of the same ruling class. As critical pedagogues, committed to social justice, we therefore have to expose and denounce Eurocentrism at every opportunity.

o That is why in Chapter Two we have highlighted the fact that some of the most fundamental philosophical building blocks of "Western" civilization, such as the dialectic, come from Africa and the Middle East. This focus on the historical roots of European civilization is not only a symbolic act of solidarity, but it also makes history more powerful, more righteous, more exciting, and most importantly, it is accurate and therefore enhances our clarity and coherence when we actively engage with the world.

o With these insights informing our conscious decisions we must actively learn to be in solidarity with one another, which requires rules of engagement, and ultimately, these "rules" serve as safeguards against Eurocentrism, that is, white supremacy (see Chapter One). In other words, we have to learn to be more fully human.

o One of the most human and unifying things we can do is listen to and make each other feel comfortable and eager to share. When we listen to one another, we show each other respect, and that is a responsible thing to do. While it is important to have spaces for healthy debate, it is equally necessary to establish spaces where everyone is listened to without being argued with. Continuingly insisting that your own ideas are the only truth does not foster solidarity (Thorpe, 2001).

o   Again, solidarity should not be confused with doing someone a favor, because that is paternalism, an aspect of colonialism. We seek solidarity because it is in the best interest of the community, and, as teachers, as servants of the people, our responsibility is to the community—community conceived holistically, but not romantically (see Chapter One).

o   This is a call to action. It requires one to be conscious of every decision one makes—clearly and coherently. The pedagogical implications of our curricular and pedagogical choices are simply too important to treat lightly without serious critical reflection.

o   When we belong to the community, we no longer belong to ourselves (Marshall, 2004). We have no choice but to counter-hegemonically resist the ideas, values, and beliefs we have internalized from being socialized in a society dominated by the ideology of the ruling class aggressor because it is in the best interest of the community to do so. This is a never-ending requirement of us if we are to take the responsibility our task demands seriously because, for example, the white supremacy we have all internalized regardless of our particular positionality prevents us from being the best teachers we can be if gone unchecked. The implications are obvious. It challenges us to unveil all illusions such as: *ancient Greece is the source of modern Western civilization* or *capitalism is the only option because history has proved it.* This simplistic determinism and coddling analysis must be critiqued and laid to waste (see Chapters Two through Four).

o   When it is all said and done, this is most certainly a call to action for all critical pedagogues to unite in critical reflection for complete transformation. All critical pedagogues, including, but not limited to, those employing the following cultural vehicles: hip hop, punk rock, poetry, activism/organizing, fine art, scholarship, and teaching/educating—all of us. This is our only way out of the crisis we are both simultaneously victims and accomplices to. This book is designed to get us thinking philosophically about what this means for us as current and/or future educators.

o　As we will see, my endeavors here have resulted in the compilation of many critical insights of the people, from many of the major regions of the world, but organized and presented in a very conscious way that challenges us to think and rethink our positions, from the perspective of solidarity, because our occupation demands it.

o　Within the critical insights and actions of the people lie our finest educators—so please let us truly engage in critical discourse and reflect on how this process challenges us to rethink our responsibilities as educators in the living, breathing, toiling, bleeding concrete world, and therefore how this critical pedagogy might look in practice—in history (as Dr. Chávez Chávez at New Mexico State University challenges graduate students to consider because it is fundamentally important for our present and future praxis, that is, to critically reflect on how *not* to coddle, or act in unison in any way with, the aggressor).

With this spirit of solidarity in mind, let us now turn to our first critical engagement in the subject matter this text humbly attempts to contribute to—that is, scholarship concerned with the advancement of thoroughly insurgent critical philosophies and pedagogies situated in the context of Native North America. In other words, let us now delve into the study of education, philosophy, and Native North America considering the many complex and often contradictory ways in which they intersect, overlap, and relate. However, before we proceed, let us consider what lies below, that is, a summary of the book beginning with Chapter Two. Chapter One introduces us to the concepts of "Western" and "Indigenous" philosophy situated in the context of North America.

* * *

In Chapter Two we begin by providing a concrete context (the American Holocaust) from which the remainder of the book can firmly stand in our effort to build and discuss philosophical relationships. I conclude the second chapter with an introductory discussion of philosophy focusing on epistemology, ontology, and metaphysics. I then provide a summary of the primary strands of philosophical thought of central importance to this book. Finally, I reflect on the implications these knowledges have for educators in the construction of our own personal and collective approaches to teaching and learning. In other words, I discuss what exactly philosophy is and why it is important for educators to be absolutely clear about what traditions inform our own practices. It is our underlying philosophies that ultimately inform whose interests we serve or do not serve as educators. That is, do we serve the interests of the occupiers, the oppressors, capital, the numerical minority, or the occupied, the oppressed, those relegated to the status of wage earners, the numerical majority? Whatever approach we take, which translates into particular interests served, we should at least be honest and clear about those choices. This is my democratic approach, confident that the majority of humanity, essentially made out of the same *stuff*, will choose freedom over enslavement, provided the necessary sense of empowerment.

In Chapter Three I deepen my analysis and focus more directly on the antagonistic relationship between Indigenous and Western philosophical traditions focusing on conceptions of land. The primary example I draw on is the restoration of salmon in the Northwest area of North America because it demonstrates the consistently complex and contradictory relationship between the occupiers and the occupied. Perhaps most importantly, the example highlights how the occupiers, in their quest to consume the land, must consume the people on *and* of the land, while the occupiers simultaneously perpetually depend upon the Indigenous knowledge of the complex ecosystems to keep the geography healthy and profitable. As the interests of the occupiers and the occupied ironically converge, we find ourselves with yet another opportunity to abolish the occupation of Native North America. Ultimately, what becomes apparent is the interconnectedness of all that is, an Indigenous philosophical worldview based on the relationships that constitute concrete material conditions. Within this discussion we therefore also look to the long history of solidarity between Europeans, Africans, and Americans (that is, Native Americans), which offers not only hope but also possible directions for work against oppression and for humanity.

Chapter Four focuses on the concrete context of schooling in both Native and non-Native communities. We therefore look at how Western and Indigenous philosophical traditions have informed schooling practices across contexts and across time periods. Within this discussion we explore the rich history of critical pedagogy and consider the ways it can enhance both native and non-native education, drawing on the work of Sandy Grande, Peter McLaren, Joe Kincheloe, Paulo Freire, and others. This chapter is primarily concerned with building a relationship of solidarity between counter-hegemonic and Native North American philosophical traditions. Within this chapter we look more closely at the legacy of the work of Marx as it informs critical pedagogy. Within this chapter we also take seriously the valuable insights offered by those not typically associated with critical pedagogies, such as Crazy Horse, because of what they teach us about liberation. Interwoven throughout this discussion are the insights offered by Indigenous knowledge.

The middle four chapters are a series of separate discussions with leading figures in critical pedagogy, critical theory, and education in general. These discussions deal with many of the same topics covered within the first four chapters. However, the discussion format offers not only a different way of understanding the content, but it offers a slightly different analysis due to the addition of voices and the manifestation of our engagement. The late Brazilian educator Paulo Freire, arguably the most important educator of the twentieth century (see Chapter Four), named this practice of restating similar ideas from different perspectives and in diverse ways "recursiveness." Freire's work demonstrates a mastery of this approach, continually posing similar challenges to his readers (for example, education should be part of the revolutionary struggle against human suffering and oppression) from different conceptual vantage points such as "democracy," "freedom," "the heart," "the oppressed," "hope," "to those who dare teach," to paraphrase a few of his book titles, which can be described as his places of departure.

In the concluding chapter, Chapter Nine, we explore how the Indigenous knowledge of the Mayan people of Chiapas, Mexico, has shaped international politics, influencing most dramatically the new, *new* Left. What this discussion and analysis point to are the invaluable insights traditional people offer those of us who are the most fully indoctrinated into the world's settler-state and imperial societies about solidarity and therefore democratic practice. It is argued that the democratic insights of Indigenous knowledge combined with critical theory offers humanity the insights we need to save ourselves from ourselves, and can therefore be described as a lifeboat. In this final chapter readers are once again called to action. This call to action is presented as a desperate plea to humanity to wake up and realize what we are doing to ourselves—we are killing each other—we are participating in a system set on self-destruction. The book therefore ends with the realization that the future is in our own hands and that, so informed, invites us to become critical educators, that is, agents of change, and thus part of the solution and no longer part of the problem. This final invitation and challenge is presented in the spirit of solidarity and support realizing that for those of us socialized to support the system, saying "no" to the bosses is one of the hardest things we could do, but the most necessary. We therefore end with a warm embrace and an outstretched hand of unconditional solidarity.

Chapter 1

Introduction: Indigenous and Western Philosophy in Native North America

This book is designed to engage you (students of philosophy such as preservice teachers, public school teachers, and teacher educators) in a discussion on the relationship between Indigenous and non-Indigenous (Western) philosophical traditions as part of the process of developing our own personal and collective philosophies (of education). In the process of reflecting on the relationship between Native and non-Native philosophies, I demonstrate how Indigenous perspectives Native to North America can assist in further contextualizing Western approaches to liberation. For example, Indigenous philosophies challenge those of us who, philosophically, are Westerners, such as myself, to consider place rather than time as our place of departure or the primary lens of analyzing events *in* time (Deloria, 1994). When considering philosophy from a place-centered perspective, we realize that philosophies are not abstract entities that exist in a vacuum waiting for the enlightened *man* to bring them into human consciousness. Rather, they are dynamic, forever-transforming products of human creativity and thus represent real people with specific cultural orientations emerging from geographical locations.

For example, progressive teacher educator Richard Brosio in *Philosophical Scaffolding for the Construction of Critical Democratic Education* (2000) begins his study with "...considering how our near and remote ancestors tried and often succeeded in making sense of their worlds" (p. 2) referring to those of ancient Greece because "my life and intellectual experiences in the West and its civilization(s) makes it natural to express myself within its framework" (p. 3). Brosio's attention to detail, he contends, and I would concur, is not indicative of a conscious bias on his part, but rather correctly represents the recognition of origin, that is, *place.* Brosio does not argue that ancient Greeks

were the *first* or the *only* people "doing philosophy" in *the old days*, acknowledging that people all over the world also have long and rich traditions in
philosophy, including Native North Americans.

However, what tends not to be discussed as frequently are the Afroasiatic
roots of Greek and thus European philosophy in general (Bernal, 1987, 2001;
James, 1954/2005; Sarton, 1952). That is, there is a relatively recent tendency
within Western philosophical discourse regarding the African and Phoenician
influences on ancient Greek civilization to downplay, deny, or avoid it all
together. For example, critical authors such as George G.M. James
(1954/2005), in effect, argue that Greek philosophy is a Eurocentric construct,
which metaphorically represents black Africa painted in whiteface. The
African roots of Greek philosophy, from this perspective, have therefore been
died blonde, or made to look like a European (blonde being the most obvious
metaphorical association). More recently, however, scholars such as Martin
Bernal (2001) contend that the early ancient Greeks appropriated their
religion, philosophy, and science from Phoenicians and Egyptians (specifically
"black" Egyptians, which is a point of contention among Eurocentric historians) because they both expanded on them and referenced their original
sources. For the remainder of this volume, when we refer to "Greek philosophy" or the "Western" tradition, this is what we mean, that is, a hybrid
approach with roots in the Middle East and Africa, as well as Europe (these
issues will be further explored in Chapter Two).

Also, contributing to the complexity of the situation, another issue that is
not always considered when reflecting on the genealogy and archeology of our
own philosophies, especially when coming from the perspective of the
occupying force (the dominant or ruling society), is the relationship between
the immigrant philosophies, consisting largely of appropriated and distorted
epistemologies, and the Indigenous traditions of the colonized, especially in
the last five hundred years in the Americas. That is, since European colonizers, referred to as "predator" by self-identified "Indigenist" scholar/activist
Ward Churchill (1995), came to American shores drawing on their Western
philosophies and theologies to legitimize genocide and an insatiable appetite
for destructive plunder (Churchill, 2004).

Contributing a slightly different analysis, Semali and Kincheloe (1999b)
locate colonization within the process of Western Cartesian-Newtonian
science and knowledge production. Western science, from this perspective,
presents the knowledge it produces as constituting a universal truth therefore
excluding other forms of knowing and knowledge production as inferior or

primitive. Consequently, from this Eurocentric perspective, non-Western, non-white, non-male, and non-middle-class people are defined as equally primitive and in need of civilizing. Considered from this vantage point, colonization/subjugation is not only inevitable but also a paternalistic favor. To avoid this trap Semali and Kincheloe (1999b) advocate against the essentialism that situates indigenous and Western knowledge as binary opposites with nothing in common or no common ground from which to create a dialogue. For example, summarizing a series of reports on Native American education produced by the "Indian Nations at Risk task force," Grande (2004) highlights the similarities between their proposals and that which is advocated by an implied Western-based critical pedagogy such as "school reform" being just one "battleground in the 'war' against colonialism" and that "the struggle for self-determined schools must be engaged alongside other revolutionary struggles, specifically those that seek to end economic exploitation, political domination, and cultural dependency" (p. 20). However, breaking from the critical school of anti-essentialism, like Grande (2004), Vine Deloria, the late internationally renowned Lakota scholar-activist-historian-theologian, seems to cautiously embrace an Indigenous-informed essentialism in much of his work. For example, in *God Is Red* (1994), Deloria makes little distinction between liberal and conservative positions within the "Western" tradition, but makes a critical distinction between Western and Indigenous philosophy and world-view arguing that:

> When the domestic ideology is divided according to American Indian and Western European immigrant...the fundamental difference is one of great philosophical importance. American Indians hold their lands—places—as having the highest possible meaning, and all their statements are made with this reference point in mind. Immigrants review the movement of their ancestors across the continent as a steady progression of basically good events and experiences, thereby placing history—time—in the best possible light. (p. 62)

Grande (2004) argues that such essentializing is an important tool Indigenous peoples use to define their own sovereignty as something unique and distinct from the settler-community, but cautions against such definitions of self and the parameters of tribal community being informed by the colonialist gaze, or the white imagination (further explored in Chapter Two). Grande's (2004) cautions encompass some of the reasons why Semali and Kincheloe (1999b) argue that essentializing portrays a too simplistic picture of a more complex concrete context.

With these distinctions and complexities in mind, how has philosophy informed the interactions between Native North Americans and those from different geographical locations? Because colleges of education in the United States and Canada, at their core, are informed by Western philosophical traditions (yet are situated on land whose people have their own unique process of knowledge creation and wisdom, which tend not to be institutionally represented, except within the schools controlled by those indigenous to North America) we must ask: "Why?" In the process of answering this question we will inevitably uncover the ongoing war waged by the occupiers against Native peoples and their cultures and philosophies motivated by an effort to extract the maximum amount of wealth and use value (such as the value of spirituality, see Churchill's *Fantasies of the Master Race*, 1998) from the people and their land, even if it means destroying everything that is (including themselves).

In the following chapters we will therefore look at the relationship between Western and Native North American bodies of knowledge and the people and the land from which they emerged. This approach, in my view, has the potential to contribute to what Kincheloe, Slattery, and Steinberg (2000) describe as a truly contextualized critically complex education and therefore contextualized or grounded philosophies. I begin this endeavor in Chapter Three by looking at what I believe is one of the biggest differences between Western and Native North American societies—a difference Vine Deloria (1994) alludes to in his time versus place analysis previously mentioned—which is embodied in competing epistemologies and epistemological relationships, the tension from which has the potential to transform the bankruptcy of the material present as evidenced by the Zapatista uprising of dialogue and communication as a process of multicultural understanding and solidarity *for* humanity and *for* radical transformation against the "death sentence" that is an increasingly globalized capitalism, neoliberal capitalism (see Chapter Four), dubbed socialism for the rich, in particular. Within this discussion we will see that while hegemonic Western traditions stand in stark contrast to Native philosophies, there is considerable overlap and room for dialogue between Western counter-hegemonic and Indigenous approaches. Embodied in this discussion are the tensions between the non-essentializing and essentializing perspectives of Native and non-Native liberationists. The antagonistic relationship between hegemonic and counter-hegemonic Western traditions is a useful place of departure in understanding these dynamics.

For example, European peoples have a long history in the development of epistemologies of domination and are therefore tragically marked by internal conflict and competing interests. Consequently, Europeans, in Europe and wherever else they have tried to re-create their homelands (i.e., *New* York, *New* Zealand, *New* England, etc.), have developed competing philosophical traditions such as theology versus science and Marxism against idealism. Brosio (2000) traces these philosophical, and ultimately material, divisions to ancient Greece and Platonic epistemology that views human intelligence as naturally rank-able serving as a justification for the division of labor and the exclusion of large segments of the population from democratic participation. Semali and Kincheloe (1999b) locate these dynamics within the scientific revolution and the Enlightenment generally. Chomsky, on the other hand, situates the seventeenth century European Enlightenment as a direct response against Platonic epistemology with the intended purpose of increasing democratic control and reducing the external command of one's labor power. We can therefore view the Enlightenment, from this vantage point, as a signpost of counter-hegemonic philosophy against an authoritarian, antidemocratic ruling class whose hegemonic interests it has been to keep the general public subordinated by either force or consent (discussed in Chapter Four). Semali and Kincheloe (1999b), again, focus on the "west-is-best discourse of colonialism" (p. 25) that characterized how the emerging ruling classes of Europe employed the rationality and reason of the Enlightenment to support their own hegemonic interests ignoring the democratic and liberatory aspects of the scientific method embodied within critical theory in general and Marxism, for example, in particular. These competing perspectives will be further explored in Chapter Two.

Again, while European peoples have created hegemonic philosophy that supports oppression and domination, they have also created and re-created philosophy intended to be counter-hegemonic in order to liberate themselves from their own ruling classes. In other words, as Westerners, we have a long history of being, in a very real sense, against ourselves, and thus full of contradictions. Commenting on the internal conflict present within Western civilizations while performing in Buffalo Bill's Wild West show in New York City in 1887, Black Elk, traditional medicine man (philosopher) of the Oglala band of the Lakota Nation, in an interview with John Neihardt (1932/2004), comments:

I could see that the Wasichus [white people, or those who represent the deceitfulness of the occupiers] did not care for each other the way our people did before the nation's hoop was broken. They would take everything from each other if they could, and so there were some who had more of everything than they could use, while crowds of people had nothing at all and maybe were starving. They had forgotten that the earth was their mother. This could not be better than the old ways of my people. (p. 167)

Like much of Deloria's work, Black Elk's position clearly represents the essentialism Semali and Kincheloe have wisely warned critical scholars against falling victim to, as it can too easily lead to romanticization, for example. Do Black Elk's sentiments represent, as critical postmodern critics would contend, as well as some Marxists, the mystical romanticism of a past that did not exist, or is there contemporary relevancy within his perspective? I believe Sandy Grande (2004) would include Black Elk's insights within what she identifies as "traditional knowledge." Making the case for the creation of a "Red pedagogy" that engages "American Indian education" in a dialectical relationship with critical theory, especially the Marxism of Peter McLaren, thereby strengthening them both, Sandy Grande (2004) notes that such an approach is imbued with an Indigenous sense of "...hope that lives in contingency with the past— one that trusts the beliefs and understandings of our ancestors as well as the power of traditional knowledge" (p. 28). The hope of which we speak is not the unrealistic, romantic hope that lives in the illusion of re-creating the past, but the hope of creating a present and future informed by the same values and ideals that were the foundation of a more democratic and egalitarian past, however imperfect.

For example, Joseph Marshall III (2001) in *The Lakota Way* documents through both story and analysis/narrative the virtues (humility, perseverance, respect, honor, love, sacrifice, truth, compassion, bravery, fortitude, generosity, and wisdom) that were characteristic of what was expected of the individual, and when functioning properly, passed on from one generation to the next through story, was (and still are) the basis of Lakota social life. Indeed, what has been widely argued and documented, and seems apparent from the most superficial analysis of historical accounts, supporting Black Elk's analysis, is that Native societies were more perfectly worked out in terms of human interaction with one another and their environment (Neihardt, 1932/2004; Zinn, 1995) than their Western relatives, negating the need for counter-hegemonic philosophies. However, things are not as they were, Western hegemony is ubiquitous, and the need for counter-hegemonic philosophy, unfortunately, is all but obvious. While some of these analyses tread on the dangerous waters of essentialism, the risks, in my view, are worth taking given the benefits such subjugated knowledge (Semali & Kincheloe, 1999b) offer education in expanding dominant *whitestream* (Grande, 2004) conceptions and formulations of knowledge production.

Adding another layer of analysis, in the capitalist present of native North America counter-hegemonies are needed in defense of, and strategies for, humanization. Grande's (2004) observation that Native American educational practices could benefit from critical theory finds evidence in Frank Black Elk's (1992) observation that "the Lakota have never had a ruling class; the leaders serve by consensus of the people" (p. 139). Black Elk's analysis, while an important observation and evidence for the current relevance of Indigenous knowledge for those of us interested in the global anticapitalist movement, evacuates the capitalist present as tribal governments based on a European model set up by the U.S. government not only resemble, but too often function, as ruling classes, and therefore vie for control of capitalist enterprises. Critical theory challenges us to better our practice as change agents through a process of reflecting on the dialectical relationship between the concrete and theoretical contexts. Rather than romantically drawing on "how it used to be" to name the present, we would do better to learn from "how it used to be" to humanize how it is. I am not suggesting that white people go to reservations to fight capitalism, but that our international struggle against dehumanization can be enhanced by not only critical theory, but by Indigenous knowledges as well. Again, the focus of struggle we are concerned with here is education, and in Chapter Four we see how Native educational practices can advance Western counter-hegemonic educational objectives.

As long as we are appropriately cautious of not falling victim of romanticization and cautious of the dangers of essentialism, there is much to be learned from the valuable insights of "how it used to be." For example, in Vine Deloria's (2006) posthumous *The World We Used to Live In: Remembering the Powers of the Medicine Men*, where he explains how native North American tribal communities, in "the old days," had not created the conditions for the need for competing philosophies, which stemmed from how humans' natural connection to specific geographies was viewed. Such knowledge offers powerful argumentation against the colonial and capitalist present. Consider his words:

Every Indian tribe has a spiritual heritage that distinguishes them from all other people. Indeed, in the past, recognizing their unique relationship to the world and its creatures, most tribes described themselves as "the people" or the "original people." Regarding themselves as unique, they rigorously followed the commands of the spirits as they had experienced them over uncounted generations and recognized that other peoples had the same rights and status as themselves. So the idea of quarreling over the traditions by which they lived was felt to be absurd. Religious wars, then, were simply inconceivable. (p. xxiii)

The philosophical traditions that have served as the foundation for the worldview described by Deloria (2006), it seems, based on my review of the literature, has provided strength and guidance for Indigenous resistance to occupation since 1492 and also the target of attack by the occupiers who understand that Native culture is what ties Native people to unique land formations, the object of much of predators' desire (Churchill, 2004). Again, Grande (2004) looks to critical theory and pedagogues for broad-based coalitions against the reeling present. In Indigenous traditions, philosophers, since time immemorial, have been medicine men engaged in the pursuit of truth and knowledge to solve problems in this material world. In Western societies, on the other hand, philosophers have tended to come from privileged backgrounds or were rebellious intellectuals seeking justice from tyranny (Deloria, 2006). It is this tradition, forged and maintained by Western rebels, that Grande (2004), as noted above, argues offers valuable tools for resisting the global encroachment of capitalism, and should therefore not be rejected outright as inherently Eurocentric and thus only capable of addressing the European condition. If my analysis is correct, Indigenous knowledge *and* critical theory offer valuable insights for Natives and non-Natives alike, because, in a sense, we are all wrapped up in some form of European capitalist condition on land Indigenous to a particular people.

However, because the primary motivation behind this work is radical social justice, it is my intention not to fall victim of treating Western counter-hegemonic or Native philosophies as pristine and untouchable relics, but rather, to hold these living and breathing knowledges to the same respectful, yet critical, analysis afforded our engagements with hegemonic traditions. Summarizing a similar perspective in his brilliantly conceptualized and executed introduction to critical pedagogy, Joe Kincheloe (2004) notes, with the vision and clarity we have come to expect from him, that:

Critical teachers explore non-Western, subjugated, and indigenous voices in order to better appreciate the nature and causes of human suffering and the process of domination. Such knowledges are very important to the critical project because of the unique perspective they bring to scholars saturated with the Eurocentric, patriarchal, and elitist ways of seeing. As important as they are, however, indigenous knowledges are not exempt from critique. Advocates of critical pedagogy always respect such knowledges but refuse to turn them into icons that are too precious to analyze and interpret. (p. 26)

Supporting Kincheloe's critical perspective, Daniel Wildcat (2001a)—while cautious of the ways in which European scientism has excluded or appropriated extra-Euro insights, Native American in particular, outlining the ways in which European science has begun to move toward a more holistic view of the world—makes the case for Native students to not disregard the knowledge passed down to them by their elders, but qualifies his position by stressing the importance of not romanticizing the past because "...everything was not perfect" (p. 8). Romanticizing the past, by Native and non-Natives alike, according to Gerald Vizenor (1990), has too often led to discursive departures from the present in what could only be failed attempts to "go back" to pre-Columbian times. As an example, Vizenor (1990) points to "Pine Ridge Reservation born Edward McGaa, law school graduate and former combat fighter pilot" and "Oglala Sioux" (p. 245) who supports efforts to return to "traditional" ways and therefore to "Mother earth," representing the essentialist "Indian" expected by whites, all the while, and most importantly, not engaging with strategies of resistance and critical pedagogies demanded by the tragic capitalist present. Theoretically situating the solution to the material conditions of the present outside the concrete context of the lived realities of Indigenous people today discursively disconnects the word from the world, thereby occluding a viable praxis (theory *in* and *of* practice) for humanization (Freire 2005).

Scholars of Indigenous knowledge (see Dei, Hall & Rosenberg, 2002; Grande, 2004; Semali & Kincheloe, 1999a; and Vizenor, 1990), on the other hand, rather than argue for a return to the past, advocate for the use of Indigenous Knowledge as a tool to resist the colonial present—that present, in no small way, includes the ways in which European thinking have assimilated Native communities resulting in what Vizenor (1990) has described as the existence of "corrupt Indian capitalists" living side by side with "corrupt white capitalists," as if there existed any other kind of capitalist—where the capitalist is someone engaged in appropriating the wealth-generating capacities and the very humanness of others—than a corrupt one. Again, this point cannot be stressed enough, Grande (2004) argues that Indigenous philosophy and ways of knowing not only have valuable insights for criticalists, but critical theory can also strengthen Native perspectives in the areas of understanding the global system of capitalism, the ways in which it is impacting Native communities, and ways to fight it. Semali and Kincheloe (1999b) offer considerable caution here. That is, unconsciously armed with the mentality of the missionizing savior, the white radical is too easily posed to impose critical theory and appropriate Indigenous Knowledge in *his* engagements with the other. The lucidness of Semali and Kincheloe's (1999b) comments in the context of the arguments presented herein renders them worthy of notable attention. When considering the following excerpt, reflect on the ways in which you (everyone, regardless of Indigeneity) have learned to think about the Indigene.

> Western scholars and cultural workers concerned with the plight of indigenous peoples and their knowledges are faced with a set of dilemmas. Not only must they avoid essentialism and its accompanying romanticization of the indigene, but they must sidestep the traps that transform their attempts at facilitation into further marginalization. Walking the well-intentioned road to hell, Western scholars dedicated to the best interests of indigenous peoples often unwittingly participate in the Western hegemonic process. The question: how can the agency, the self-direction of indigenous peoples be enhanced? must constantly be asked by Western allies. What is the difference between a celebration of indigenous knowledge and an appropriation? Too often Western allies, for example, don't simply want to work with indigenous peoples—they want to transform their identities and become indigenous persons themselves. (p. 20)

Semali and Kincheloe's (1999b) challenges are relevant to all of those indoctrinated with European/"Western" thinking, Native and non-Native alike, as evidenced by the discussion above on Native peoples who have internalized the "romantic Indian" of the colonial gaze. However, because 90% of teachers in North America are "white," we will gear the following discussion toward the white Europeans of the present era, "members" of the dominant group. Because of the implications for white teachers when this issue is not resolved, it is worth taking a moment to consider why "whites" seem to be so susceptible to identity crises and a retreat from their European American present. The late Detroit radical Fredy Perlman (1985) situates the weakness of whiteness within the lie upon which it was/is based—racism—and the guilt associated with the ongoing atrocities committed in its name from international wars to the multitude of domestic policies informed by the white supremacist Indian

Reorganization Act that led to the official termination of many federally sanctioned tribes that, in effect, told thousands of Native Americans that they were no longer recognized as a distinct human group and therefore were no longer eligible for claims to land rights of national sovereignty (see Chapter Two). Written in the humorous yet painfully clear prose of revolutionary populism, reminiscent of Black Panther Party co-founder Dr. Huey P. Newton, with the honesty and vividness of independent radicals such as Noam Chomsky, Perlman (1985), in the following excerpt, offers a perspective on the emergence of whiteness useful for our present discussion. Again, because of the relevance of his analysis of whiteness as only ever racist and, as such, a tool of nationalism, and the pedagogical value of *hearing* his voice, we will not attempt to use his words sparingly:

> The North American colonizers broke the traditional bonds of fealty and feudal obligation but, unlike the French, they only gradually replaced the traditional bonds with bonds of patriotism and nationhood. They were not quite a nation; their reluctant mobilization of the colonial countryside had not fused them into one, and the multilingual, multi-cultural and socially divided underlying population resisted such a fusion. The new repressive apparatus was not tried and tested, and it did not command the undivided loyalty of the underlying population, which was not yet patriotic. Something else was needed.... The American settler-invaders had recourse to an instrument that was not, like the guillotine, a new invention, but that was just as lethal...racism, and it would become embedded in nationalistic practice.... Human beings were mobilized in terms of their lowest and most superficial common denominator, and they responded. People who had abandoned their villages and families, who were forgetting their languages and losing their cultures, who were all but depleted of their sociability, were manipulated into considering their skin color as a substitute for all they had lost. They were made proud of something that was neither a personal feat nor even, like language, a personal acquisition. They were fused into a nation of white men....and mobilized...into white mobs, lynch mobs, "Indian fighters." (pp. 15–16)

Perhaps it is the pedagogical and curricular bankruptcy of whiteness and the guilt associated with its unjust privileging and the countless atrocities committed in the name of its un-reasoning, alluded to above by Perlman, that account for the many mistakes well-intentioned white people too often make when relating to people of color. This is important for white teachers, who are not a part of the ruling class (their wealth does not come from surplus value expropriated from the labor power of their fellow humans); they themselves are workers, however glorified, because they rely on a wage for survival. While white teachers are part of that shrinking and terrified "middle-class," they are not like poor whites that tend to be too preoccupied with their own suffering to think of "helping" people of color, whom they are led to believe are part of the source of their own problems. The issues that arise from white "do-gooders" are therefore largely the problems of those who suffer from excessive guilt. However, mobilized around whiteness, all white people, including white teachers, have been conditioned to support the ruling class and are therefore rewarded for their role in maintaining the basic structures of power, however meagerly, and feel guilty for it because their support is a sellout—the sellout of their fellow human beings. White progressive and radical teachers who want to be a part of the solution have to get over their white guilt, and the only way that can be genuinely done is to *fight the bosses*, as it were, and not fall into the trap of nationalism or romanticism. In other words, if white people want to be a part of the solution, they need to save themselves by reflecting on and challenging their own internalized white supremacy and support for wealth and power. Only then will they be fit to fight for freedom as a process and not as an end point, paraphrasing Freire (2005).

Another point in need of serious consideration is where some white Marxists come into conflict with contemporary tribal leaders who advocate for a tribal sovereignty in the form of a nationalism of the oppressed for cultural and individual freedom (Perlman, 1985). For example, the dominant crux of Ward Churchill's massive body of work, cited widely throughout Chapter Two, is based on movement toward Native Nationalism. Such an approach is based on the perspective that nationalist liberation struggles, such as the Cuban Revolution, is a way to break up the capitalist empire. However, independent Marxists such as Perlman (1985) argue that nationalism is just the most current form of capitalism, and hopefully the last, when defeated by the world's vast majority relegated to the status of worker. While this discussion needs to be open and honest, white people need to be cautious not to let their white supremacy get the best of them, and therefore attempt to tell Native Americans, for example, what they arrogantly think is best for them. White teachers in particular would do better by demonstrating a pedagogy of humility by listening to those who have traditionally been oppressed. Marxists such as Peter McLaren exemplify this humility while simultaneously arguing for a socialist future, however undetermined, by supporting Native treaty rights. In a personal communiqué, McLaren summarizes his position:

> I support the land claims of First Nation peoples, those land claims recognized by treaties with the U.S. government but never actually carried out. I would also support

the notion that unceded territory belongs to the First Nations peoples under international treaties. I support, for instance, the Black Hills being returned to the Sioux Nation. Ultimately, as a socialist, I believe a post-capitalist world would be such that all land would be shared in common by all peoples of the world with appropriate steps being taken to protect and respect sacred sites.

While McLaren's position provides considerable insight for democratic socialist practice and encompasses a post-nation future, the notion of nationalism still needs to be problematized. The idea of nationalism is a European construct and can be viewed as having supplanted indigenous relationships to land, which were, and in some instances still are (see Chapter Three for a discussion of the efforts by the Warm Springs Native American Reservation to restore wild salmon runs), based more on common usage and guardianship, rather than ownership and control. Out of fear of critique, much of the non-Native North American Left has therefore tended to avoid critical inquiries and engagement with Indigenous traditions, alluded to by Kincheloe (2004) and Wildcat (2001a), retarding the dialogue between Western and Indigenous peoples that is increasingly important as we enter the twenty-first century facing not only perpetual war and global poverty, but environmental devastation as well. Even though the most well-intentioned study of Native philosophy is Europeanizing, contend Semali and Kincheloe (1999b), non-Natives who want to be a part of the solution have little choice but to "...understand the dynamics at work in the world of the indigene" (Semali & Kincheloe, 1999b). In Chapters Five through Eight, very humbly attempting to be a part of this discussion, I engage Native and non-Native critical educators/pedagogues in a series of informal e-mail inquiries and recorded interviews about how they view their work in relationship to these and other related issues.

* * *

The primary question serving as the driving force behind this book, again, is how can students of philosophy (teachers) better our practice by considering the relationship between Native and non-Native philosophies? The question of philosophy, to be sure, is of the utmost importance for educators because every decision we make as curricularists and pedagogues, whether we are conscious of it or not, emerges from philosophy. That is, the choices we make about curriculum and pedagogy reside in our beliefs and understandings about

how knowledge is created and who creates it, and what constitutes truth and
beauty, for example.

This book is unique in that it is designed to engage both current and future teachers in exploring the relationship between peoples and our philosophies and the many ways in which such an approach can inform the creation
of our own philosophies of education and, ultimately, our practice in not only
the classroom but in the world in general. I would consider this work a dismal
failure if it became another tool the settler-community used to continue to
plunder native North America, that is, philosophy as one more thing of value
to steal and employ against those who created it to maintain the occupation.
Why? That is, what is my own personal motivation?

First and foremost, it is my belief that the global movement against human
suffering, engendered by the bloody hands of capital, can best be served by a
complex theory informed by the invaluable insights of not just critical theory,
that is, counter-hegemonic Western knowledge, but Indigenous knowledge as
well. In other words, combining Western-based counter-hegemonic and
Indigenous knowledges, in my view, offer the most powerful insights informing
an educational practice against capitalism and its attendant hegemonies such as
white supremacy, homophobia, and patriarchy. This call for unity and
solidarity apply equally to everyone regardless of positionality. The motivation
I have as a white person is slightly different because it focuses on what I feel I
need to do to keep my own white guilt in check so it does not immobilize me.

Again, while I myself am a descendant of European settlers and am writing
from the perspective of the settler-community, my own personal philosophical
foundation is based on counter-hegemonic Enlightenment-based thought
(Marxism in particular), which is grounded in notions of self-rule, democratic
control, and social justice. These values and principles inform my own practice
as a teacher educator and scholar (Malott, 2006). Because there is virtually
nothing socially just about how Anglo-American officialdom, in both the
United States and Canada, in general, have and continue to engage with Native
North America, in an effort to avoid hypocrisy (and guilt), it is my responsibility to use my own limited power as an education professor to challenge future
teachers to take seriously, with as much intensity as they can muster, the land
on which they stand, every square inch of which in North America is indigenous to a particular group of people, to paraphrase Ward Churchill (2003a).

What this *could* and perhaps *should* mean for myself and other "white"
North American "settlers" is to take on the role of twenty-first century John
Brown abolitionists—that is, to be part of abolishing the illegal occupation of

the Americas by the colonialist governments of Canada and the United States. This, for me, translates into being part of the movement to globalize the resistance against capitalism. In the chapters that follow I will demonstrate that it is in the interests of everyone within North America to become abolitionists. Ward Churchill (2003a), and many others such as Peter McLaren, offers considerable insight into what this might look like in practice. For example, Churchill argues that siding with Native Americans on environmental issues is a matter of self-preservation because pollutants created on reservations, such as the highly toxic tailings from uranium mining, contaminates watersheds, which eventually becomes an issue for those both on and off reservations. The physical act of writing this book, and therefore engaging you in these debates, is part of my own personal action toward anticolonialist praxis, and hopefully, for you, as current or future educators, either an affirmation of an already-existing practice or the beginning of a new practice.

* * *

Before we jump into Chapter Two I would like to engage you in one more brief discussion on the interrelated topics of discipline and indignation as informed by the late Paulo Freire (2005) in *Teachers as Cultural Workers: Letters to Those Who Dare Teach* first published in 1997 and *Pedagogy of Indignation* (2004) also by Freire, and in fact his last book. Our biggest challenge as educators is *engaging* the students we have the privilege of working with in the indispensable lifelong journey of teaching and learning. At the same time, my biggest challenge as an author is engaging my readers (many of whom are reading these very words not because they possess an internal drive to learn about critical theory and Indigenous peoples and knowledges, but because they have to, that is, it is a course requirement, it is assigned reading) in a genuine desire to know and learn from what I have written.

However, I will take a considerable amount of liberty and a good dose of optimism and assume, however naively, that you have placed yourself in the position of "student" and are therefore being assigned readings, such as this one, because you want to either become a good teacher or because you want to better your existing practice. If you are here because you feel you had no other options and are becoming a teacher until something better comes along, to paraphrase Freire (2005), hopefully this book will help you either rethink your attitude toward teaching or it will persuade you to immediately decide *not* to teach because our profession is already undervalued and we therefore need fully committed teachers fighting as political militants to gain the respect our task deserves (Freire, 2005).

The struggle to gain the respect that the task of educating is justly due, to be sure, requires tapping into the same source of internal discipline needed to fully engage with this book. Freire (2005) argues that discipline is most effectively nurtured by an internal desire to know, "the passion to know," as it were. Such a passion most forcefully comes from the emotion of anger/indignation/outrage. It is my hope that what you have read thus far has sparked your epistemological curiosity and that Chapter Two will make you angry, and that your anger will inspire you to actively engage with the rest of the book. In other words, I want you to talk back and challenge what you read while objectively respecting that which is quantitatively and qualitatively sound. Put yet another way, I do not want you to engage with these chapters passively and mechanically simply regurgitating what you have consumed.

The question I want you to hear loud and clear, and reflect on, is How are the arguments and points of view presented within this book informing your future and/or current practice? To paraphrase my colleague and former teacher Rudolfo Chávez Chávez at New Mexico State University, asked in a slightly different fashion, what does it mean to your responsibilities as an educator that the concrete conditions of the material world demands not only outrage and anger but a critical pedagogical project with the theoretical tools embodying the ballast needed to not only understand and denounce that which exists but to create an undetermined future freed from the interconnected oppressions of human suffering and environmental destruction? It is my hope that your active engagement with this book leads you to what I believe are the "right" questions, away from the "wrong" questions, and on to new unasked questions.

For example, it is my hope that dominant society (i.e., white middle class) students do not walk away from the discussion in Chapter Two on the ongoing genocide waged against Native Americans by a predominantly European settler-community asking this historically oppressed group what can we do to help you? While such a position is obviously better than thinking you get what you deserve, it is not as useful as asking yourselves what can we do to better ourselves so we can (1) Fight the motivations behind genocide, that is, capitalism generally and white supremacy within the dominant group from which we come specifically, and (2) Create broad-based coalitions between diverse groups for systemic change? At the same time, it is my hope that those from oppressed groups do not leave these discussions asking, What can we do to return to a less oppressive past, but rather how can we become an effective part of overcoming the oppression of the capitalist, white supremacist, patriarchal, homophobic, xenophobic present in the interests of creating a more humanized future?

Following Grande (2004) and Semali and Kincheloe (1999a), the book before you is informed by the belief that everybody, regardless of positionality, can become more humanized and better suited for the educational task of transformation by both Indigenous knowledge and critical theory, Marxism and progressive postmodernism in particular. This is a useful lens, I believe, that will assist you in successfully making it through the remaining eight theoretically intense and emotionally provocative chapters that follow. Enjoy, and do not fear anger or let it immobilize you. That is, draw on it as a source of pedagogical strength with the capacity to fuel your ontological right to possess hope—hope for a world without suffering and degradation of any kind.

Chapter 2

The Building Blocks for a Philosophy of Education in Native North America

This city was built on the backs of the brave...
Some got the nerve to say go back to where you came from
Same ones who stole the land from chief [Seattle] and then named the city after him
as if to say we honor you
Right after we conquered you and pillaged your home, soil fertilized with indigenous
bones

Blue Scholars (2006), "Evening Chai"

Before we begin exploring what exactly a philosophy of education *is* and what it means to create our own personalized approach as educators by way of considering the relationship between Native and non-Native philosophical traditions, we need to come to terms with the American Holocaust (Churchill, 1995, 1997, 2003a, 2004; Deloria, 1985; Stannard, 1992; Thornton, 1987), however uncomfortable that may or may not be. Our place of departure in creating a philosophy of education on Native land is when and where it all began, which is Columbian contact in the Caribbean Basin from which came the Columbian spirit of conquest, wealth extraction, depopulation, and repopulation. After this initial discussion of Columbus and the philosophy informing his campaign of terror, I focus the remainder of my attention on Anglo-America, that is, the United States and Canada, because it is within this space that I teach and which therefore encompasses my target audience. It is not until Chapter Nine that we consider how our practice as current and future educators can be enhanced from the many democratic lessons offered by those indigenous to the southern most part of Native North America, that is, Mexico.

However, the theoretical framework developed throughout this book can be applied and is therefore equally relevant to any place where the Native population and their land is being occupied by an originally foreign European force, such as Africa, the Philippines, Ireland, South America, Central America, New Zealand, and Australia, to name but a few places and regions. The primary purpose of this initial chapter is therefore to establish a holistically conceived concrete material/philosophical context from which our discussion of Indigenous and Western philosophy as applied to our own approaches to education can firmly stand with the integrity afforded those who speak with honesty and *truth*, a concept associated with certainty, which we can reflect on in our discussions as we actively engage the remainder of this book, comparing and contrasting both Western and Indigenous perspectives.

Columbian Pedagogy

> There is one particular figure whose name looms large, and whose specter lingers, in indigenous discussions of encounters with the West: Christopher Columbus.... He has come to represent a huge legacy of suffering and destruction. Columbus 'names' that legacy more than any other individual. He sets its modern time frame (500 years) and defines the outer limits of that legacy, that is, total destruction. (Tuhiwai Smith, 2005, p. 20)

In contrast to aboriginal scholar Linda Tuhiwai Smith (2005)—speaking from the vantage point of the colonized, from the perspective of the occupiers—the arrival of "predator" in the Americas (Churchill, 1995, 1997, 2002) is viewed as the "great discovery" representing the heroic adventurism of crusading against infidels or, in the case of the Americas, the "unknown," the "wild" and "untamed." It is thus celebrated as representing not only a monumental advancement in social progress but also the very essence of human greatness and respectability largely because, through Columbus, Christianity was fulfilling its global, apocalyptic destiny to serve the "common good." However, the common good, in fifteenth-and sixteenth-century Christian Europe, was conceived as the return of Christ, which was believed would not happen until the gospel was "...spread throughout the entire world, and the entire world was not yet known [as the early Christians, informed by the ancient Greeks who themselves were informed by Egyptian Africans, knew]. Spreading the gospel throughout the world meant acceptance of its message by all the world's people, once they had been located—and that in turn meant the total conversion or extermination of all non-Christians" (Stannard, 1992, p. 192).

One of this fledgling religion's central messages to be globally exported, and either accepted or face the military capacity of the crusaders, was that the "pleasures" of the "flesh" are not only inherently "sinful," but "the very nature of humankind" and "nature itself" is "corrupt." It therefore followed that "only a rigid authoritarianism could be trusted to govern men and women who, since the fall of Adam and Eve, had been permanently poisoned with an inability to govern themselves in a fashion acceptable to God" (Stannard, 1992, p. 155). The idea that *man* is naturally evil is based on the dichotomy between the mind (things of the spirit, thought to be pure, and thus superior) and the body (things of the world, thought to be corrupt, and therefore inferior), the two of which exist in an antagonistic relationship where the barbaric and savage flesh wages constant war (i.e., sexual desire) on the sacredness of the soul. This hierarchical division between the mind/spirituality and the body/the material world is alive and well in not only Christianity, but in Western science and theories of learning and educational practices, which can be traced back to ancient Greece (explored, in brief, at the end of this chapter and at length in Chapter Four).

The dominant form of Christianity that informed Columbus' worldview and pedagogy, in other words, was based on the belief that the psychologically healthy act of embracing one's sexuality, as those native to North America were guilty of, was a sign of witchcraft and devilry. There is a long tradition in European thought dating back to at least the ancient Greeks and Romans that see themselves as somehow divinely chosen and at the center of the civilized world. For Columbus, who saw himself imbued with "divine destiny in an age of apocalyptic promise" (Stannard, 1992, p. 195), this translated into bringing "civilization," slavery, or extinction to the barbaric worshippers of the flesh within the unexplored margins of the world still under the rule of Satan (Stannard, 1992). The core of this reasoning can be traced back to ancient Greece and Plato's ideas of intelligence as naturally unevenly distributed where the small minority (the "gold metal" people) were endowed with a special gift for ideas, reasoning and therefore leading and managing the affairs of commerce, the gods, and governance. The silver metal people, although not as advanced as the gold metal people, were still honorable and able to demonstrate a respectable level of intellectual capacity.

The "bronze metal" people of ancient Greece, the brutes and slaves (labor), on the other hand, were considered to be exclusively of the body or the flesh, and therefore had no capacity for intelligence, humility, and self-control, and could thus not be trusted to participate in the democratic process, relying on people of higher quality and moral fiber to make decisions for them (Brosio, 2000; Stannard, 1992). If non-Christians were of the quality of "brass" and thus unable to reason, then they could not be expected to be saved because only humans capable of reason could accept Christ as their savior. If the colonizers were to view non-Christian brutes as capable of reason, then they could be saved. If, however, they chose not to accept Christianity, thereby waging war on God, then killing the body was not only in the service of protecting the Lord, but it was seen as the only way to save the soul from the sinful temptations of the flesh. All the while it was acknowledged by Christian thinkers that carnal temptations were inescapable and that the noblest of holy men remained imprisoned by their own internal sinful desires—the wilderness within.

The notion of wilderness came to represent all that Christian priests and soldiers fought to eradicate, which was the creative impulse of life itself. In lofty medieval anecdotes of Christian idealism the world was depicted as free from the wildness of nature and untamed men through a systematic process of conversion or extermination. Such sentiments reflected official policy in Columbus' day, for those deemed inconvertible to Christianity were slain with impunity as the will of God. However, as we will see, it seems that exporting Christianity, as the will of God, was used by Columbus as a convenient justification to extract wealth and commit "the most massive act of genocide in the history of the world" (Stannard, 1992, p. x) rather than to save souls.

In effect, Christianity came to be held by its adherents as "...an abstract, worldwide, theology-based religion" (Wildcat, 2001b, p. 54), that, as alluded to above, can be understood as an extension of ancient Greek idealism, and thus an immutable ideology based on a Platonic epistemology that views knowledge/spirituality as disconnected from material existence and naturally unequally distributed. Columbus' greatest humanitarian achievement is therefore said to be embodied in his having brought "civilization" (i.e., Christianity) to the "new world" (i.e., those and that which is untamed) because it is believed to be part of the process in which the "chosen" people must engage to facilitate the Second Coming of Jesus signaling the end of the world and God's judgment of humankind. The discursive choice of the term "discovery" to describe the European invasion of the Americas connotes images of an empty continent, if not empty of people, then empty of civilization, which was equated with Christianity. Eurocentric historians, writing in the service of the aggressor/colonizer, therefore speak of "the vast empty spaces of the new world," which they often describe being characterized by "the absence of roads, towns, laws and kings" (Edmondson, 2000, p. 8). However, according to Howard Zinn (1995),

> Columbus and his successors were not coming into an empty wilderness, but into a world which in some places was as densely populated as Europe itself, where the culture was complex, where human relations were more egalitarian than in Europe, and where the relations among men, women, children, and nature were more beautifully worked out than perhaps any place in the world... Perhaps there is some romantic mythology in that. But the evidence from European travelers...is overwhelmingly supportive of much of that "myth." (Pp. 21–22)

Columbus in fact commented at length in his journals on his impressions of the Indigenous people he encountered, the description of which hardly seem like they were viewed as barbaric or ungodly, but rather looked at with admiration. Coming from a Europe wrought with "violence, squalor, treachery and intolerance" (Stannard, 1992, p. 57) Columbus was astonished with amazement at the Native peoples lack of jealousy, unrelenting generosity and their matter-of-fact embrace of sexuality.

> They exhibit great love toward all others in preference to themselves. They also give objects of great value for trifles.... I did not find, as some of us had expected, any cannibals among them, but, on the contrary, men of great deference and kindness. (Columbus, quoted in Bigelow, 1998a, p. 18)

However, for Columbus, his possible desire to understand these curious people was no competition for a much stronger desire for the accumulation of wealth and fame. Many of his comments speak volumes to the less than admirable purpose behind these voyages, which highlight his adherence to what would become a reductionist (versus holistic) Western science that Deloria (2001) describes as "...disjointed sterile and emotionless... [having] no moral basis and...entirely incapable of resolving human problems except by the device of making humans act more and more like machines" (pp. 2-4). After reading his journals it seems apparent that Columbus' Christianity and Western philosophy in general was little more than an elaborate justification, in the name of the Holy Trinity of course, for the naked and brutal accumulation of wealth, which, in the process, reduced millions of people into mechanistic slaves, and ultimately, led to their extermination, rather than engaging in a genuine soul saving mission, for it is abundantly obvious that the souls in need of saving were in fact Columbus, his men, and the Europe for whom they represented.

For example, Michele de Cuneo, who joined Columbus on his 1494 expedition, reflecting on Columbus' quest for riches, wrote, "after we had rested for several days in our settlement, it seemed to the Lord Admiral that it was time to put into execution his desire to search for gold, which was the main reason he had started on such a great voyage" (quoted in Loewen, 1995, p. 43). Columbus' savage search for wealth is entirely understandable not only within the philosophical context of fourteenth-century Christian fanaticism, but in the material context of fifteenth-century Europe, with reference to the Spanish nobility in particular, who served as the Admiral's primary investor, all of whom were facing bankruptcy due in part to a largely fruitless series of very costly Holy Crusades, and having been expelled from their last strongholds in the holy land, Jerusalem, from Muslim defenders. Christianity, and the generation of "Christian" wealth, was therefore, at the moment, confined to a decaying Europe plagued by disease, specifically what became known as the Black Death, which claimed the lives of one out of every three Europeans, contributing to escalating rates of famine, poverty, and intra-Christian conflicts. Mumia Abu-Jamal (1997), languishing from what he has poignantly described as the State's (U.S.) man-made "bright, shining hell" (death row), summarizes the role of Christianity in the Americas, noting that:

> It was used not so much to distinguish believers from unbelievers, but civilized, light-skinned colonists from uncivilized, dark-skinned natives—the so-called primitive Africans, savage Indians and other such heathen. It was a convenient spiritual underpinning for the sociopolitical order, that is, the "order" of white supremacy and domination. In such a context, the conversion of a non-white to the dominant, European faith meant next to nothing... (p. 44)

While it has not been an arduous task to demonstrate that Columbus' high moral Christian ideals—the same ideals that held dominant political sway in the Europe from which he was a dedicated participant—were of the most fundamentalist and fanatical nature so intolerant of non-Christians and, as noted by Abu-Jamal (1997), non-Europeans, and later between Christians of different sects (i.e., Protestants and Catholics), that its theological leaders openly advocated for the violent slaughter and extermination of non-believers, or those believed to be unable to convert (or those they did not want to convert), as the rational will of God. Columbus' role as occupier/predator can therefore be viewed as within the epistemological and metaphysical framework of his religion that not only dichotomizes the mind/religion/spirituality from the body/science/material existence, but is also based on an Aristotelian categorization of knowledge and experience obsessed with controlling and dissecting therefore impeding a holistic understanding that demonstrates the interconnectedness of all material and spiritual existence. Reflecting on the potential material value he saw within the Taino people, indigenous to what is now the Dominican Republic and Haiti, and in the process demonstrating the bankruptcy of his own spirituality, the "great adventurer" notes:

> They...brought us parrots and balls of cotton and spears and many other things, which they exchanged for the glass beads and hawks' bells. They willingly traded everything they owned... They do not bear arms, and do not know them, for I showed them a sword, they took it by the edge and cut themselves out of ignorance... They would make fine servants... With fifty men we could subjugate them all and make them do whatever we want. (quoted in Zinn, 1995, p. 1)

Providing further insight into the reductionist intentions informing the former African slave trader's "adventurous" pedagogy, Columbus boasts, "as soon as I arrived in the Indies, on the first island which I found, I took some of the natives by force in order that they might learn and might give me information of whatever there is in these parts" (quoted in Zinn, 1995, p. 2). Contrary to popular opinion that paints Columbus as a noble sea traveler bringing civilization to the "new world," Columbus was ultimately interested in slaves, gold, and the extraction of wealth regardless of the human costs. After exaggerating to his Spanish investors, who guaranteed him 10% of all he could plunder, about the vast gold fields he had "discovered," which in fact did not exist, Columbus had to fill his ships with *something* of value. It is therefore not surprising that Columbus took hundreds of Indigenous people to Europe as slaves, the majority of whom died en route or upon arrival. Desperate for gold, Columbus ordered every capable man to pay the invaders a gold tax every week for those who did not pay the gold, the vast majority because there were no vast tracts of gold, brutal punishments were imposed such as cutting off hands and leaving the victims to bleed to death.

Indigenous men were forced to work in mines under the most ghastly conditions that resulted in a life expectancy of just three to four months. The miners were chained together and lowered into shafts as far as 750 feet below the surface for a week at a time with nothing more than a small bag of corn and all the while being exposed to the toxic gases that are a by-product of mining. When a man died, of toxins or exhaustion, his head was typically severed from the chains and his body left to rot while another *Indio* was brought in as a replacement. If he survived his weeklong shift, he was usually beaten when returned to the surface for not mining enough gold. Physically exhausted, beaten and bloodied, as a final act of humiliation and conquest, the men, left shackled and helpless, were then often discarded under their own beds while Spaniards raped their wives directly above them. As the men were forced to work in mines, the women were made to toil in the fields to do the grueling job of erecting countless hills for cassava plants (Stannard, 1992).

Native peoples who attempted to flee were hunted down like animals by the invaders' bloodhounds and systematically butchered with an unrivaled barbarism. Native resistance was attempted but in the long run proved unsuccessful. Suicide rates were high as people chose death over enslavement. Mothers routinely killed their newborn babies to save them from Spanish cruelty. Indigenous peoples also suffered catastrophic loss through the diseases brought from Europe. Within twenty-one years of Columbus' arrival in the Caribbean, the once densely populated islands were desolate. Nearly eight million people perished as a result of violence, disease, or despair. Commenting on the bewildering atrocities he had witnessed, documented in his book *History of the Indies*, Bartolomé de las Casas, Spanish missionary and former plantation owner gone staunch critic, offers a sobering account of what took place:

> ...Our work was to exasperate, ravage, kill, mangle and destroy... Thus husbands and wives were together only once every eight or ten months and when they met they were so exhausted and depressed on both sides...they ceased to procreate. As for the newborn, they died early because their mothers, overworked and famished, had no milk to nurse them, and for this reason, while I was in Cuba, 7000 children died in three months. Some mothers even drowned their babies from sheer desperation.... In this way, husbands died in the mines, wives died at work, and children died from lack of milk...and in a short time this land which was so great, so powerful and fertile...was depopulated.... My eyes have seen these acts so foreign to human nature, and now I tremble as I write.... (quoted in Zinn, 1995, p. 7)

The horrors that caused Bartolomé de las Casas to "tremble" as he documented them, which he had not only witnessed but, to some extent, been a willing accomplice, can only be understood as the logical consequence of a philosophy that views non-Christians as "uncivilized" and thus a part of nature, and nature a utilitarian thing whose sole function is to serve the narrowly defined material-interests of "civilized" *man*. What took place in the Caribbean Basin was only the beginning. Despite the utter disregard for humanity as possessing an intrinsic right to exist free from tyranny and oppression, Columbus is touted as a hero from virtually every segment of U.S. and Canadian society (and much of the Western world), even from the one area that is institutionally designed to foster intellectual development—education in general and history textbooks in particular. For example, Columbus, with few exceptions, if any, is portrayed as one of the greatest sailors of his time who engaged in a "great adventure" demonstrating his nearly unprecedented bravery, courage, and determination (Bigelow, 1998b).

The nearly universal textbook story holds that Columbus was seeking a more direct trade route to India. However, many critical scholars (Loewen, 1995; Zinn, 1995) have refuted this claim arguing that Columbus was in fact lost, therefore questioning common assertions that he was perhaps the greatest sailor of his time. Still yet another historical account has been put forth that suggests that Columbus was not looking for India *or* lost, but rather knew exactly where he was going as a result of what he had learned from the West Africans he had been engaged with as a slave trader. It was, the argument goes, Europe's technological advancements, military warfare, and arms in particular that brought Columbus to the Americas with the specific purpose, again, of obtaining gold and enslaving the Indigenous population. A final speculative account put forth by Native professor Daniel Wildcat (2001b), summarizing Kirkpatrick Sale's argument in *The Conquest of Paradise,* is that "Columbus was not so much trying to discover a new land but escape from a declining, chaos-ridden old land" (p. 55). Whatever the reasons or motivations behind Columbus' travels were, what is certain is that his arrival in the Americas marks the beginning of a new era of European barbarism, which, for many Native peoples, was the end. Ward Churchill (2003a) identifies this new age of unprecedented brutality and deception as "predation" (discussed below), that is, the process of plundering and destruction.

In "Deconstructing the Columbus Myth," Ward Churchill (1997) summarizes the legacy of Christopher Columbus as setting "in motion" the "crystallization" of a "European culture" whose "dominant themes" are nothing less than "racial supremacy, conquest, and genocide" manifesting itself internationally from the Nazis in Germany to "the French against the peoples of Algeria" (p. 92). In the following passage Churchill (1997) underscores what this *Columbian pedagogy* has meant and continues to mean for Native peoples, which, because of its poignancy, is worth quoting at length:

As a symbol...Christopher Columbus vastly transcends himself. He stands before the bar of history and humanity, culpable not only of his deeds on Hispañola [modern day Haiti and the Dominican Republic], but, in spirit at least, for the carnage and cultural obliteration which attended the conquests of Mexico and Peru during the 1500s. He stands as exemplar of the massacre of Pequots at Mystic in 1637, and of Lord Jeffery Amherst's calculated distribution of smallpox-laden blankets to the members of Pontiac's confederacy a century and a half later. His spirit informed the policies of John Evans and John Chivington as they set out to exterminate the Cheyenne in Colorado during 1864, and it road with the 7th U.S. Cavalry to Wounded Knee in December of 1890. It guided Alfredo Stroessner's machete-wielding butchers as they strove to eradicate the Aché people of Paraguay during the 1970s, and applauds the policies of Brazil toward the Jivaro, Yanomami, and other Amazon Basin peoples at the present moment. (p. 92)

Howard Zinn (1995) and other scholars, whom I would classify as "radical" or "counter-hegemonic," such as Ward Churchill (1995, 1997, 1998, 2002, 2003a, 2003b, 2003c, 2004), Vine Deloria (1985, 1994), Rodolfo Acuña (1988), and David Stannard (1992), to name but a few of the more widely read authors, go to great lengths to document, "with clinical precision" (Churchill, 2003a), the impact of predator on the civilizations of the Indigenous populations of the Americas. What follows is therefore a summary of the damage that has been done and continues to be done to Native North America. Because genocide is a serious concept not to be taken lightly or used casually, I will proceed from here with a conceptual definition to ensure that we deal with it in an appropriate manner for the remainder of this discussion.

Genocide in Native North America: The Legacy of Columbian Pedagogy

Raphaël Lemkin (1944), a Polish-Jewish lawyer, developed the concept of genocide (which literally means race/tribe killing) in the years proceeding World War II and the Nazi Holocaust. However, Lemkin began the monumental task of defining the horrendous processes and attempts to depopulate and then repopulate entire regions much earlier after becoming interested in the subject upon learning of the horrific Turkish genocide of Armenians during World War I. Lemkin understood that eliminating a people included more than physical murder, but encompasses "...any policy undertaken with the intention of bringing about the dissolution and ultimate disappearance of a targeted human group" (Churchill, 2004, p. 3). In the following definition Lemkin therefore makes a clear distinction between three modes of genocide: physical, biological, and cultural, which have and continue to be used against

Native North Americans. Drawing on Lemkin's definition I will analyze, mode-by mode, Native American genocide, which will provide us with a concrete material context from which we can engage in philosophical discourse. Lemkin's (1944) definition, as quoted in Churchill (2004), is as follows:

1. *Physical Genocide* includes both direct/immediate extermination...and what are referred to as "slow death measures": i.e., "subjection to conditions of life which, owing to lack of proper housing, clothing, food, hygiene and medical care or excessive work or physical exertion are likely to result in the debilitation [and] death of individuals; mutilations and biological experiments imposed for other than curative purposes; depravations of [the] means of livelihood by confiscation, looting, curtailment of work, and the denial of housing and of supplies otherwise available to the other inhabitants of the territory concerned."

2. *Biological Genocide* includes involuntary "sterilization, compulsory abortion, segregation of the sexes and obstacles to marriage," as well as any other policies intended to prevent births within a target group.

3. *Cultural Genocide*–which encompasses the schema of denationalization/imposition of alien national pattern...[and] includes all policies aimed at destroying the specific characteristics by which a target group is defined, or defines itself, thereby forcing them to become something else. Among the acts specified are the "forced transfer of children...forced and systematic exile of individuals representing the culture of the group...prohibition of the use of the national language...systematic destruction of books printed in the national language, or religious works, or the prohibition of new publications...systematic destruction of national or religious monuments, or their diversion to alien uses [and] destruction or dispersion of objects of historical, artistic, or religious value and of objects used in religious worship." (p. 6)

Physical Genocide

Physical genocide includes the crimes most commonly, often exclusively, associated with the vast subject area of genocide. In his much acclaimed *A Little Matter of Genocide: Holocaust and Denial in the Americas, 1492 to the Present* (1997), Ward Churchill meticulously documents the physical genocide waged against American Indians, offering one of the most comprehensive and well-researched summations of the subject, which, among other monumental works of his, such as *Perversions of Justice* (2003b) and *Struggle for the Land* (2002), I draw on heavily in the pages that follow. Initially, physical genocide was the primary mode of extermination employed by predator. It has been estimated that there were upwards of 125 million Indigenous people living in the Western hemisphere when Columbus first arrived in "Hispaniola" in 1492 (Churchill, 1997; Stannard, 1992). By 1892, a mere four centuries after Columbian contact, a relatively short period of time in the context of Indigenous existence, the U.S. Census Bureau reported that there were just a quarter million Native inhabitants remaining within the claimed borders of the United States. In all, at least 90% of the lives of the original people have been lost. Two points of demographic concern, the original size of the Native population, and how much of the loss was due to unintentional factors such as disease, are hotly debated issues. Churchill (1997) argues that there is a tendency among mainstream demographers and anthropologists to err on the side of unintentionality because it removes blame from the settler-community and places it on the inevitability of history itself. In this chapter I focus on the philosophical implications of both Native and immigrant traditions of the unintentional genocide that occurred as a result of infectious diseases. This section, however, deals exclusively with the *intentional* genocide that has painted, and continues to paint, the Americas red for all time (Churchill, 1997).

What follows is a list of European and Euro-American genocidal atrocities committed against the many peoples Native to North America outlining the gruel and utterly barbaric nature of predation (defined below). This list will continue to assist our development of comprehending the concrete context from which we must engage in our development of the theoreti-cal/philosophical context. In other words, for our philosophies of education to hold concrete relevance, we must concretely deal with the following reality, for it is within this breathing, living reality that we live and work, and ultimately, support or transcend. There have literally been volumes of work dedicated to documenting the physical genocide that has occurred in the Americas, and is therefore far too vast a subject to encompass en masse here. What follows is thus a summary highlighting a number of cases indicative of the overall pattern of physical genocide. These examples are neither fantasy nor exaggeration, but represent perhaps one of the ugliest manifestations of human expression that has painted the whole of the Americas red with Native blood for eternity. Please remember that the following accounts are merely a brief sampling of what has occurred. If I were to embark on the construction of an exhaustive list, it would surely consume the entirety of this book, and perhaps a stack of such volumes:

o 1637—British forces surround Mystic, an ancient Pequot town situated in current-day Pennsylvania, set it ablaze and with axes and swords, brutally butcher eight hundred or more fleeing men, women, and children (Churchill, 1995). Such practices increased in frequency as the colonists learned how to survive in North America from the helpful Indigenous nations in which they encountered. The motivation? To take over the well-cultivated farmlands and other geography of those native to what is now the United States and Canada and engage those lands in the sterile and alienating process of value production, and with those indigenous to these specific places exterminated or forcefully removed, stripping the geography of its native culture and ignoring its spiritual power and significance (Deloria, 2006; Loewen, 1995).

o 1763—Lord Jeffery Amherst orders subordinate Bouquet to give smallpox-laden blankets from the smallpox hospital to Pontiac's Algonquin confederacy as a gesture of friendship intended to "extirpate this execrable race." When his people begin to get sick, U.S. army doctors suggest that they seek refuge with their healthy relatives with the desired effect of spreading the highly infectious disease. It works. As many as 100,000 Native Americans die in the epidemic rendering "westward expansion" considerably less arduous. The target of attack and ultimate extermination was not just Pontiac's military forces, but more importantly, the people as a whole (Churchill, 1995, 2003a).

o 1779—"An army commanded by John Sullivan undertakes a campaign against the Seneca and other members of the Haudenosaunee (Six Nations Iroquois Confederacy) in upstate New York to "punish" the Indians for siding with England (*in George Washington's successful insurrection of wealthy colonists against England to emerge as the new ruling class within the settler-community*). Sullivan orders a "war of extermination against even the very orchards," and his men comply with gusto, laying waste to every native town, field, and human being they encounter. Much weakened by the onslaught, the Haudenosaunee are rapidly disposed of their land." (Churchill, 2003c, p. 44)

o 1780—"An offensive similar to that conducted against the Haudenosaunee a year earlier, and against the Cherokees in 1776, is undertaken against the Muskogee (Creeks) and Chickamauga. The Muskogee suffer damages comparable to that incurred by their predecessors. The Chickamauga are all but totally exterminated" (Churchill, 2003c, p. 44).

o 1836—The U.S. Army may have distributed smallpox-infected blankets to the Missouri River Mandan in an effort to not just neutralize a military opponent, but to wipe out the entire society. If so, the U.S. Army is responsible for the deaths of more than a quarter million Indigenous people who perished in the pandemic (Churchill, 1995).

o 1864—Colonial John Chivington orders his troops to exterminate men, women, and children alike because "nits make lice" (Churchill, 2004, p. 14). At least two hundred and fifty Natives perished at the hands of Chivington's troops. The Sand Creek Massacre was part of a series of such acts over a thirty-year period aimed at "taming the west."

o 1890—The Wounded Knee Massacre, committed by the U.S. seventh Cavalry where three hundred unarmed Lakota were slaughtered, proved to be the finale in the list of slayings designed to subjugate the western tribes (Churchill, 1995, p. 175).

o 1890—The U.S. Census admits that the Native population of California had been reduced from 300,000 in 1800, considered far greater now, to less than 20,000 in 1890 largely due to massacres committed by white settlers and miners. Killing Native peoples was a viable, if not entirely savage, way to supplement a miner's income during the off-season when water levels and flow were not conducive to mining.

o 1800-1895—The great herds of bison provided the primary source of nutrition for many Native Americans of the Great Plains, the Lakota and Crow most notably. During "aboriginal times," it has been estimated, these herds were as great as sixty million strong. By the beginning of the nineteenth century they had been reduced to forty million. The most dramatic decline occurred between 1800 and 1895 when the buffalo, reaching their nadir of less than one thousand, were brought to near extinction resulting in "...widespread starvation and the social and cultural collapse of many Plains tribes...(Thornton, 1987, p. 52). Demonstrating the interconnectedness of the buffalo and the Lakota way of life, and in turn, indigenous philosophy, traditional Lakota philosopher Joseph Marshall III (2001) in

The Lakota Way notes, "the bison was the greatest nomad on the plains and our association with and dependence on it turned us into nomads as well. As the bison went, so did we" (p. 211). It was understood by the U.S. Army that the Plains Indians existence was intimately connected to that of the bison, and the extermination of the bison would advance the policy of Indian extermination, that is, genocide. Because the culture of the Lakota, for example, was so intimately connected to the bison, it can be argued that the destruction of the great herds was not only an act of physical genocide, but cultural genocide as well. For example, General William Tecumseh Sherman encouraged hundreds of white buffalo hunters and sportsmen to slaughter the great herds by the tens and hundreds of thousands as part of a systematic effort to tame "...the wild Indians by killing off their lifeline" (Marshall III, 2001, p. 217).

The pedagogical ghost informing these ghastly practices can only be that of Columbus. Employing the graphic imagery necessary for comprehending the physical genocide just laid out, that is, the unfathomable magnitude of these crimes committed against humanity in the last five centuries by predominantly European colonizers and settlers, Ward Churchill (1997) notes:

> The people had died in their millions of being hacked apart with axes and swords, burned alive and trampled under horses, hunted as game and fed to dogs, shot, beaten, stabbed, scalped for bounty, hanged on meat hooks and thrown over the sides of ships at sea, worked to death as slave laborers, intentionally starved and frozen to death during a multitude of forced marches and internments, and, in an unknown number of instances, deliberately infected with epidemic diseases. Today, every one of these practices is continued, when deemed expedient by the settler population(s)... (p. 1)

Drawing on the perspective offered by Native activist/poet John Trudell and the work of radical Chicano activist/scholar Rodolfo Acuña (1988) in *Occupied America: A History of Chicanos,* Churchill (2003a) has consistently situated the analysis of physical genocide embedded within the above quote in a larger context by describing "the moment predator washed up on American shores" as the beginning of predation, that is, *the act of plundering and preying.* We might also refer to the effects of physical genocide as perdition— *complete and irreparable loss and ruin.* The completeness and irreparability of the loss and ruin has been all but total for many indigenous societies (outlined below). However, as described in Chapters Three and Four, other nations native to North America have been engaged in the arduous task of countering perdition through rebuilding their societies since the 1950s and after. However, as we will see below in the sub-section on native resistance and in Chapter Three, this process of struggling against colonization has been very complex and can therefore not be understood by the simple occupiers versus occupied dichotomy.

In *American Indian Holocaust and Survival: A Population History Since 1492,* renowned demographer Russell Thornton (1987) concludes that the American Indian population within the United States reached its nadir of a mere 4%/5% of its pre-Columbian population, a figure that has since been revised to 2%/3%, and subsequently began its continuing resurgence around the beginning of the twentieth century. While these examples will provide us with a rich source of hope for the future of humanity, we must first continue our mission to comprehend the American genocide/Holocaust more fully.

William Carlos Williams, quoted in Stannard (1992), reflecting on the physical genocide represented in the preceding examples from Columbus onward, speaking from the perspective of the settler-community, or predator, mournfully comments with indignation, "we are the slaughterers. It is the tortured soul of our world" (p. xvi).

Biological Genocide

Most recorded instances of biological genocide have been waged specifically against women, and can therefore be understood as the ultimate manifestation of European misogyny. If the policy is extermination, as it has been in regards to Native Americans, then it makes sense to target those who are responsible for reproducing the next generation—women. Underscoring this twisted logic in *Conquest: Sexual Violence and American Indian Genocide* (2005), Andrea Smith, Cherokee activist and scholar, gets straight to the point in her observation that "the notion that...Native communities pollute the body politic continues to inform the contemporary population control movement...Women of color are particularly threatening, as they have the ability to reproduce the next generation of communities of color" (p. 79).

o   1970s—The Bureau of Indian Affairs' (BIA) own "Indian Health Services" (IHS) instituted a policy of involuntary sterilization of Native American women of childbearing age. Reports on the percentage of Indigenous women sterilized differ from region to region, but estimates range from

25% to 100%. For example, it has been estimated that 25% of all Native women in Oklahoma were sterilized and 100% of "pureblood" Kaw women. WARN (Women of All Red Nations) reported that between 40% and 50% of all Indigenous women were sterilized during the 1970s (Churchill, 1995, p. 32; A. Smith, 2005, pp. 82–84). Smith (2005) notes that the Native population did increase during this period, which suggests to her that estimating the sterilization rate to be 50% is probably too high. On the other hand, Smith notes that many of the women involuntarily sterilized already had three or four children obscuring the effect of the highly illegal practice on population growth. This analysis is by no means intended to belittle or downplay the genocidal intentions of a policy of involuntary sterilization (A. Smith, 2005).

o   1977—Situating U.S. sterilization policies in an economic context (i.e., conducive to the profit motive) R.T. Ravenholt representing the U.S. Agency for International Development when referring to the Indigenous peoples south of the U.S./Mexico border, commented: "population control is necessary to maintain the normal operation of U.S. commercial interests around the world..." Otherwise Native peoples "...would rebel against the strong U.S. commercial presence" (A. Smith, 2005, p. 80).

o   1982—Hepatitis B trial vaccinations were administered to Alaskan Native children without parental consent because it was argued that hepatitis B was on the rise, while it was actually on the decline with a 0-.05% prevalence rate indicating that Alaska Natives are not at risk at all. Health care activists have questioned the validity of vaccinations in general, noting, for example, that Disease Control reported that between 1973 and 1983 87% of all cases of polio in the U.S. were caused by the vaccine. Given the available data, why do doctors continue to administer the vaccines? Most doctors receive a commission from the pharmaceutical companies for each child they vaccinate. It is therefore not surprising that Native communities, deemed not only expendable, but in the way of developing the natural resources within their ancestral lands, are not only highly vaccinated, but are the all-too-often unknowing recipients of often deadly trial vaccines (A. Smith, 2005).

o 1990s—Native activist groups such as WARN have put the necessary pressures on the IHS to curb sterilization abuses. However, the problem still lingers as Smith (2005) documents: "one woman I know went into IHS in the 1990s for back surgery and came out with a hysterectomy" (p. 85).

o 1990s–present—The IHS now uses long-lasting contraceptives such as Norplant and Depo-Provera, often involuntarily, to prevent Native pregnancies despite the dangerous side effects associated with the drugs, including heart attacks, blindness, sterility, and cancer. Nearly 90% of these hazardous materials are used on poor and women of color. The message sent by IHS officials is that Native women are inherently "dirty" and in need of cleansing and purification (A. Smith, 2005).

Cultural Genocide

...Of all the malignancies embodied in twentieth-century U.S./Canadian Indian policy, the schools were arguable the worst. The profundity of their destructive effects upon native people, both individually and collectively, not only in the immediacy of their operational existence but in the aftermath as well, was and remains by any reasonable estimation incalculable. Ultimately, neither the nature nor the magnitude of the genocide suffered by Native North Americans can be truly appreciated unless the impact of the residential schools is understood. (Churchill, 2004, p. xlv)

Whenever I have introduced the notion of cultural genocide, drawing on the example of "Indian" boarding schools, and the detrimental effects on the ongoing longevity of native North American sovereignty to my teacher education students, regardless of national, ethnic, or cultural background, with few exceptions, I am inevitably met with confused looks of bewilderment. "Assimilation does not kill you" I am frequently reminded. I will typically use this "spark" as a springboard into a discussion on what exactly "constitutes the 'death' of a group" (Churchill, 1995, p. 96), and also what does it mean to be an "Indian," should it be the right of Native Americans to decide, as international law commands, or should such operational definitions be externally imposed as is the practice in the United States and Canada (Churchill, 2003b)?

The point to which my statements and questions are designed to lead is an understanding of "assimilation" as intended to "...bring about the dissolution and ultimate disappearance of a targeted human group" (Churchill, 2004, p.

3). Put another way, a policy or practice can be said to be an act of cultural genocide if it is "aimed at destroying the specific characteristics by which a target group is defined, or defines itself, thereby forcing them to become something else" (Lemkin, 1944, quoted in Churchill, 2004, p. 6). The following list of actions, all of which were designed to destroy targeted groups by cultural means, did not universally achieve their desired results. It seems that while it is more difficult to successfully engage in cultural genocide than physical or biological genocide, once achieved, as Churchill (2004) asserts, it is far more destructive in the long run. It is worth noting that the choice to engage in cultural genocide (i.e., boarding schools) was ultimately an economic one because it was estimated by the U.S. government that it was more expensive to physically kill "Indians" than to "educate" the "Indian" out of native peoples (Adams, 1995).

o   1492-present—The foundation for which Native American cultural identity is firmly grounded is specific land formations. Native spirituality is part and parcel of the land from which it emerged. To divest native peoples of their land is to strip them of their source of cultural expression. While land theft has most assuredly resulted in physical genocide (as demonstrated above), I have included it here, under the sub-section *cultural genocide*, for the philosophical implications most relevant to this book. Churchill (1995) notes that as of 1992 Native people, within the contiguous United States, have been divested of 98% of their original land base, which, as of 1492, included every square inch of North America. In other words, as a result of at least forty "Indian Wars" waged by the U.S. and the "negotiated agreements" that ensued, Native America has been "...constricted to about 2.5 percent of its original 2 billion-acre land base..." (Churchill, 1995, p. 112). The physical and biological genocide outlined above, the cultural genocide underscored below, as well as a series of extra-legal manipulations (see, for example, Churchill, 1995, and Deloria, 1985, for a discussion outlining the implications and precursors of the "Marshall Doctrine"), have been part of an elaborate scheme fabricated by European, Euro-Canadian, and Euro-American colonialist/expansionists to steal Native land by whatever means necessary, the very act of which is genocidal in nature—an attack on the culture of the people resulting in the death of a specific human group. In other words, without a landbase sufficient to build and sustain an independent and sovereign community, a people lose the capacity to exist as such.

o   1784—As payment for their assistance to the British government against the American colonialists during the American revolutionary war, the Six Nations Confederacy was granted an unusually large portion of land that had been alienated from the Mississauga—six miles deep on either side of the entire length of the Grand River. Just as the people of the Six Nations had lost land to the Americans and were subsequently provided a new land base in Canada by the imperialist forces of Great Britain, many white loyalists had also been stripped of their land claims and were therefore granted Canadian land for their services to the British Crown. However, unlike the lands belonging to the Six Nations, when the lands of these whites were encroached on, the invaders were removed. As a result, the Six Nations have been stripped of nearly all their lands. In 1841 the Canadian government promised that if the Nations gave up most of their lands, the depredations would cease. Feeling like they had no recourse, the chiefs hesitantly agreed, but the intrusions and the Canadian government's unwillingness to enforce the law did not stop. Today the Six Nations, like most other nations native to North America who still have a landbase, are fighting tooth and nail to hold onto the last few scraps of geography still under their jurisdiction (see below under *Native North American Resistance*).

o   1818—The U.S. House Committee on Indian Affairs, in an early and unsuccessful attempt to divest Native peoples of their land-based culture, with the intended effect of accessing Native-held ancestral lands, encouraged Congress to take steps to socialize native peoples in the ways of Western commerce and productivity, referred to as "civilization," resulting in the creation of a Civilization Fund, allotting an annual budget of $10,000 under the supervision of the first Superintendent of Indian Affairs, Thomas L. McKenny (Adams, 1995).

o   1880–1980—Churchill (2004) lists 129 Indian boarding schools operating within the United States with the intended purpose of killing the Indian and saving the man, to paraphrase Richard Henry Pratt, who was selected to build and maintain the compulsory school system for Native Americans. His background was not in education, but in killing. That is, he was an officer in the U.S. Army.

o   1880–1980—Churchill (2004) lists 87 Indian boarding schools in Canada designed to achieve the same results as their U.S. counterparts where children were forcibly removed from resistant parents and taken sometimes thousands of miles from home for years on end, and prohibited from speaking their native tongue or practicing any of their other cultural traditions. In other words, they were prohibited from being "Indian," and made, sometimes with deadly force, to be something else, that is, "white."

o   1887—U.S. Congress passed the General Allotment Act to divide reservations into parcels of land to be distributed among their Indigenous occupants, "160 acres to each family head, 80 acres to single persons and orphans over eighteen years, and 40 acres to single persons under eighteen" (Adams, 1995, p. 17). Allottees were granted US citizenship. The intended result was to dissolve traditional communal ways of cultural organization. "Full-blooded Indians" were granted a privileged land granting status resulting in the erosion of cultural conceptions of "Indianness" and tribal membership intended to divide and thus conquer the targeted group (Churchill, 2003b). Finally, "leftover" land, the very basis of traditional native culture, was sold to white settlers.

The settler-community's official history curriculum subjects all students of all racial and ethnic backgrounds, from the elementary to secondary levels, to a form of indoctrination that is steeped in denial and victim blaming. In his classic work, *Lies My Teacher Told Me: Everything Your American History Textbook Got Wrong*, James Loewen (1995) documents, at considerable length, these distortions, omissions, and outright lies that have led to an endless list of misunderstandings among non-Natives and Natives alike about Indigenous peoples.

For example, as a response to a mini lecture I gave on the American Holocaust, a "white" Canadian student in my *Critical Issues in Education* course shrugged it off arguing that "Indians are lazy. They will do anything to avoid their responsibilities... They live off the welfare system and don't contribute anything to society because they choose not to." His classmates did not show any signs of outrage or protest to his victim blaming. Many, in fact, chimed in to defend their colleague from my probing questions regarding what I considered to be central issues to the discussion such as land theft, colonization, illegal occupation, and genocide, which point to the structural factors that contribute to the alienation that they have observed with their internalized white gaze, which is not only oppressive and dehumanizing to native peoples, but it is self-destructive because it prevents us from forming broad-based coalitions needed to overcome the capitalist present that exploits everyone dependent on a wage for survival, the vast majority of humanity.

Bill Bigelow and Bob Peterson (1998), in their edited volume *Rethinking Columbus: The Next 500 Years,* offer teachers real alternative practices to counter the system of indoctrination that has successfully blamed the victim, and therefore created a "friendly" non-Native populace to support, or at least not actively oppose, the ongoing attacks on native North Americans/America. These counter-hegemonic approaches, situated in the context of a massive system of hegemonic indoctrination, will be explored at length in Chapter Four.

I would be doing the long history of native struggle and survival, and the human spirit of self-determination more generally, a considerable disservice if I did not provide a summary of indigenous resistance before I move on to discuss the basic tenets of philosophy in the context of educational practice and preparation. What follows is therefore a list of examples of past and present oppositional movements to predation engaged in by those native and some not native to North America. The last thing I wish to leave my readers with new to this subject matter is the impression that indigenous peoples have passively "took it," as it were, or were "too stupid" to devise effective means of resistance.

Native resistance, however crafted, as demonstrated below, has almost always been met by predator with the most barbaric actions to put it down as evidenced by the FBI's domestic Counter Intelligence Program (COINTELPRO) that have a long history of operating in a covert fashion to disrupt, misdirect, and otherwise neutralize political dissident groups within the U.S., to paraphrase J. Edgar Hoover, the FBI's founder and director between 1918 and 1972 (Churchill & Vander Wall, 1990). With the "passing" of the U.S.A. Patriot Act, after being submitted for review at three in the morning, COINTELPRO-style operations are now being conducted in broad daylight.

Before I begin to list examples of native resistance in my standard institutional bullet format, we must pause and consider the extremely complex and contradictory nature of this history. Theoretically, this is one of the most important sections of this book. The cultural genocide documented above and the federal relocation programs after WWII resulting in more than two thirds of all Native peoples living in urban communities away from tribal centers (Fixico, 2001), are the main culprits, in my estimation, of the contradictory nature of indigenous survival and resistance. Drawing attention to the impact the "urbanization" of "Indians" has had on "intertribal" organization, Terry Straus and Debra Valentino (2001) note that in the past,

> Indians in urban areas were negatively stereotyped by reservation people as "fallen" or diminished Indians, "sell-outs" who abandoned tribal homeland, practice, politics, and problems for the good life in the city. Such stereotypes affected communication between members of urban and reservation communities and made it difficult for urban residents to return to their home reservations. (p. 89)

Gerald Vizenor (1990) drew attention to this tension between "reservation" and "urban" "Indians" in the early 1970s in his analyses of the American Indian Movement (AIM) noting that AIM was created by "urban Indian militants" dreaming of returning to a romanticized reservation as the "new tribal warriors" (p. 183). Vizenor (1990) notes that the majority of AIM members have been some of the most oppressed and alienated Native youth both on and off the reservation, and that AIM has defined the "enemy" as both white people and those they identify as corrupt tribal leaders resulting in deadly conflicts between the predominantly urban AIM and tribal governments. Contributing to these tensions argues Vizenor (1990) is the fact that many urban "Indians" do not speak their tribal languages and their largely symbolic militant tactics (highlighted below) do not reflect the values and beliefs of tribal people on reservations. In addition, many tribal leaders were raised in BIA boarding schools and reflect the interests of the U.S. government, causing AIM to push for their resignation, but ironically calling on the federal government to take them out of office (Vizenor, 1990).

What these issues speak to is what Freire (1998) refers to as "the duality of the oppressed: they are contradictory, divided beings, shaped by and existing in a concrete situation of oppression and violence" (p. 37). Freire (1998) argues that it is common for the oppressed when engaged in resistance against dehumanization, shaped by the ideology of their oppressors, to act in dehumanizing ways because of their internalized oppression. In an in-depth study on the hegemonic and counter-hegemonic manifestations of punk rock cultural spaces created as a means of social protest, Milagros Peña and myself (2004) made similar observations (see *Punk Rockers' Revolution*) in that punk rockers, while resisting the ideas, values, and beliefs of the mainstream society, inevitably reproduce them in ways strikingly similar to those described above by Vizenor (1990) of **AIM**. Consider our words, which are worth quoting at some length because of their relevance:

> ...Punk and mainstream are not dichotomous but continuous. Alternative cultural spaces and those who occupy them, are woven together by overlapping contradictory ideas and actions with extremism on both ends. Indeed, those reared in a "smoggy" (i.e. racist, capitalist) place cannot be free of the effects of that smog (Tatum 1997). Thus, in our efforts to create a more humane way of life there will no doubt surface traces of the old system, for unlearning and becoming is a lifelong process (Freire 1970). According to Freire, revolution is made possible only through the love of humanity and human liberation. In an unloving, dehumanized society, it is love that we are deprived of, and which is needed to become more human, but in coming to that realization we must unlearn oppressive ideologies. (p. 98)

In our research we found a strong tendency among punk rockers to focus on identity politics and therefore overly concerned with who the "real" punkers were and were not. Similarly, the split between reservation and urban Native Americans, in Vizenor's (1990) narratives, seems to point to a similar issue, that is, who is a real "Indian" and who is a poseur. In our analysis of punk rock we argue that it would be far more constructive for punk rockers to concern themselves with focusing on their own internalized oppressions and construct creative ways to challenge the commodification of humanity and therefore the process of value production (i.e., fight capitalism) rather than pointing the finger at those they think do not fit the mold, so to speak. I see this position not dissimilar to that advocated by Grande (2004) in her discussion on identity politics and Native Americans. However, Grande adds a layer of complexity challenging multiculturalists' position against essentialist conceptions of identity and at the same time contesting the U.S. federal government's monopolization of what a "real Indian" is arguing that part of Native sovereignty should include the ability to determine who is a tribal member cautious not to fall victim of reproducing "whitestream" conceptions of Indigeneity. Summarizing her position Grande (2004) notes,

> ...American Indian intellectuals must be careful, in their own assertions of what constitutes American Indian-ness, to avoid reenacting the divisive logic of colonialist domination—one that not only pits Indian against non-Indian, but also Indian against Indian and tribe against tribe. Thus, while the clearly defined categories of essentialism provide the necessary protection against cultural encroachment and colonialist absorption, it is important to recognize that they also confine American Indian stu-

dents to narrowly prescribed spaces, ossifying indigenous subjectivity to the chasms of the whitestream imagination. (p. 106)

With these theoretical insights in mind, let us now turn to a few examples of Native American resistance. Based on my review of literature, at its core, Native resistance, it appears, has been designed to hold onto and reclaim as much land as possible, and is therefore not only material in nature but cultural because it is Indigenous culture that seems to tie the self-defined, sovereign Native community to specific geographical locations, from this outsider's perspective of course. Interrogated in Chapter Four is what also seems to be a renaissance in specific Native cultural practices, including an emphasis on language and traditional philosophy, within tribally conceived, operated, and controlled schools (Cleary & Peacock, 1998; Deloria & Wildcat, 2001; Skinner, 1999).

Native North American Resistance

o 1876—Having come to the realization after a series of broken treaties and accompanying massacres that the only effective way to engage with the U.S. is militarily, Sitting Bull, Hunkpapa Lakota Leader, sends a message to other leaders calling for a summer gathering. Six thousand to eight thousand respond, a quarter of the Lakota Nation. The group first camped at Ash Creek, then Greasy Grass River, better known as the Little Big Horn. With both victories and defeats, the Lakota resisted the U.S. military onslaught, and ultimately "white" encroachment, for thirty five years (Marshall III, 2004).

o 1968—The American Indian Movement (AIM) is officially established in Minneapolis, Minnesota, with the organization and implementation of what was aptly named the "Minneapolis AIM Patrol," designed to counter state-sponsored terror manifesting itself as police brutality. From its inception AIM articulates itself as part of the Native struggle that has existed since the arrival of predator five hundred years ago. AIM articulates its primary focus as moving "...toward a renewal of spirituality which would impart the strength of resolve needed to reverse the ruinous policies of the United States [and] Canada...." On their official web page AIM leadership describes what their focus has looked like in practice noting that "AIM has repeatedly brought successful suit against the federal government for the protection of the rights of Native Nations guaranteed in treaties, sover-

eignty, the United States Constitution, and laws. The philosophy of self-determination upon which the movement is built is deeply rooted in traditional spirituality, culture, language and history."
http://www.aimovement.org/ggc/history.html

o   1969—Alcatraz Island is occupied for nineteen months in an act of symbolic resistance bringing the predominantly urban militant AIM leadership not only international recognition, but the all too familiar wrath of the United States government (as documented in the above summation of the genocide that has been waged against Native peoples informed by what I identified as a Columbian Pedagogy of Predation) in the form of the FBI's deadly COINTELPRO. In its wake, the FBI left many prominent AIM members either dead or indefinitely imprisoned, and the American Indian Movement deeply divided. To this day AIM is distinctly divided into two camps that can be physically located in Minnesota and Colorado chapters. Both groups claim to represent the "real" AIM, accusing the other of either posing or corruption.

o   1970—Minnesota AIM establishes the Legal Right Center to provide Indian people with legal representation where there had previously been none. As of 1994, the Center had provided nineteen thousand Native people with legal representation

o   1974—Native American women involved in the American Indian Movement form WARN (Women of All Red Nations) based in Rapid City, South Dakota. WARN has been especially active in combating the federal government's involuntary sterilization programs and other policies that contribute to biological genocide, as outlined above (A. Smith, 2005).

o   1993—The Annual Assembly of the World Council of Indigenous Peoples agreed, without dissension, to reject the Human Genome Diversity Project's (HGDP) attempts to collect the DNA of Native peoples described by Grande (2004) as the "...most egregious form of capitalist profiteering to impact indigenous communities..." (p. 111). The Assembly argued that the 20 million dollars to be used annually to collect and store Indigenous DNA could more usefully be used on social programs that would better protect Native biodiversity. The group also called for the dissolution of the HGDP more generally (Grande, 2004).

o 2000–INCITE! Women of Color Against Violence, co-founded by Cherokee activist and professor Andrea Smith, was born out of the success of a conference at the University of California at Santa Cruz that dealt with multiple issues related to "the color of violence," such as immigration and treaty rights. INCITE! is currently the largest grassroots, multiracial, feminist organization in the U.S. and Canada (A. Smith, 2005)

o 2000–The Boarding School Healing Project (BSHP) was formed to work towards repairing the damages inflicted on Native communities through the Indian boarding school era. For example, numerous men who were sexually abused in these schools later committed suicide. BSHP is therefore dedicated to healing through a number of means such as educating the general public, holding those responsible accountable, and documenting the innumerable abuses and examples of cultural genocide (A. Smith, 2005).

o 2005-present–Distinguished scholar and Colorado AIM activist Ward Churchill is terminated from Colorado State University at Boulder for academic misconduct and questions concerning his ethnic origins, "posing" as Native American, issues which surfaced after an essay he penned wherein he made the case that 9/11 can be understood as a military response to the long history of U.S. intervention throughout the world, the Middle East in particular. The controversy has brought attention to the over four thousand plus pages of academic, predominantly historical, text Churchill has published, the majority of which document the specific manifestations of predator in Native North America. While this example clearly represents another attempt to silence a powerful voice against the long legacy of atrocities the U.S. government has committed against countless peoples throughout the world, focusing primarily on Native Americans, I have included it here because it seems to have somewhat solidified a broad-based community of resistance, therefore representing an example of the struggle to create coalitions between different cultural groups for social justice. In Churchill's defense, some of the most esteemed Native and non-Native scholars in the U.S. have written letters in support of not only Churchill's academic freedoms, but in support of the specific arguments, conclusions, and methodologies of his voluminous body of academic work (cited heavily throughout this first sub-section of this chapter). The following list summarizes their overall sentiment:

- o   Noam Chomsky: Without reservations, I support Churchill's right to free speech and academic freedom, and regard the attack on him as scurrilous - and by now craven cowardice as well, as the state authorities and other critics pretend that the issue is (suddenly) his academic credentials and ethnic origins. That's a real disgrace.

- o   Mumia Abu-Jamal: This is in defense of Ward Churchill, historian... Churchill is now under fire for an essay penned shortly after the events of September 11th.... In his 2002 essay, Some People Push Back: On the Justice of Roosting Chickens, Churchill recalls the famous comment by Malcolm X after the assassination of President John F. Kennedy, "It was but a case of Chickens coming home to roost". Both Malcolm and Churchill know something about U.S. actions abroad, its export of violence abroad, and its demonstrated hatred of dark peoples the world over.... It is not enough for us to merely, dumbly intone that Churchill has the right to write what he does, no we must do more, we must insist that Churchill is right...

- o   Kathleen Cleaver: ...Having suffered during the late 1960s and early 70s the stings of disinformation, infiltration, political repression and the murder of members of my political organization, my take on current political development may differ from many. In the massive campaign to oust Churchill, I cannot help but detect the fine trace of an operation designed to appear 'spontaneous' but actually manipulated to attain a larger political objective.

- o   David Stannard: The sentiments of his new book [*A little Matter of Genocide*] are extraordinarily compassionate and humanitarian, while its overall argument is eminently fair, deliberative, and reasonable.... It is only because of troublemakers like him that the deadened conscience of this nation might some day begin to stir. May his kind multiply.

- o   Barbara Alice Mann: Over my several years as a practicing scholar of Native American Studies, I have had countless occasions to note Churchill's citations. In tracking down points referenced by him, I have always found that what he said was there, exactly where and as he said it was. I therefore find the recent, incendiary attacks on his scholarship to be highly dubious. http://wardchurchill.net/blog/statements/statements-of-support/

- o   In response to the accusation that Churchill has no Native American ancestry in his genetic composition, Scott Richard Lyons (2005), Leech Lake Ojibwe, speaking with the authority of a "real Indian," and with the power of being an assistant professor of Writing and Rhetoric and Native American Studies at Syracuse University, comments:

> If Churchill is in fact 100 percent white - which no one will ever know for certain then what exactly would that make him? Seems to me he would then occupy that time-honored position of a colonizer "going Native;" that is, taking on the habits and perspectives - not to mention the politics - of the colonized. He would be what racial theorists call a "race traitor;" one who denies and decries "white privilege" by refusing to participate in "whiteness" as a system of privilege. How exactly would that harm Indian people? (p. 1)

o 2005—Led by the clan mothers of the Six Nations Confederacy in Caledonia, Ontario, the tribe stopped construction of high end housing, Douglas Creek Estates, successfully blocking this example of a twenty-first-century attempt by moneyed interests within the white settler-community to encroach on their territory, the land granted to them in 1784 by Lieutenant Governor Haldimand. Unique about this land grant was the fact that it was land previously alienated from the Mississauga Nation, in part by the Six Nations themselves, who received ownership of it as payment for their military service to the British government during the American Revolutionary War at which time they lost their lands to the United States government.

The Six Nations were granted six miles on either side of the Grand River, which became prime real estate. When whites, oftentimes U.S. citizens, would decide to take a piece of this land, the Indigenous would most commonly appeal to the government to protect their right to their granted land, the Canadian authorities apparently never did anything about it, as was the case when in 1995 the Six Nations Confederacy filed a lawsuit against the 1992 acquisition of Douglas Creek Estates by Henco Industries Ltd. With no support from the Canadian government, despite an International ruling in the Six Nations' favor, left with no alternatives, the tribe barricaded incoming roads and reclaimed their lands. Like every other example since 1784 when Native peoples have attempted to stop the theft of their land, the Canadian authorities have intervened, and like so many other times, violently.

On Thursday, April 20, Hazel Hill of the Six Nations was physically assaulted by the Ontario Provincial Police, who unsuccessfully attempted to end their blockade. The Six Nations people continue to hold their reclamation with twenty four hour patrols. The Confederacy has publicly made an open invitation for people to come to the site of their struggle and express their solidarity through standing with the Six Nations both physically side by side, or materially with video cameras, camping equipment, and provisions (Podur, 2006).

These examples of Native resistance and solidarity constitute just a brief smattering of the long history of Indigenous struggle for the basic right to exist. Just as it would take multiple volumes to fully document the abuses suffered by Native peoples at the hands of a deadly and deceptive enemy, so too would it take multiple volumes to fully document every instance of resistance conceived and put into practice by Indigenous communities. In the chapters that fill up the remainder of this book you will learn more about the complexities and contradictions of the manifestation of Native struggle that tend to characterize colonized and oppressed peoples (explored in Chapter Three, for example). The contradictory tendencies that too often plague colonized communities, as we will see in Chapter Three, are a direct result of the process of colonization, that is, predation, and therefore nonexistent before invasion and conquest. We have already seen how the reductionist philosophy informing Columbus' fundamentalist Christianity gave way to a Columbian pedagogy of death and destruction as an integral part of the process of wealth extraction that continues to inform ruling class governments around the world.

In Chapters Three and Four the psychological effects of cultural genocide (the imposition of philosophical doctrines) are explored in relation to their educational implications. The importance for educators and future educators to develop educational philosophies with the power to assist *all* of our students in developing the skills to not only survive in the world that exists, but to transform it, is all but total. It is not hard to comprehend the relevance of such an endeavor for educators of Native students. However, the majority of our students are not and will not be native to North America, but we are all on Native land, the vast majority of which is currently, as you read these very words, being illegally occupied, and, historically, it has been the non-Native community, people of European descent especially, that has had the greatest, and most negative, impact on Indigenous communities.

It is therefore urgently important that all teachers have the opportunity to develop philosophies, individually and collectively, that are conducive to not only the process of healing, ensuring future atrocities do not occur, but ending the genocide that is currently under way. What has been laid out before you are therefore the philosophical building blocks that could be a part of your own lifelong engagement with theory and practice (i.e., praxis). Remember, this discussion is meant to whet your intellectual appetite and spark a passion to know within you, taking you in new (or old) theoretical directions, and ultimately, new (or improved) ways of teaching and learning.

The Building Blocks of Philosophy

The role philosophy plays and has played in our interactions with ourselves, each other, physical places, and the manifestation of cultural expression should be abundantly obvious after the preceding accumulation of pages on the American Holocaust and resistance. Consider: as a future or current educator in Native North America (or any other colonized land), why is it significant that we understand that every choice we make and every action we take is philosophically informed? The following outline of the basic building blocks traditionally associated with philosophy is designed to further challenge us to consider what it means to be educators in occupied places—that is, land that is held against the will of its original inhabitants. Another important interrelated consideration for educators is the colonization of Native and non-Native minds. We will begin with a brief discussion of what are considered to be the essential building blocks of any worldview or philosophy—epistemology, ontology, axiology, and metaphysics. When considering the following arguments, think about their relevance as they relate to teaching against white supremacy and capitalism—the two main enemies of Indigenous sovereignty.

After providing a foundation for understanding these basic tenets of philosophy, I provide a contextualized description of each of the philosophical traditions that play a significant role in the remainder of this book. I begin the discussion in pre-Columbian America and then take our discussion off to ancient Greece, because, for Western philosophy, that is where it all began, or so we are told. I then move into a discussion of the Enlightenment, followed by a brief account of the work of the German philosopher Hegel, and then into Marxism. Because I expand on Marxism and focus on neo-Marxists such as Gramsci in Chapters Three and Four, this section only includes the basics. I then turn to postmodernism, but again not in great detail as I return to this mode of analysis in Chapter Four, especially in regards to the Frankfurt School. Finally, I describe the major components of philosophy native to North America after Columbian contact.

o   *Epistemology:* The study of knowledge. What is knowable? How do we
      come to know? How is knowledge created? Is it static? Does it transcend
      time, history, and culture? Are knowledge and truth relative to situa-
      tions/circumstances? Are there universal truths that are qualitatively dis-
      tinct from situational truths? What is truth? What does it mean for
      something to be regarded as true? Do God(s) or spirit powers determine
      what is true? Is truth determined solely by empirical evidence? On what
      do we base our knowledge of the world?

            What pedagogical practices are most conducive to our understandings
      of how knowledge is created (Kincheloe, Slattery, & Steinberg, 2000)?

o   *Ontology:* On being and existence. What are the relationships that define
      the existence between entities? What is reality? What is the nature of
      identity? Descartes' famous "I think, therefore I am" exemplified Enlight-
      enment ontology.

            How should curriculums be organized in relation to each other (Kin-
      cheloe, Slattery, & Steinberg, 2000)?

o   *Axiology:* Typically divided into ethics and aesthetics and therefore
      concerned with notions of "beauty" and "good." For example, is beauty
      universally applied across contexts, or is it culturally specific? Debates sur-
      rounding ethics are typically viewed as axiological issues. Just think of the
      slogan and heated exchanges surrounding the notion of "family values."
      Manifestations of these concerns can be witnessed in questions such as:
      what is valued as beautiful art? What books should be censored, or should
      any books or ideas be withheld from public discourse, or from particular
      age groups (i.e., youth) in specific contexts (i.e., schools).

            What behavior, dispositions, attitudes, expressions, etc. are most con-
      ducive to learning and engaging with the specified curriculum (Kincheloe,
      Slattery, & Steinberg, 2000)?

o   *Metaphysics:* What does it mean to be in and of the world? What is the
      structure of the universe? What forces are at work in the universe? What
      is the ultimate nature of reality? For example, what is the relationship be-
      tween the spiritual world and the material world?

            What knowledge has the most worth and should therefore be in-
      cluded in the curriculum (Kincheloe, Slattery, & Steinberg, 2000)?

What follows is the final set of philosophical building blocks we will need to begin work on constructing our own approaches to curriculum and pedagogy. I begin this section with a summary of philosophy native to North America, which, because of its vast difference to Western traditions, should make those of us who are Westerners acutely aware of our own worldviews. I follow this section up with ancient Greece because these two traditions developed unaware of the concrete existence of the other. There might have been an awareness that something else exists, but no real knowledge of what that looked like in practice. I follow up these two initial sub-sections by roughly tracing the genealogy of Western philosophy post-1492 beginning with the Enlightenment, many of the thinkers of which were intimately aware of the existence of the philosophical traditions native to North America. For example, in "Perceptions of America's Native Democracies," Donald Grinde Jr. and Bruce Johansen (2001) underscore this point noting that the predominantly hegemonic, Enlightenment-based architects of the United States, such as Benjamin Franklin, Thomas Jefferson, and Thomas Paine, as well as counter-hegemonic revolutionaries like Karl Marx and Friedrick Engels, all drew on the example of Native Americans "to judge society's contemporary ills" (p. 85). The philosophical and material picture that emerges from this discussion is the history of hegemonic and counter-hegemonic schools of Western thought antagonistically related to one another representing the conflict between what we can crudely refer to as *the bosses* and those relegated to the status of *worker/slave*. As you read, think about the forces that have influenced your own ideas about learning and teaching, and how these discussions challenge or reinforce your own perspective.

Traditional Thinking

Philosophy in Native North America: Relational Since Time Immemorial

Semali and Kincheloe (1999b) in "What Is Indigenous Knowledge and Why Should We Study It?" offer a broad definition of Indigenous knowledge/philosophy underscoring what they understand to be the similarities between traditions from across the globe. While we are primarily concerned with the knowledges native to North America, beginning with a wide lens helps to situate our discussion in a larger context:

> The term, indigenous, and the concept of indigenous knowledge has often been associated in the Western context with the primitive, the wild, the natural. Such represen-

tations have evoked condescension from Western observers and elicited little appreciation for the insight and understanding indigeneity might provide. But for...indigenous peoples...indigenous knowledge is an everyday rationalization that rewards individuals who live in a given locality. In part, to these individuals, indigenous knowledge reflects the dynamic way in which the residents of an area have come to understand themselves in relationship to their natural environment and how they organize the folk knowledge of flora and fauna, cultural beliefs, and history to enhance their lives. (p. 3)

The philosophical traditions native to North America developed in their own concrete and theoretical contexts uninfluenced by the Western traditions described below. What follows is a summary of Indigenous philosophy in its theoretical and concrete contexts, as it existed before Columbian contact as described by scholars of native North America. In Chapter Three I explore the relational manifestations of Native and Western European immigrant philosophy as they have interacted and transformed one another in North America in both their concrete and theoretical contexts.

Summarizing what he perceives to be the most important similarities between not only Native North Americans, but between all Indigenous peoples, based on the definition of Indigenous as naturally originating from specific places, Ward Churchill (1995) argues:

The universe as a relational whole, a single interactive organism in which all things, all beings, are active and essential parts; the whole can never be understood without a knowledge of the function and meaning of each of the parts, while the parts cannot be understood other than in the context of the whole. The formation of knowledge is, in such a construct, entirely dependent upon the active maintenance of a fully symbiotic, relational—or, more appropriately, *inter*relational—approach to understanding. This fundamental appreciation of things, the predicate upon which a worldview is established, is common...to all American Indian cultural systems. (p. 312)

Central to this relational philosophy is the explanatory power of spirituality, which is viewed as just as much a part of the material world as the plants and animals that inhabit specific physical places. Frank Black Elk (1992) reiterates this point asserting that "everything in the universe is related within Lakota spirituality; everything is relational and can only be understood that way" (p. 148). If everything is connected/interrelated, then everything in the world is simultaneously and inseparably spiritual *and* physical. From this perspective the spiritual world and the material world are not two separate entities but are part of the same whole. While Indigenous epistemology values the use of human senses to study nature and observable phenomena as a key source of knowledge about the physical world, it also values knowledge obtained through intangible spiritual/sacred avenues, the source of power within matter, as important sources of information about material reality. Summarizing this relational/holistic position, Daniel Wildcat (2001a) notes:

> Human beings, in all our rich diversity, are intimately connected and related to, in fact dependent on, the other living beings, land, air, and water of the earth's biosphere. Our continued existence as part of the biology of the planet is inextricably bound up with the existence and welfare of the other living beings and places of the earth: being and places, understood as persons possessing power, not objects. Traditional American Indian cultural practices actively acknowledge and engage the power that permeates the many persons of the earth in places recognized as sacred not by human proclamation or declaration, but by experience in those places. (p. 13)

Vine Deloria's (2006) *The World We Used to Live In: Remembering the Powers of the Medicine Men* provides perhaps one of the most comprehensive accounts of Wildcat's (2001a) theoretical description of how the spiritual powers of traditional Native societies were (and are) derived from and dependent upon very specific physical places underscoring the relevance of spirituality as an important source of knowledge about geographical locations. Drawing attention to the very specific place-centered nature of Native spirituality, Frank Black Elk (1992) offers insight into such "spiritual traditions" as "born of and continued by such things as the geography from which they sprang; they are truly indigenous to certain areas and are the only forms of spirituality appropriate to those areas" (p. 138). The documented accounts of the ancient powers of the medicine men of yesteryear highlighted by Deloria (2006) serve to "...demonstrate to the present and coming generations [of Native Americans] the sense of humility, the reliance of the spirits, and the immense powers that characterized our people in the old days" (p. xx). Similarly, the philosophy of ancient Greece has served as an invaluable source of knowledge concerning the power of inquiry for countless generations of Westerners. However, while Native traditions are grounded in a relational, holistic conceptualization of the world, Western thought is based on the dichotomy between the material and spiritual worlds, that is, between science and religion.

Philosophy in Ancient Greece: The Dualism Between Science and Religion

Because it has long been noted that the archeology of Western philosophy can be traced to ancient Greece, it is worth noting that much of the Greek interest in philosophy and science can be traced to the Egyptian schools in which many of these scholars studied. Situating this analysis in a larger social-historical context of European white supremacy, Haroon Kharem (2004) notes:

> Western history...claims that Europe brought civilization to the "dark continent" of Africa. Most Western historians would agree that the first civilized Europeans were the Greeks, who created the knowledge they later passed on to the Romans...[However] Greek civilization was profoundly influenced by Afroasiatic civilizations and that this knowledge was (and to a great extent still is) deliberately obscured by unbridled Eurocentric racism. Such a perspective has consistently refused to acknowledge that the Greeks always recognized the Afroasiatic roots of their civilization and culture.... Africans from the Nile Valley freely gave the Greeks their knowledge. (p. 120)

Kharem's (2004) analysis and approach can be understood as part of a long legacy of African American resistance to the psychological trauma of white supremacy that can be traced back to the lives and works of African American freedom fighters such as Frederick Douglass and W.E.B. DuBois (Bernal, 2001). That is, highlighting the African roots of Greek civilization, touted by Europeans as the bedrock of civility, exposes the extent to which ruling classes and their supporters have gone to cover up the racial ideologies created to legitimize their own hegemonic barbarism (i.e., the enslavement of Africans). For example, many African as well as non-African abolitionists in the United States have been keen to note that bringing light to the African influences on ancient Greek civilization would expose the absurdity of the declaration put forth in the U.S. Constitution that an African is only three fifths of a human being. George G.M. James's *Stolen Legacy*, first published in 1954, despite its errors (Bernal, 2001), was designed to bring attention to the relationship between Egyptian and Greek traditions in an effort to boost the self-esteem of African Americans suffering from the deleterious effects of internalized oppression. Summarizing the African influence on Western philosophy, Crawford (1995) leaves no room for ambiguities, commenting, "...if the Western philosophical tradition is in any significant sense a series of footnotes to Plato, and if Plato was working within a tradition whose basic conceptual format was Egyptian, then the Western philosophical tradition is a series of footnotes to Egypt" (p. 138).

If one were searching for something of lasting importance to be proud of within this ancient Egyptian philosophical tradition, what could be more important than the dialectic? According to Martin Bernal (2001), "Plato's theory of ideas and moral dialectic were anticipated in Egypt by over a thousand years" (p. 390). For example, the late Senegalese scholar Cheikh Anta Diop, drawing on primary ancient Egyptian sources, made possible by his ability to read and translate hieroglyphic literature, writing through the 1950s until his death in 1986, noted that "there is no doubt that the theory of the dialectical movement due to the action of opposite couples (thesis, antithesis, synthesis) originates from the Hermopolitan cosmology, which explains all the phenomena of the universe by the action of the law of opposites" (quoted in Crawford, 1995, p. 137). David James (1995) provides a detailed description of what this dialectical movement looked like in practice through his analysis of a discussion between an Egyptian father, Any, and son, Khonshotep, on the nature of moral instruction written before or during the fourteenth century B.C. on papyrus. The banter begins with Any equating moral instruction with the taming of a wild animal (thesis) similar to Freire's (1999) critical description of the banking model of education (see Chapter Four). Khonshotep returns fire holding that only with reason and inward acceptance can one truly learn the virtues of morality (antithesis) alluding to an active rather than passive engagement with ideas. The debate continues, and the tension from which gives way to new understandings (synthesis). By highlighting the root source of this theoretical and philosophical framework, the dialectic, conceptualized more than a thousand years before the Socratic Method, James (1995) sheds considerable light on the broad and generous shoulders from which Greek philosophers stood.

These African and later Greek traditions, the dialectic in particular, were preserved by Islamic (black) Berbers (Moors) and used to bring Europe out of the Dark Ages after the Moors conquered Spain in 711 and ruled it and much of the region until 1492 (Kharem, 2004). The dialectic, as part of that African tradition, went on to influence the likes of Hegel and then Marx and Engels. The dialectic continues to inform critical philosophical heavy-hitters as you read these very words, as argued below. Again, what more needs to be said than the whole of European philosophical thought has roots in the dialectic, which existed for more than a thousand years in Africa before it eventually spread to Europe via Islamic intellectuals and their efforts in preserving ancient Greek, African, and Chinese philosophy, and subsequently creating new knowledges through these endeavors?

Beyond the dialectic and intertwined in complex and contradictory ways with its positive influences for social justice is a central tenet of Greek thought that has survived through the ages and has flourished in the current era, relevant for the purposes of this discussion, which can be understood as an elaborate discursive justification for those with wealth and power to maintain their privileged position against democratic peasants seeking the full rights of Greek citizenship. Greek aristocratic thinkers were interested, to lesser and greater extents, in formalizing elite rule through the uncertainty of science rather than through what they understood to be the certainty of myth or magic—hence, the genesis of the Western philosophical dichotomy between science and religion (Brosio, 2000; McNally, 2001). Their tools were scientific reasoning and theories of math and science, for example, and their place of departure was the quest for knowledge, assumed by Plato to be predetermined and knowable, but known, ironically, only to those who already know.

The self-identified primary concern of these ancient Athenians was with uncovering laws of pure thought through reason and scientific inquiry. According to David McNally (2001) in *Bodies of Meaning: Studies on Language, Labor, and Liberation,* in his critique of idealism as separating the mind from the body as a bourgeois discursive tactic to deny the existence of human suffering and exploitation, places its origins in ancient Greece noting that "...for Plato, the aristocratic male body is to be freed from the realm of sense experience itself, so as to enter the sphere of mathematical and formal reasoning, of knowledge uncontaminated by sensible contact with the things of the empirical world" (p. 11). It is therefore not surprising that Plato and other Greek philosophers, distrustful of the senses as a source of pure thought, were skeptical of natural science that relied quite heavily on sensual experience (Brosio, 2000).

Similarly, other thinkers, most notably Plato's mentor Socrates, were less concerned with science, and more interested in ethics and morality (the just, the true, and the good), that is, pure thought or philosophy. The source behind unjust and immoral actions, argued Socrates, was ignorance, an affliction many did not have the faculties to overcome, according to the powers that were. Those few and fortunate citizens conveniently born with the capacity to obtain knowledge, acquired through purely mental functions, were therefore deemed as natural leaders and decision makers possessing the cure for social ills, such as an unruly class of slave laborers. Such forms of circular logic provide justification for inequality, especially when the rulers decide who has been endowed with intelligence, and who has not. For Socrates, knowledge and truth were obtained through the dialectics of questioning and answering mediated by the reason and logic of the endowed sage—Socrates himself of course! Through this method of inquiry, reasoned Socrates, false claims would be exposed, such as slaves should be afforded the full democratic rights of citizenship, giving way to wisdom and *man's* "true" hierarchical nature.

The educational goal of the Socratic Method was to develop the mind of *man* in the ability to reason and achieve truth through the dialectical engagement between pupil and teacher. The ideal world of thought was the object of desire, which gave way to what is known as idealism, which is based on the assumption that truth and knowledge exist in the realm of the mind, largely ignoring the body and material reality. In effect, language and the mind came to represent everything of value, and the body, the realm of the majority of the population, constituted nothing but brute force to be controlled by those endowed with the capacity to reason and achieve true knowledge.

In Western philosophical lore the place of the ancient Athenians is traditionally painted as a beacon of democratic utopianism and a bastion of intellectual discourse and thought. However, for five sixths of the people who lived within the cities of Greece, such as women and slaves, daily reality could not be further from the truth. Greek society was largely based on the ideas of one of Socrates' most famous students, Plato, who argued that intelligence is naturally unequally distributed. Plato used the metaphor of metals to describe the innate ranking of *men* where gold people were deemed superior, silver humans civilized, but not ideally intelligent, and those of brass quality representing barbarians who possessed nothing of value but brute force, which needed to be externally commanded by those more ideally endowed. In short, what was put forth was the hierarchy of metals, which would carry over into Christianity and provide the philosophical underpinnings needed to commit acts of genocide a desperate and declining (and religiously fundamentalist) Europe was ripe for. Platonic epistemology is therefore based on the assumption that human intelligence is naturally rank-able serving as a justification for the division of labor and the exclusion of large segments of the population from democratic participation. Underscoring this Platonic epistemology that assumes those relegated to the status of worker are intellectually inferior therefore rationalizing the division of labor, Marx (1867/1967) notes, "With

Plato, division of labour within the community is a development from the multifarious requirements, and the limited capacities of individuals. The main point with him is, that the labourer must adapt himself to the work, not the work to the labourer" (p. 365).

However, those who did receive the democratic rights of citizenship in Greek society enjoyed great democratic freedoms based on Aristotle's *Politics*, which was informed by the understanding that a true democracy should be fully participatory as the most logical path to achieve the common good. To reach these ends it was assumed that a relatively equal distribution of power had to be maintained among citizens so they could operate as equals, which translated into opposition against practices that lead to the emergence of a class of super rich *men* and the vast majority left in the misery of poverty. Aristotle was also keen to warn that if a small wealthy ruling class did emerge, the majority, overtaken by their barbaric tendencies, would use their democratic rights to redistribute the wealth. To prevent such atrocities Aristotle suggested either reducing poverty or limiting democracy, and to his credit, privileging the former over the latter (Chomsky, 2001, p. 6).

"Western" Traditions (and Native Thought Post-1492)

The Enlightenment

> Many Eurocentric historians portray the Dark Ages as an exceptionally barbaric period of human existence. This notion, however, is an ethnocentric one that arises from historians who claim that Europe was the only civilized part of the world. The Dark Ages were dark for Europe, but not all human civilization was thrown into this period of turmoil and savage brutality brought about by a supposedly superior civilized region of the world. In fact, at the time European rulers were preoccupied with religious tyranny, wars among themselves, [and] keeping the masses in utter poverty...the Moors brought Islamic civilization and culture to Europe and essentially ended the Dark Ages. (Kharem, 2004, pp. 120–121)

Kharem situates the period in Europe after the Dark Ages, the Renaissance, in a context unfamiliar to those of us *miseducated* in North American Eurocentric schools. While the Islamic-inspired Renaissance occurred roughly fifteen centuries before the Enlightenment, it arguably paved the way for the Enlightenment by (re)-introducing the ancient African, Phoenician, and Greek foundations of science, reason, and philosophy into the European context. Eurocentric history, on the other hand, portrays both the Renaissance and the Enlightenment as emerging from strictly European sources avoiding the determining role non-Europeans have played in curbing a most intransigent European barbarism. Such insights are especially unsettling for those of us reared in the Islamaphobic context of the West.

For example, Ibrahim Abukhattala (2004) in "The New Bogeyman Under the Bed: Image Formation of Islam in the Western School Curriculum and Media" documents with compelling precision the way in which Islam has replaced communism as the new enemy of the West. Abukhattala (2004), as well as Steinberg (2004) in the same volume and Steinberg (2007), document the negative, essentialist portrayal of Islam in Western, dominant-society media as sexist, backward, irrational, primitive, grossly superstitious, enslaving of the human spirit, fundamentalist, and altogether uncivilized perpetuating a public pedagogy conducive to the West's seemingly perpetual war against the oil-rich countries of the Middle East. Unfortunately, however, the misrepresentation of Islam in the West is not confined to the media alone.

Abukhattala (2004), for example, documents the ways in which the official curriculum of the West's public schooling contributes "...to the perpetuation of fundamental misconceptions about Islam as a religion, culture, and civilization" (p. 164). Connecting this discussion back to the Enlightenment, Abukhattala (2004) notes that "even Islamic contributions to world civilization are either briefly discussed or totally overlooked" (p. 164) in the history textbooks that dominate Western institutions of education from kindergarten through university. The result of this miseducation is not only the creation of a Western populace easily persuaded to go to war and commit unspeakable atrocities against Islamic nations, but it is damaging to the self-esteem of Muslim immigrants exposed to the resulting lies, distortions, and omissions who come from countries that tend to provide a more balanced view of the world's religions and the ancient sources of philosophy and science (Abukhattala, 2004).

Like the section above drawing attention to the African roots of Greek philosophy, here too we are challenged to consider the Islamic contributions to the European Enlightenment. The Enlightenment, from its inception, began in the direction Aristotle's Phoenician-influenced ideas were pointing towards—that is, greater democratic rule and the struggle against ones labor power being externally controlled. Again, this Greek inspiration should be understood as largely existing through other influences, such as Islam. Muslim scholars were responsible for preserving ancient Greek thought, combining them with Chinese and Egyptian traditions as argued above. For example, Wilson (1993) notes Islam's influence on the Enlightenment noting:

> A general impression of Islam's freedom from any authoritative priesthood or even dogma had percolated into European culture, or would soon do so. A long line of European intellectual Islamophiles began to appear...which influenced the Enlightenment... (Wilson, 1993, p. 20)

For example, in *Radical Enlightenment,* Jonathon Israel (2002) notes that "...the most striking example of the ideological deployment of Islam, and the life of Mohammed, in the European Early Enlightenment" (p. 571) can be found within the French radical Henri de Boulainvilliers's *La Vie de Mahomed,* which remained unfinished at the time of his death in 1722. Within the text Boulainvilliers's favorable treatment of Mohammed lies in stark contrast to accepted Christian conceptions of the prophet and Islam more generally. Israel (2002) summarizes Boulainvilliers's portrayal of Mohammed as "...a true prophet and philosopher...[who] emerges as a great teacher of man, the power and grandeur of [his] thought [is] characterized by its rationality and freedom from superstition and 'mysteries'" (p. 572). In his final analysis, comparing Christianity with Islam, Israel (2002) argues that Boulainvilliers held that "...no other religious doctrine would seem to conform so completely to the light of reason as that founded by Mohammed" (p. 572). In general, while not all Enlightenment thinkers possessed equally positive analyses and attitudes of Islam as Boulainvilliers, as argued by Israel (2006) in *Enlightenment Contested,*

> ...Traditional antipathy yielded in radical texts to an image of Islam as a pure monotheism of high moral caliber which was also a revolutionary force for positive change and one which from the outset proved to be both more rational and less bound to the miraculous than Christianity or Judaism. (p. 616)

As suggested above, it was the Islamic Berber's occupation of Spain until 1492 that brought philosophy and thus reason to the dark barbaric continent of Europe. However, from this punk rockers' perspective, one of the more intriguing mediums through which Islam, and as a result the ancient Greek materialism of Aristotle, reached European Enlightenment thinkers were "Renegadoes," that is, former European Christian maritime workers who converted to Islam because of its more democratic tendencies and/or employing the logic "the enemy of my enemy must be my friend." Other European maritime workers, men who had been commissioned by the emerging nation states of the French, Dutch, and English to engage in acts of piracy against the Spanish, eventually turned their piracy skills against the ruling classes who had employed their services. Both pirates and Islam-converts, that is, *Renagadoes*, and the *real* pirates of the Caribbean, were engaging in acts of resistance against a Europe who placed them on the bottom rung of the social hierarchy and had therefore been treated as less than human experiencing conditions on merchant vessels far more savage and barbaric than even the early English factories of the Industrial Revolution. Hakim Bey (2003) sheds light on this early influence of the Enlightenment, noting these pirates, informed by the conditions they were subjected to and the emancipatory messages of Islam, developed a profound sense of respect for human rights and dignity:

> Fleeing from hideous "benefits" of Imperialism such as slavery, serfdom, racism and intolerance, from the tortures of impressments and the living death of the plantations, the Buccaneers adopted Indian ways, intermarried with Caribs, accepted blacks and Spaniards as equals, rejected all nationality, elected their captains democratically, and reverted to the "state of Nature." Having declared themselves "at war with all the world," they sailed forth to plunder under mutual contracts called "articles," which were so egalitarian that every member received a full share and the Captain usually only 1¼ or 1½ shares. Flogging and punishments were forbidden—quarrels were settled by vote or by the code duello. It is simply wrong to brand the pirates as mere sea-going highwaymen or even proto-capitalists. (p. 116)

The raiding parties they launched against the merchant ships transporting cargo between the so-called *old* and *new* worlds were so successful that they spawned an imperial crisis nearly crippling the emerging system of value production based on slavery, war, and outright thievery. The renegade pirates who engaged in this form of resistance and the ways in which they understood themselves in the world, it has been argued (Rediker & Linebaugh, 1993), helped lay the groundwork for the Enlightenment, the architects of which sought to be the "spokesmen for the revolutionary bourgeoisie of eighteenth century Europe..." (Eagleton, 1991, p. 64), informing anarchist and socialist traditions, for example. The foundation for such movements rests in the notion that ideas rather than emerging from innate or transcendental sources have roots in the certainty of material reality, which can be brought into view through scientific reason, the scientific study of ideas, coined ideology. Summarizing the Enlightenment through the changing concept of ideology, Terry Eagleton (1991) argues that

Ideology in our time has sometimes been sharply counterposed to science; so it is ironic to recall that ideology began life precisely as a science, as a rational enquiry into the laws governing the formation and development of ideas. Its roots lie deep in the Enlightenment dream of a world entirely transparent to reason, free of the prejudice, superstition and obscurantism of the ancient regime. To be an 'ideologist' – a clinical analyst of the nature of consciousness – was to be a critic of 'ideology' – in the sense of the dogmatic, irrational belief systems of traditional societies. (p. 64)

The Enlightenment project did emerge, as Eagleton (1991) suggests, as a counter-philosophy and practice against the mystic certainty of the old European monarchs and papal that relied on a religious doctrine with roots in Athenian idealism based on the dichotomy between the spiritual or intellectual, the realm of the rulers, and the material or physical, the realm of the bewildered herd, the untamed wilderness, the unruly throng. Enlightenment thinkers argued that truth and wisdom are not divinely determined and bestowed by the will of God to a select few whose purpose is to rule the less-fortunate masses, but can be known through scientific analysis and reason. What follows is therefore the notion that people, trained to think scientifically and act democratically, can control their own labor power and create a democratic society for the common good. Again, Islamic thinkers, many of whom were seemingly addicted to Aristotle (Israel, 2006), played no small role in bringing these messages to a reeling Europe strung out on mysticism and lashing out in an endless cycle of persecutions.

The Aristotelian notion that the democratic imperative (Brosio, 2000) is dramatically hindered by the existence of concentrated wealth assumed a central role in the works of prominent Enlightenment thinkers such as Thomas Jefferson, David Hume, and Adam Smith (Chomsky, 2001) writing in an England overcome with the barbarism of poverty, disregard for humanity, and the social chaos of a nascent capitalism (see Chapter Three for more discussion of Enlightenment thinkers). The Enlightenment project of reason and science in the reductive search for order, to be sure, had at its core concerns with overcoming the tyranny of a European ruling class consisting of Christian and noble officialdom whose mountain of corpses left in its wake made the bloodshed committed in the name of Islam so insignificant that it rendered it virtually unnoticeable in comparison (Israel, 2006).

Enlightenment-informed thinkers in the U.S. have tended to be less concerned with place than their European counterparts. While U.S. Enlightenment-based educational philosophers, such as John Dewey, rejected the tendency within Western philosophy to dichotomize the material and cognitive worlds because humans are part of both, they avoided the issue of dichotomizing the spiritual and material worlds by denying the former's existence, as was customary in the Enlightenment generally. Summarizing this popular position, Brosio (2000) argues that Dewey "...rejected the religious and philosophical claims based on transcendent guarantees of truth and rightness, arguing instead that knowledge could emerge only from the application of the scientific method to problematic situations" (p. 124). By claiming that the spiritual is not a part of the material, and thus not a source of knowledge about the physical, Dewey falls victim to the either/or philosophy he laments.

In other words, using Dewey's logic, we would argue that just because religious doctrine has been used to distort peoples' understanding about the physical world, does not mean spiritual knowledge cannot teach us anything about the world and humans' relationship in it beyond how it gives us false consciousness. To deny the relevance of spirituality is to deny one of the foundations of Indigenous philosophy, and that which connects Native people to their lands, that is, their places of origin. Consequently, Enlightenment thought does well to challenge Western hegemony, but can be theoretically strengthened by Indigenous knowledge. This issue will be taken up and further explored in Chapter Three.

Hegelian Dialectics and Idealism

With Hegel we see a return to Greek dialectics and the notion of achieving knowledge of absolute truth as the manifestation of the unhindered human spirit (idealism). In other words, truth is assumed to exist in the realm of pure thought unhindered by the sensual experience of the material world. Hegel achieved this by replacing that which is concrete with the idea of it, discursively transforming that which is finite into the infinite. Summarizing this inversion in Hegel's thought, Marx (1843/1978) notes how he "...gives the predicates an independent existence and subsequently transforms them in a mystical fashion into their subjects" (p. 18).

Unlike Aristotle who believed that knowledge and thus reality had to be separated and categorized to be fully comprehended, Hegel, influenced by the Socratic dialectical method of inquiry, argued that everything was in fact related and true understanding comes from comprehending reality in its entirety. Hegel argued that the absolute truth could be achieved by the enlightened mind through the dialectical process of thesis, which represents a position put forth for argument; then a counter-argument, the antithesis, is presented; what then develops is a new idea, the product of the interaction of the original two, the synthesis. The synthesis then becomes the new thesis, and the cycle repeats itself. This crude explanation of the dialectic is not meant to represent a mechanical process but is intended to demonstrate the dynamic relationship between ideas. This historical process/engagement was thought to develop infinitely until the absolute idea emerged. Hegel held that the ultimate and absolute idea or philosophical tradition was embodied within the Prussian state, representing the will of the people. For Hegel the state was the most evolving reality of history and the ultimate manifestation of the idea, and thus the producer of history itself. Within this reasoning, a person's capacity to be socialized is a civilizing process whereby men and women are expected to bend to the will of the state, for it is the state that represents the final synthesis and thus the end of history (Torres, 1998).

If we were to except Hegel's idealism, then we would stand on the notion that it is just ideas that prevent *men* from achieving absolute truth and their full potential, and therefore the struggle against oppression exclusively exists at the level of discourse. Marx and Engels (1932/1996), critiquing this idealism, comment that the "phrases" Hegelians fight "...are only opposing other phrases, and that they are in no way combating the real existing world when they are merely combating the phrases of this world" (p. 41).

Marx's New Paradigm: Dialectical Materialism

Informed by not only ancient Greek dialectical thinkers like Aristotle and Heraclitus; the materialist focus on history and development of the Enlightenment embodied in the works of Adam Smith, David Hume, and John Locke, for example; as well as Hegel's dialectics of historical development; but also the material conditions engendered by the barbarism of a nascent industrial capitalism, Marx's philosophical contributions to Western traditions are numerous including dialectical/historical materialism (roughly outlined below). Marx's contributions to theory and practice have been so immense and hopeful that they have informed, in one way or another, every revolution and every revolutionary movement of the twentieth century from Russia, China, Cuba, Nicaragua, El Salvador, England, the United States, and the Congo, to name just a few hotbeds of Marxist-informed activity, some more progressive/democratic than others. Karl Marx is therefore one of the most well known figures throughout the world, and perhaps one of the most misunderstood, for he has been demonized by the world's ruling classes as the devil incarnate himself. Reflecting on the rejection of Marx's class analysis in colleges of education, world-renowned Marxist teacher educators Peter McLaren and Ramin Farahmandpur (2005) comment on how Marxism tends to be "dismissed...as a form of ideological Neanderthalism or as a crusted-over antediluvian memory..." (p. 19) and "to identify your politics as Marxist is to invite derision and ridicule from many quarters, including some on the left" (McLaren, 2002, p. 36). In Chapter Four, I return to these critiques, which predominantly come from postmodernists, and highlight some of the more intriguing rebuttals by Marxist educators as they pertain to educating against occupation. First, however, we need to develop a rudimentary understanding of how Western philosophy (and the world, discussed in Chapter Three) was transformed by the vast body of Marx's work. What follows is therefore a summary of Marx's philosophical contributions to Western traditions.

Marx embraced Hegel's developmental notion of dialectics (although replacing his idealism with materialism) because it went beyond the common linear cause-and-effect mode of analysis by considering the inter-contradictions within thought and the interrelatedness and tension between all that is charging social annalists with fomenting misunderstanding when they studied and discussed phenomena as if they exist in isolation disconnected from the larger totality in which they are naturally situated. From this perspective everything is a contradiction and embodies its own negation. For Marx, capitalism can therefore only be understood as always in a particular stage of its own development, and thus historically contextualized. Capitalism, like feudalism and slavery before it, embodies the contradictions within it that ultimately lead to its own negation. That is, as the engineers of capitalism strive to achieve ever-higher levels of profit, externalizing the costs to the working class and the public more generally, while the promises of industrial progress seem increasingly unlikely, the challenge of the dominant class to freeze the historical development of the relations of production within the current structure becomes increasingly difficult. In this light, capitalism is clearly not an abstract ahistorical concept, but defines a particular set of contradictions that exist as relationships between people and the natural environment that develop as a result of the interaction between opposing interests—the proletariat and the bourgeoisie.

The history of capitalism can therefore be understood as the development of the class struggle through time, each part of the dichotomy vying for an upper hand. The capitalists' main interest can be understood as embodied in the desire to maintain the labor/capital relationship, the source of *his* wealth/profit/capital, and labor's interests as embodied in abolishing capitalism—a relationship for which only a small numerical minority of the population benefit economically. Contrary to popular belief that has tended to describe Marxism as a dogmatic formula predicting the natural unfolding of human affairs according to rigid economic laws of development, Marx's work acknowledges the unpredictability of the outcome between competing forces that exist within specific modes of production in particular historical periods. While there are historical tendencies, in other words, there are few certainties.

Marx's dialectical place of departure was thus the human being (referred to as *man*, which we can use interchangeably with woman as a gender-neutral referent). Hegel, on the other hand, began with the state, which citizens were expected to accommodate themselves to because the Prussian state was believed to represent the ultimate manifestation of the highest form of human thought, critiqued by Marx as an abstraction disconnected from the material conditions of the sensual world. For Marx, on the other hand, the state existed *for* man, and should therefore be analyzed from a human-centered perspective, as demonstrated above. Critical of the ruling class interests served by the hierarchical tendencies of the state and its indoctrinating functions needed to manufacture consent, Marx advocated for a more horizontally structured communism/socialism where revolutionary proletariats can develop as individuals in communion with one another working toward common interests of survival and culture governed by the simple principle "from each according to his ability, to each according to his needs" (Foster, 1996, p. 26). Human labor power for Marx, unhindered by the alienating nature of the labor/capital relationship, represents the creative expression of human needs and powers, suppressed in a class society. Marx's humanism is therefore concerned primarily with the development of the full woman.

Marx sought out to build a relational philosophy geared towards facilitating the development of a holistic global epistemology designed to not only understand the world, but more importantly, to transform it. That is, Marx set out to connect the realm of the mind with the realm of material existence. In the process, Marx theorized the question of religion/spirituality out of existence by denying its relevance as a source of knowledge about material conditions. It is therefore not surprising that scholars making a case against the relevance of Marx's work have equated it with religion, and its adherents as seduced by its emotional appeal, and ultimately falling victim to an irrational blind faith (Foster, 1996). Marx referred to religion as the opium of the people, which is typically, and incorrectly, interpreted as something that is given to the oppressed by the bosses to keep them passive and misinformed about the true nature of the world. However, after witnessing the utterly barbaric conditions workers lived in under the industrializing capitalism of England, Marx saw religion being used as a drug by poor people to help ease the suffering they experienced as fodder in the process of value production. Marx therefore saw religion not as something given to the oppressed, but taken by the exploited to ease the pain and suffering of their mental and physical existence. According to Marx (1844/1978), "religious suffering is at the same time an *expression* of real suffering and a *protest* against real suffering. Religion is the sigh of the oppressed creature, the sentiment of a heartless world, and the soul of soulless conditions. It is the opium of the people" (p. 54).

As a result of his rejection of religion, however sympathetic he was to those who sought its refuge, Marx avoided reconciling the ancient science/religion dichotomy in Western thought by explaining away religion as a barrier to critical consciousness, thwarting the revolutionary energy of the proletariat. To his credit, however, Marx's rejection of spirituality and religion as a valuable source of knowledge can be understood as a logical conclusion given the real bankruptcy of European metaphysics. Commenting on this subject matter Friedrich Nietzsche in *Beyond Good and Evil* observes that "we northerners are undoubtedly descended from barbarian races, also in respect to our talent for religion: we have little talent for it" (quoted in Abu-Jamal, 1997, p. 34). Countless Native American observers have come to similar conclusions in their analysis of the all-too-frequent theft of Indigenous spiritual traditions by those of European ancestry.

Postmodernism: Critiquing the Enlightenment

The origins of postmodernism can be traced to German critical thinkers of the Frankfurt School, whose most influential and well-known place of departure can arguably be traced to the Italian neo-Marxist Antonio Gramsci. Adorno, Marcuse, and others were skeptical of the Enlightenment's promises of human progress and social justice as the natural result of reason and the scientific method due to their general sense of hopelessness and cynicism engendered by the working class' support of Nazism, fascism, and WWII, all of which relied heavily on the grand narratives of science and a rhetoric of social progress and the common good. Informing their skepticism was what they interpreted to be the use of the concept and scientific method of "reason" for not only good but evil as well. Summarizing the critiques of modernism that animated the post-WWII minds of the Frankfurt School scholars, Brosio (2000) observes, "They realized that the Enlightenment's championing of reason included a dichotomy that threatened its stability. They worried about how 'objectivist' science could be guided by 'subjectivist' moral claims" (p. 97). Postmodern scholars have concluded that because of the inherent subjectivity of human thought, objectivity is an impossible objective. What is more, postmodern critics have accused the creators of the notion of objectivity of having more sinister intentions than naively striving for the unattainable, that is, they claim it has historically served to disguise the subjectivity of the white, male, Christian, moneyed interests of science. In other words, by claiming to hold the keys that unlock true understanding of the social totality in the form of what has been dubbed "grand narratives" or "meta-narratives," such as Marxism, social scientists create an exclusionary discourse that does not value the multiple voices of, and the many ways oppression is experienced by, not only white working class men and women, but the many tribal communities native to North America, those of African descent and all peoples not included in current conceptualizations of whiteness.

The postmodern rejection of grand narratives has resulted in contributions to critical theory and educational practice even the world's leading Marxist educators have embraced. Summarizing postmodernism's advancements from a Marxist perspective, Peter McLaren and Ramin Farahmandpur (2005) offer the following analysis:

> ...Postmodern theory has made a significant contribution in helping educators grasp the politics that underwrite popular cultural formations, mass-media apparatuses, the technological revolution's involvement in the global restructuring of capitalism, the ideological machinations of the new capitalism from Schumpeter to Keynes, and the reconceptualization of schooling practices in the interests of making them more related to (racial, gender, sexual, and national) identity formation within postcolonial geopolitical and cultural spaces. (p. 17)

In practice postmodernism has manifested itself in identity politics and is often associated with feminism. The emergence of identity politics has resulted in a fractured left more concerned with our gendered and racialized differences, for example, than with creating broad coalitions around similar class-based interests. Marxist commentators have therefore charged postmodern politics with being debilitating. The generally agreed upon solution by humanist Marxists is to build a broad-based movement against the labor/capital relationship informed by an anti-racist/anti-homophobia/anti-sexist pedagogy that can unite those who depend on a wage to survive while respecting and finding strength and vision within the many voices of the world's oppressed peoples (Hill, McLaren, Cole & Rikowski, 2002).

Supporting their theory with a material referent, postmodern annalists describe the contemporary social universe as characterized by the postmodern condition or postmodernity. Joe Kincheloe (2001) offers perhaps one of the most comprehensive descriptions of the phenomena known as the postmodern condition. In his description of the contemporary social universe Kincheloe (2001) includes: "the increased importance of the sign...; an exaggeration of the power of those who hold power...; the fragmentation of meaning...; the growth of cynicism in a climate of deceit; the celebration of surface meanings...; the substitution of fascination for analysis...; the reorganization of capital/economic power in a global context...; [and] the change of change: everything is different or at least it feels that way" (p. 62). The picture Kincheloe paints of the world is one where people are simultaneously more connected, through technology, and less connected due to the superficiality of public knowledge and discourse permeating our social universe. What emerges is an image of the world dominated by a socially unjust civic subjectivity fueled by the seeming neutrality of scientific reason that has given birth to technological innovations such as the Internet and satellite television saturating our lives with information—information that hides behind a false sense of objectivity concealing the gendered, racialized, classed, and colonizing interests it ultimately serves. The antagonism within Western traditions, as well as the tension between Western and Indigenous philosophy, is explored in Chapter Three. However, before we move on to that study, we will consider the implications of the content presented thus far for us as educators and the creation of our own approaches to teaching and learning. First, we will briefly reflect on the impact Columbian pedagogy has had on Indigenous philosophy, as alluded to above in our discussion on the complex and contradictory nature of Native resistance.

Native Philosophy Since Predator Came

In terms of education, the thievery began in 1611 when French Jesuits opened the first mission schools expressly aimed at educating Indian children [as the French]. Not to be outdone, Spanish and British missionaries soon followed, developing full-service educational systems intent on "de-Indianizing" Native children. By the mid-eighteenth century Harvard University (1936), the College of William and Mary (1693), and Dartmouth College (1769) had all been established with the charge of "civilizing" and "Christianizing" Indians as an inherent part of their institutional missions. The American school was therefore a well-established weapon in the arsenal of American imperialism long before the first shots of the Revolutionary War were ever fired. (Grande, 2004, p. 11)

What have been the long-term implications of this four hundred year-long educational attack on Native philosophical traditions? When searching for evidence to answer this question, we find two distinct issues that need to be understood dialectically, that is, as they relate to one another. The two interconnected issues are Native philosophy and the philosophy of Native people. On one hand, you have the pre-Columbian Indigenous Philosophy communally in practice. On the other hand, you have the Native person so completely assimilated into the settler-community society that he himself, or she herself, philosophically, is a Westerner. These are the two opposite ends of a continuum with every possible combination in between as representing the social reality that has developed as a result of the antagonistic relationship between the oppressor and the oppressed. However, this analysis is not sufficient. What we must isolate are tendencies within the continuum.

First and foremost, this forced assimilation has been successful at gaining access to Native lands. If philosophy defines the relationship between specific human groups to specific masses of land, then transforming peoples' relationship to land is not just a physical endeavor, but is a philosophical one as well. Education as indoctrination has therefore been the place of concentration for such mind work. It is therefore not surprising that Native scholars have overwhelmingly focused on cultural and spiritual rejuvenation as the primary goal of Indian education rejecting theory, according to Grande (2004), as "definitively Eurocentric." Grande (2004) summarizes her analysis noting that "American Indian scholars have largely resisted engagement with critical educational theory, concentrating instead on the production of historical monographs, ethnographic studies, tribally centered curriculums, and site-based research" (p. 1). While stressing the importance of this work, Grande (2004) argues that the rejection of theory has limited Native resistance because it can serve as a way of building broad-based coalitions and as a tool to resist the "global encroachment" on "indigenous communities" (p. 2), and in so contribute to the rebirth of North American critical pedagogy. Part of this process has been major Native Relocations during the 1950s. The result has been urban and reservation Indians often engaged antagonistically and conflicted with one another, manifesting itself in gunfights, as was the case during the early AIM days on the Rosebud Sioux Reservation in South Dakota, as described above. The attack on philosophy has made it difficult for Native peoples to come together and fight for their common interests and create broad-based coalitions between Native peoples and between Natives and non-Natives. The situation has made it confusing for the settler-community Left to know who to stand with in solidarity when both "sides" are represented by hegemonic and counter-hegemonic figures and positions. Andrea Smith in *Conquered* (2005) focuses on the psychological implications of these processes for native peoples noting the problem of the internalization of self-hatred.

These issues will be further explored throughout the remainder of this book focusing on the deleterious effects of white supremacy and those whose identity it is most centrally based, that is, white people. For now, however, let us reflect on the discussions we have been presented with thus far.

Building Educational Philosophy:
An Individual and Collective Endeavor

The focus of discussion thus far has been designed to get you, the reader, interested in and thinking about the relationship between the theoretical contexts of philosophy situated in the concrete context of Native North America. This dynamic is not to be taken lightly as it often is in today's anti-intellectual environment. In other words, in the current sociopolitical context the ancient Western dichotomy between the mind (philosophy/theory) and the body (humans teaching and learning in physical places) is alive and well as if the two are completely unrelated and therefore have no business being in the same place (classrooms on Native land) at the same time (during class). Following Indigenous *and* critical traditions, theory and practice are *only* relevant when they are in the same place at the same time informing each other in a never ending process of reflection and action.

Creating philosophy to form educational practice is at the same time an individual and collective endeavor because education is part of creating and re-creating societies/communities while the act of teaching is a very personal and thus intimate undertaking. Teaching for social justice tends to manifest itself as a complex and contradictory tension-filled endeavor highlighted by competing interests. The challenge of progressive education is therefore to connect the personal interests of educators and the collective goals of schooling to the common interests of marginalized communities. Again, this process is not to be taken lightly. As previously mentioned, every decision we make as educators, pedagogically and curricularly, is philosophical in nature. For those of us interested in the inherently political nature of education, it therefore makes sense, when engaged in the preparation of teaching and learning, to begin with philosophy. There are two components to educational philosophy that we will concern ourselves with here—theory and practice. The first component of philosophy that is relevant to our current endeavor is the theory of the particular tradition(s) under consideration. For example, the first step in becoming a particular *kind* of educator, let's say Marxist, is deciding that *that* is what we want to become, which requires some form of motivation or inspiration (preferably in the form of a rudimentary understanding of the central concepts of the theory giving way to new, empowering readings of the world, rather than romanticized conceptualizations that betray the spirit and essence of a given text).

The next step is to learn the theory, which can take many years of research, study, discussion, and successful and failed attempts to teach from that particular perspective; hence, the second, interrelated, component of becoming a (fill-in-the-blank) educator is practice. In other words, knowing a specific theory is one thing, but putting it into practice is quite another. Chapters Three and Four not only expand on the theories discussed thus far, but they further situate them in the concrete context in which they have drawn and continue to draw breath. These chapters should therefore not only contribute to your theoretical understanding of the philosophies in question, but they should also help you understand what they could look like for you in practice based on what they have looked like in practice for others.

This book is therefore designed to introduce the novice philosopher to different *kinds* of philosophies, and therefore different *kinds* of educators. However, because this book takes an unmovable stance against genocide and oppression and human suffering generally, I privilege those Western traditions most conducive to counter-hegemonic praxis, and Marx's scientific analysis of capitalist society offers the most comprehensive account of its inter-most workings, a necessary component of informed action. While native scholars, especially those actively engaged in the politics and practice of land reclamation, do tend to agree with Marx's description of capitalism, they extend his mode of relational analysis challenging the Western dichotomy between the spiritual world and the material world thereby adding a layer of complexity to

European conceptions of land. In practice this has translated into a difference in objectives.

For example, it has been argued that Marxists are concerned with seizing control of state power where Native traditionalists want to abolish the occupying government. Churchill (2002) summarizes this difference in objectives arguing that the goal of Marxist revolution is to create a state apparatus whereas those seeking to "...free themselves from the yoke of settler-state oppression" represents Indigeneity which include "certain segments of the European population" (p. 372), namely, Ireland, Wales, and parts of Spain and France (the Basques), and of course the Americas, large portions of Africa, New Zealand, Australia, Palestine, East Timor, the Philippines, and Tibet, for example. The goal of Indigenous resistance, from this perspective, is therefore to expel alien occupation and rebuild societies (Churchill, 2002) dealing with the concrete conditions of the capitalist present careful not to romanticize the past and therefore falling victim to whitestream conceptions of Indigeneity (Grande, 2004).

However, both paths seem to share common goals: the disempowerment and disillusionment of the existing regime and the abolishment of the capitalist relations of production. Is there room for collaboration? Can the subordinate classes of the settler-community conceive of a way to liberate themselves from the grip of their own ruling class (the same ruling class that has exploited the labor power of the settler-community in not only putting them to work in production, but as slaughterers and wealth extractors of everyone from American Indians to Iraqis) without continuing to deny Native Americans their Native American ancestral lands? Or, will a liberated settler-community working class continue to occupy 98% of Native land? If bona fide collaboration is something worth pursuing, how might educational practice serve those ends? In other words, how could these collaborations translate into our educational philosophies—the theoretical frameworks that we consciously draw on to inform the curricular and pedagogical choices we make as educators? These questions will be both directly and indirectly addressed throughout the remainder of this book.

As we move into Chapter Three, let us keep in mind the psychological implications of the unprecedented loss and trauma outlined above on Native peoples in the twenty-first century. The feelings engendered by such monumental world-altering experiences are unfortunately not unique to those native to North America as noted above. There seems to be a tendency embodied

within a collective sentiment of great loss and a yearning to transform the
bankruptcy of the contemporary moment. Grande (2004), Vizenor (1990),
and many others, while embracing change, caution Natives and non-Natives
alike against romanticizing the past. There is also a tendency among white "do-
gooders" to position themselves as "white saviors," which should also be
adamantly resisted as just another manifestation of white supremacy. The
following lyric, from the song "Laura," sung by Dave King (Flogging Molly,
2006), who came of age during the 1970s in the heart of Dublin's most run-
down slums and the center of the IRA's (the Irish Republican Army) recruiting and training grounds against "settler-state oppression," captures a common
sentiment echoed by colonized peoples the world over:

> Feel the words from my lips
> To your harsh finger tips
> Then you know where I come from
> Cause I know, yes I know
> Everything there is to know
> Cause I have lost everything I had
> See, I could have danced on the sun
> But meh world came undone

Reflecting on his IRA-informed background, King (Flogging Molly, 2006) has
commented that music, and ultimately Flogging Molly, became *his* IRA. The
power and the passion within not only King's but the many voices that give
birth to these kinds of heart-wrenching words every day continues to find its
strength in the deep sense of injustice stemming from the loss of one's land,
people, and way of life, as well as from the power of hope derived from
remembering, unromantically, how it was, and therefore how it could be (i.e.,
life after capitalism, colonialism, and white supremacy). With this insight in
mind (the existence of collective mourning and resistance), let us now consider
more intensely the antagonistic relationship between Western philosophy and
the traditions native to North America and paths toward collaboration and
coalition building. The indigenous philosophers, scholars, and musicians
outlined thus far, and in Chapter Three, speak with such an intense conviction
that *that* emotion itself talks, telling those that can relatively accurately decode
the emotion that philosophy is as vital to culture and the substance that makes
a people a people as water is to the survival of fish.

Knowledge that comes from emotion tends toward the spiritual and is
therefore not recognized by Western scientific traditions that privilege the

quantifiable, the readily tangible over that which is more elusive and thus more difficult to grasp, in short, the spiritual (metaphysics). The lessons and understandings about the world offered by the spiritual, as demonstrated by Native traditions (Deloria, 2006; Erdrich, 2003; Marshall, 2004, 2001; Neihardt, 1932/2004), are far too significant to be disregarded by those whose role in society it is to introduce people to ideas and ways of thinking, such as teachers. I am not suggesting that secular teachers and institutions of education should adopt religious doctrine and preach from the Scriptures, but I am saying that if education, like philosophy, is about pursuing knowledge and seeking wisdom, then it would be wise to consider all ideas, where they came from, and how they were derived, the best we can tell. Only then can education, collectively and individually, leave the murky waters of indoctrination and enter the clear springs of discovery unhindered by the fear of what dangerous knowledge might be lurking around the next corner.

Chapter 3

Beyond the Antagonistic Relationship Between Indigenous and Western Philosophy in North America: Toward a Pedagogy of Unity

The most relevant place of departure for our discussion of the antagonistic relationship between Western traditions and those native to North America, based on a review of the literature (highlighted throughout Chapter One and Chapter Two), seems to be *land*. Before we proceed, however, I would like to pause for a moment and respond to the critique that will inevitably be leveled against the dualistic analysis I have set up between Native and Western traditions—a form of empirical analysis that is a product of Enlightenment-based positivist science that many postmodernists have argued distorts the highly complex and unpredictable nature of human interaction. This argument has been made against Marx's dialectical analysis that focuses on the internal relationship between two opposing forces, one positive (capital) because it benefits from the arrangement and one negative (labor) because it is severely limited *in* it. While aware of the complex and contradictory nature of the manifestations of class relations, Marx sought to isolate what he thought were the most essential elements of capitalism—a method of scientific inquiry he referred to as abstraction—so as to thoroughly interrogate them.

However, while honing in on the root structure of the system he was investigating, Marx was not blind to the complexity engendered by the messiness of human subjectivity as well as the ruling elite's tendencies to foment divisiveness as part of the process of subjugation. Just as "Marx does not...overlook the multitude of 'middle and intermediate classes' between the bourgeoisie and proletariat, or the possibility of all kinds of alliances in the class struggle" (Foster, 1996, p. 23), I do not overlook the various "kinds" of class, cul-

tural/ethnic, and gender "alliances" that have formed as a result of colonization, such as people within settler-communities of imported labor abandoning
their invasive settlements for the many benefits of Native communities
(Churchill, 1995; Zinn, 1995), reflected upon below. Marx's discussion of
primitive accumulation as part of the historical development of the capitaliza-
tion of humanity, which began in England roughly a decade before Columbus
set foot in present-day Haiti, is useful here in understanding Europeans'
engagement in the Americas in particular and global affairs in general. Because
of the light it sheds on the discussion that follows, a sizable excerpt taken from
Volume One of *Capital* (Marx, 1867/1967) is presented here for analysis:

> The so-called primitive accumulation...is nothing else than the historical process of
> divorcing the producer from the means of production. It appears as primitive, be-
> cause it forms the pre-historic stage of capital and of the mode of production corre-
> sponding with it.
>
> The economic structure of capitalistic society has grown out of the economic
> structure of feudal society. The dissolution of the latter set free the elements of the
> former.
>
> The immediate producer, the labourer, could only dispose of his own person
> after he had ceased to be attached to the soil and ceased to be the slave, serf, or bond-
> man of another. To become a free seller of labour-power, who carries his commodity
> wherever he finds a market, he must further have escaped from the regime of the
> guilds, their rules for apprentices and journeymen, and the impediments of their la-
> bour regulations. Hence, the historical movement which changes the producers into
> wage-workers, appears, on the one hand, as their emancipation from serfdom and
> from the fetters of the guilds, and this side alone exists for the bourgeois historians.
> But, on the other hand, these new freedmen became sellers of themselves only after
> they had been robbed of all their own means of production, and of all the guarantees
> of existence afforded by the old feudal arrangements. And the history of this, their
> expropriation, is written in the annals of mankind in letters of blood and fire....
>
> The starting point of the development that gave rise to the wage labourer as well
> as to the capitalist was the servitude of the labourer. The advance consisted in a
> change of form of this servitude, in the transformation of feudal exploitation into
> capitalist exploitation....
>
> The expropriation of the agricultural producer, of the peasant, from the soil, is
> the basis of the whole process. The history of this expropriation, in different coun-
> tries, assumes different aspects, and runs through its various phases in different orders
> of succession, and at different periods. (pp. 714–716)

From Marx's work we can begin to gain a slightly different understanding of
the process of predation from the European colonialist perspective. Winona
LaDuke (1992), recognizing the accuracy of Marx's description of primitive

accumulation, challenges us to extend Marx and consider what type of society is possible on primitively accumulated real estate when the people and the land itself have suffered not only physical trauma, but spiritual damage as well. Keeping indigenous people in a permanent state of separation from the very land that gave life to their culture, argues LaDuke, is to prevent the healing of wounds. What is more, the very process of primitive accumulation, in some cases, has rendered the effects irreversible as the land has been so abused and contaminated that it is uninhabitable. One only need to begin to follow the glowing trail of hazardous waste sites throughout the U.S., concentrated around "Indian Reservations" to begin to understand the sobering truth behind the analysis provided by LaDuke (2005, 1992). After reflecting on the usefulness and limitations of Marx's analysis of primitive accumulation, LaDuke wonders if Marxism can be reformulated or altered so as to be made into a more useful tool in dealing with the issues central to "...the remaining land based peoples of the North American continent" (p. vii). Some years later, as LaDuke's essay was first published in 1983, Sandy Grande (2004) presented the world with a special gift, *Red Pedagogy: Native American Social and Political Thought* (referenced throughout the above preface and first chapter), which answers LaDuke's inquiry with a thunderous affirmation looking to the Marxism of Peter McLaren. The revolutionary alliances forged out of the struggles informed by such analyses are explored below.

However, not all alliances have been as subversive as the unity between democratic Marxism and Indigenous philosophy as outlined in *Red Pedagogy* (Grande 2004), which must be interrogated so as to transgress their limitations. Destructive alliances have included members of Indigenous communities taking up with the invaders and waging war against their own traditional ways and peoples (Churchill, 1995, 2002). Marshall (2004) argues that these "negative" alliances began to emerge between whites and some of the Lakota almost as soon as Fort Laramie was established on the outskirts of Lakota territory in the 1830s marking the permanent presence of whites in their region. Attracted to "white-man things" and later (roughly the 1840s) U.S. government "annuities," such as "free" meat (beef), a few Lakota "pitched their lodges within bow shot of the fort" (p. 37) resulting in a state of dependency as traditional hunting practices were forgotten as they ceased to be used or passed on as they had been for thousands of generations. The Lakota named these people "Loaf About the Forts" or simply "Loafers," which, notes Marshall (2004), in the beginning were the exception and by no means the rule, as evidenced, in part, by the core aspects of Lakota culture, such as the Lakota language, persisting to the present day. One of the consequences of the Loafer phenomenon is what we might call "Native-on-Native" violence.

In his demographic analysis of American Indian population decline and resurgence Russell Thornton (1987) attributes a small percentage of the overall deaths of the physical genocide to warfare and genocide (the number one cause was far and away European diseases), sometimes tragically manifesting itself in Native peoples being "...killed by other Indians in intertribal wars resulting from European involvement in tribal relations" (p. 49). These *dark alliances* are not new phenomena as colonizers, as part of the process of colonization/primitive accumulation, have actively sought to establish them as part of the process of seizing control of Native land and labor power, most negatively manifesting themselves as deadly inter-Native tribal wars.

For example, the Grand River Valley of current day Ontario, Canada, was originally inhabited by the Attawandaron (referred to as the Neutrals by the French), a people descended from the Iroquois but who did not join the Confederacy (the Mohawk, Seneca, Cayuga, and Onondaga, who fought with the British, and the Oneida and Tuscarora, who remained neutral or offered occasional assistance to the colonialists), refusing to side with either of the competing colonialists, the French or the British. Lying to the northwest of themselves were the French-allied Huron (Wyandot), between 25,000–35,000 strong at one time covering an estimated 340 square miles (Thornton, 1987), and bitter enemies of the Six Nations, who, at the time, still occupied not only their ancestral lands but far beyond, reaching west into the Ohio valley and to the Eastern Seaboard including current day western New York, which is south of the Grand River Valley, due to their military dominance of the Indigenous fur trade with primarily the French and British (Banks 2003). To secure control over their lucrative fur trade among the twenty eight farming villages of the Huron against the Six Nations of the Iroquois Confederacy, the French established an alliance and built missions to spread Christianity beginning in 1639. With the arrival of the French, between 1634 and 1640, the Huron (as well other Native American societies in the region such as the Six Nations) experienced catastrophic smallpox epidemics reducing their numbers by two-thirds or more in just a couple of years. Vulnerable from disease, the French-allied Huron quickly fell to the British-allied Six Nations. Caught in the middle, the Attawandaron were eventually destroyed as a body politic with an established land-base. It seems as though part of the Confederacy's motivation for overrunning their northern neighbors was not only to gain access to valuable furs, but also to replenish their own populations, which had also been severely decimated by disease. Thornton (1987) summarizes the events as follows:

> ...The Iroquois suffered particularly from smallpox during the eighteenth century. They had been depopulated earlier by mid-seventeenth century smallpox epidemics, but had partially recovered and were even regaining population at the beginning of the eighteenth century. Mooney went so far as to assert that the Iroquois had doubled their post-smallpox population size by conquering and sometimes adopting other tribes such as the Huron, the Neutral, the Erie, and the Conestoga, as well as by intermarrying with non-Indians. But smallpox struck the Iroquois again. (p. 78)

However, the Six Nations survived, and having sided with the British during the American Revolutionary War, was eventually granted the Grand River Valley by Colonel Governor Haldimand in the Haldimand Tract. Their land has been gradually eaten away by white settlers, but the Confederacy still exists and remains committed to fighting for their land and therefore their right to be (Podur, 2006). Taking note of these contradictions is not a critique of Native philosophy, but rather is a documentation of the acceptance or surrendering to external control when, for the moment, there appear to be no other options, which paved the way for the incorporation of the colonizers' thinking, too often manifesting itself as internalized oppression. Andrea Smith (2005), for example, attributes these alliances with the internalized oppression that is a direct consequence of the process of colonization drawing on sexual violence as an example, complicating the issue of violence more generally in Native communities: "In Indian country...community members will argue that sexual violence is 'traditional.' This phenomena indicates the extent to which our communities have internalized self-hatred" (p. 13).

The self-hatred described by Smith (2005) can, in part, be attributed to the hegemony of Eurocentric historians taught to all school-aged children, including Native Americans (see Chapter Four). Representing this Eurocentric history in *Niagara Frontier: A Narrative and Documentary History,* Merton Wilner (1931) alludes to the colonization of Six Nations land, which includes present-day Buffalo and Niagara Falls, New York, as the inevitable manifestation of the spreading of the superior European "civilization," conveniently ignoring the sophisticated democratic knowledge of governance "barrowed" from First Nations confederations such as that of the Six Nations (see Chapters Two and Nine). As you read the following quote listen and look for the philosophical underpinnings in Wilner's (1931) coddling discourse of manifest destiny:

> The reclamation of this continent from a primeval wilderness was an achievement in which each separate locality became a scene of action. This marvelous forward sweep of civilization can be understood best when its details are read in localized history. The Niagara Frontier has been one of the most vital points in this continental development... The Niagara region forms...a natural gateway between the eastern seaboard and the western prairies. Here the terminus of unbroken lake navigation concentrates commerce, and here science has found means to convert the natural energy of nature into mechanical power...It presents the triumphs of peace and progress. (p. iii)

A year after the Eurocentric *Niagara Frontier* was released, Alice Williams (1932) published *A Child's Story of the Niagara Frontier,* also written from the conqueror's perspective reproducing the same coddling arguments, yet translated, in a sense, for children—providing an even closer look at the curriculum designed to normalize and naturalize a system and process inherently undemocratic. In the first two chapters Williams (1932) paints with broad strokes her largely invented history of the Niagara region portraying Native Americans as part of the past whose time has inevitably come and gone as a result of the emergence of the superior European civilization. Williams accomplishes this by offering a comparison between pre-European Native North America and Europe. Consider her white supremacist fiction:

> At last men with red skins and strange ways came and built their huts on the edge of the river where the fish and game were plentiful...They Scratched the hard soil with their clumsy tools...It does not seem a good life to us for fear always ruled it. Fear of hunger, for food was often scarce; fear of cold, for the winds over Lake Ontario were bitter during the long winter; and fear of the terrible Indian neighbors, the Iroquois... (pp. 10–11)
>
> Now we must leave Indians and wild woods for a while, and from this window see a very different picture, for we are looking far away across the tree tops and across the sea, which is so wide and deep, to the lands in which our ancestors lived when this country was an undiscovered wilderness. It is to the land of France that we must especially look, for it is from that country that the white men who first saw this river came. France was a good country. Cities and villages had comfortable houses and beautiful churches. Rivers were bridged and easy to cross. The fields were cultivated and the roads were hard and straight. (p. 12)

After setting up this false dichotomy Williams addresses the inevitable question it elicits, *if Europe was so great, why did so many Europeans leave?*, by arguing that "men loved adventure more than ease" (p. 12). This perspective, advanced throughout the entirety of Williams's story, reflects her own positionality as she served in the city's government for thirty one years. In the above two short passages Williams not only inverts the oppressor/oppressed relationship but also inverts the reality of material conditions outlined in Chapter Two. For example, Daniel Wildcat (2001b) argues that "Columbus was not so much trying to discover a new land but escape a declining, chaos-ridden old land" (p. 55).

The hegemony of Williams's (1932) and Wilner's (1931) white supremacist discourse of "discovery," which represents the perspective of the bosses, has not only long affected the self-concept of Native peoples, but can also tragically be found within the labor movement of the settler-state's official publications since at least the late 1800s, if not before. For example, in the September 7th, 1896, edition of the *Official Programme and Journal of the United Trades and Labor Council of Erie County and Vicinity,* WM. J. Taggert's (1896) essay, "History of the United Trades and Labor Council," decries the unfair practices of "the Bosses" because they are responsible for "robbing the people of our country" and "of their inalienable rights; namely, the right to combine to better protect themselves against the encroachments which are constantly being placed upon the people by the greedy and avaricious capitalistic combinations of our country" arguing that it is therefore the necessary task of the people to "take hold of the reins of Government and do for themselves what the cunning and crafty politicians of the past and present day have refused to do for them; namely, to make laws for the benefit of the whole people and not for the few" (pp. 13–15).

It is undeniable that the immigrant working class in North America in general and in the "Niagara Frontier" in particular was assembled and put to work against itself, that is, for exploitation, and their history is therefore the history of resisting such subjugation, for itself, their call for justice has tended to ignore the injustice embodied within the land upon which they stand—land Taggert (1896) refers to as "our country" without mention of the Indigenous populations, the Haudenosaunee (Six Nations), who had been reserved in the region roughly just one hundred years prior in a series of two treaties, one in 1784 at Fort Stanwix in upstate New York and the other in 1789 at Fort Harmar securing themselves much of their traditional lands (six million acres) in the Niagara region providing a buffer between the U.S. and British interests in Canada (Churchill 2002). Almost immediately after the Haudenosaunee secured their lands with the United States federal government, the State of New York began "leasing" lands from the Six Nations under the false premise that this was the only way to ensure the protection of "Indian lands" from the federal government. As a result of the success of this deception, by 1889 the Six Nations had been dissolved of more than 80% of their reservation land.

Situating these histories in a relational context we can therefore begin to understand that as the United Trades and Labor Council, for example, was fighting the abuses suffered by the region's largely imported workingclass, the same government and corporations responsible for these atrocities were busy appropriating Haudenosaunee reservation land. As a result, the working class has too often presented itself as in competition with the elite few for a "fair" share of the wealth their labor has been used to extract from the land— Indigenous land. In the present era there is still much progress to be made within the realm of solidarity. As we will see below the labor movement's support for industrialism, and therefore the bosses' vision of how appropriated Native land is to be used and abused, represents perhaps the biggest mistake of organized labor, for they have suffered greatly for it.

In other words, the general sentiment embodied in Wilner's perspective, that Europeans brought civilization to an untamed wilderness, remains the official settler-state perspective. For a contemporary example one only needs to examine Brad Edmondson's (2000) recent essay "Environmental Affairs in New York State: An Historical Overview," produced for the New York State Archives. Through his analysis, and by omission, Edmondson seems to mark the beginning of history in the Niagara region with the arrival of European immigrants, commenting that

> The history of environmental affairs in New York is the story of how New Yorkers decided to use their natural resources, and how they still struggle to use soil, timber, water, air and wildlife in ways that do not decrease their value...European immigrants began spreading across the state about 200 years ago. In that relatively brief time, New Yorkers have developed the state's 976 miles of ocean coastline and dug 524 miles of state-maintained canals. (p. 2)

The history of environmental issues from the colonizers' perspective, as demonstrated by Edmondson, is the history of predator and the mathematics of plundering. Environmentalism, from this referent, is the science of extracting the maximum amount of wealth over the longest period of time from occupied lands. To be wild is therefore to be outside the process of value production. To "tame" is thus to incorporate into the process of production.

The goal of this system is simple: maximum amount of profit by any means necessary. The very high human cost has never been part of the equation—only the economic cost of extermination and subjugation is considered by predator, which ignores completely the cost to humanity of losing part of our rich diversity. It should therefore not be surprising that the immigrant labor colonizers brought into places like western New York, some of whom, at times, were made to feel special/entitled for being "white" while they were fulfilling their externally commanded role in the process of value production, have since been largely left to rot because predator has his sights on plundering other parts of the world such as Mexico and China (Porfilio & Hall, 2005). Not only rotting but also dying of cancer.

That is, in Niagara Falls the rate of cancer among the working class settler-population who work and live around the many chemical plants is exceedingly high, facts that the bosses, the supposed allies of white workers, have bent over backwards to deny and avoid responsibility of—leaving the people not only impoverished, but sick. Niagara Falls, New York, is the infamous location of Love Canal, which was used as a toxic waste dump in the 1940s and 1950s where 20,000 tons of material was deposited. The canal was then filled in and given away to the city for housing and an elementary school as a tax write-off for the chemical company responsible for the crime. By the 1970s the waste "sealed" in metal containers began to leak and subsequently rose to the surface. The large amounts of toxins that began to saturate the area's soil was found to be responsible for the region's unusually high rates of not only cancer, but birth defects, miscarriages, and chromosome damage. The predominantly white Love Canal population was evacuated in 1978 and in 1980 the location was declared a national emergency (Mokhiber & Weissman, 1999). While many of these corporations are no longer engaged in the plunder of the region's "natural resources" and exploitation of the local, predominantly imported, populations, and a few costly clean-up attempts, the ground remains highly contaminated, and the rates of disease are still far above average.

However, this is not to suggest that the spirit of Columbus has left the Niagara region all together. The sweet smell of cereal coming from the massive humming General Mills factory still fills the air of Buffalo's downtown lakefront area. General Mills, using imported grains, puts Lake Erie to work in its production process. General Mills is just one example of how predator is extracting wealth from the land appropriated from Native Americans. Further down the shore toward Niagara Falls one can find another use of this "natural resource" in Mohawk Power Corporation's profitable power plant mockingly named after one of the Six Nations in the customary fashion of the occupiers, of the settler-state ruling class. Through their power plants, especially the Huntley & Dunkirk coal burning plant near Buffalo, New York, Niagara Mohawk is one of the state's leading polluters. In 1998 alone, according to their own reports, they spewed nearly six million tons of toxic chemicals into the environment (Associated Press, 1999). Another way predator is extracting wealth from the Niagara region is through drinking water. Managed by American Water, a for-profit corporation, the Buffalo Water Authority provides water to over 290,000 "customers," billing each one an average of roughly $325 a year. In 2006 alone American Water/Buffalo Water Authority processed and distributed 27 billion gallons of water averaging 73.5 million gallons per day (Buffalo Water Authority & American Water, 2007).

What this analysis suggests is that it is self-destructive for anybody, Native and non-Native alike, to form an alliance with predator/colonizer/capitalist. Such alliances can only be viewed as a form of procrastination for what must be done—engage in critical solidarity and fight the bosses. It requires that the settler-community, which today includes both immigrant (including forced immigrants) and Indigenous people, to transcend the revolutionary goals of the proletariat to seize control of the means of production as part of the process of democratizing the economy, and completely subvert the entire process of predation, that is, wealth extraction and accumulation. The examples related to the damage corporate polluters have been consciously inflicting on human and animal populations are staggering. Taking just one example from Mokhiber and Weissman's (2005) essay "The 10 Worst Corporations of 2005" proves to be indicative. DuPont Corporation's twenty year cover-up of a grease-resistant chemical they developed to be used in processing paper food packaging has been shown to be in the blood of as much as 95% of the United States population, contributing to an untold number of cancer victims. When the primary motivation of private producers is profit, and the human and environmental costs are ignored, then we should not be surprised when disaster ensues.

Again, understood from this perspective, it is in the interest of every living person concerned with the health and well-being of themselves, and their friends and family, to resist the perpetuation of the capitalist industrial system that can only ever lead to crisis. The only sane thing to do in this context is to denounce and lay to waste that which has only ever proven to be insane—the process of value production (as demonstrated in Chapter Four, critical educators can and have played a crucial role here). Underscoring the insanity of capitalism, Joel Bakan (2004), in his study of one of the most central units of analysis of this system, the corporation, notes that "the irony in all of this is that the corporation's mandate to pursue its own self-interest, itself a product of the law, actually propels corporations to break the law. No corporation is exempt from this built-in logic, not even those that claim they are socially responsible" (p. 80). Drawing on the largest corporation in the world as an example, General Electric (GE), who portrays themselves as environmentally friendly in their advertising campaigns, Bakan (2004) outlines "some of the company's major legal breaches between 1990 and 2001" (p. 75). The following examples bring to light the utter disregard GE has for the environment and therefore the health and well-being of not only their employees, but the people who live in the communities in which their production facilities are located. A few examples from the 1990s:

March 23, 1990: Shepherdsville, Kentucky: GE and others ordered to clean up PCB contamination of soil and water.

March 27, 1990: Wilmington, North Carolina: GE fined $20,000 for discrimination against employees who reported safety violations.

May 11, 1999: Fort Edward/Hudson Falls, New York: GE ordered to clean up PCB contamination of Hudson River.

October 11, 1990: Waterford, New York: GE fined $176,000 for pollution at Silicone Products plant.

March 4, 1992: Orange County, California: GE fined $11,000 for violating worker safety rules on handling PCBs.

March 2, 1993: Riverside, California: GE and others ordered to pay $96 million in damages for contamination from dumping of industrial chemicals.

September 15, 1995: Brandon, Florida: GE fined $137,000 for groundwater contamination.

September 9, 1996: Waterford, New York: GE fined $60,000 for Clean Air Act violations.

February 22, 1997: Somersworth, New Hampshire: GE and others ordered to clean up contamination of groundwater and public water supply.

September 17, 1999: Moreau, New York: GE ordered to build drinking water system after PCB contamination of water supply. (Bakan, 2004, pp. 75–78)

While many of these examples, especially the alliances between the oppressors and the oppressed, highlight the fragmented, decentered, and contextually relevant nature of power, there are not only identifiable concentrations of power within dominant classes/colonizers/occupiers/invaders, but there are also concentrations of disempowerment/subjugation/oppression within colonized communities. We can therefore abstract from the complex nature of colonization the essential elements of the dialectical relationship between the occupied and the occupiers in order to better understand the internal philosophy and workings of the system while keeping in mind the complexities that emerge as a result of the historical development of the relation.

This Marxist method is perhaps best represented in classic works associated with colonialist studies such as Franz Fanon's *The Wretched of the Earth* (1963), Albert Memmi's (1965) *The Colonizer and the Colonized*, and Paulo Freire's (1970) *Pedagogy of the Oppressed*, and more recently, in Churchill's many works such as *A Little Matter of Genocide* (1997) and *Struggle for the Land* (2002). While Churchill would most assuredly frown upon his work being associated with Marxism, like many works of Marxist scholarship, much of it, if not all of it, focuses on the dialectical relationship between the colonizers and the colonized and its historical development, including purposeful action against the relation toward utopia, and the psychological barriers engendered by indoctrination leading to contradictory alliances forged out of false consciousness and other ideological forms of deception. From indigenous *and* Marxist relational perspectives, the complexities are essential in understanding the whole; anything short of the full picture will lead to distortions and misunderstandings and at the end of the day a misguided direction for the future.

While the similarities between a Marxist and an Indigenous dialectical (relational) study of human affairs are not hard to discern, there is one area of contestation less easily resolved, which brings us back to the central focus of this chapter: *land*, which also tends to be presented dualistically by Native scholars and activists. For example, Winona LaDuke (1992) describes industrial society, the result of primitive accumulation, as synthetic because it has been disconnected from the natural organic connection between people and the land where the settler-community represents the violent imposition of the inorganic. At the end of Chapter Two, I put it like this: can the subordinate classes of the settler-community conceive of a way to liberate themselves from the grip of their own ruling class (the same ruling class that has exploited the labor power of the settler community in not only putting them to work in production, but as slaughterers and wealth extractors of everyone from American Indians to Iraqis) without continuing to deny Native Americans their Native American ancestral lands? Or, will a liberated settler-community working class continue to occupy 99% of Native land? Because North America's working class seems far from liberating itself from its ruling class, the cause of which has been associated with many interconnected factors including whiteness (see McLaren & Farahmandpur, 2005), such a consideration is a moot point. What is not a moot point, however, is how to work together. Winona LaDuke (1992) has addressed this issue situating the solution within a process of collective relearning and collaboration:

> I would argue that Americans of "foreign" descent must become Americans. That is not to become a patriot of the United States, a patriot of the flag, but a patriot to the land of this continent.... You were born here, you will not likely go away, or live anywhere else, and there are simply no more frontiers to follow. We must all relearn a way of thinking, a state of mind that is from this common ground.... If we are in this together, we must rebuild, redevelop, and reclaim an understanding/analysis which is uniquely ours. (p. 1)

What this has, does, and could look like in practice is explored in detail here and in Chapter Four. Ultimately, LaDuke is challenging all of us to rethink the philosophies that inform the way we *read* the world and subsequently the choices we make *in* the world, which, for educators, translates into curriculum and pedagogy (what we teach and the way we teach it). For Churchill (2002) LaDuke's "common ground" is a unified (settlers and Natives) movement against the colonialist governments of the United States and Canada in support of Native land reclamation as dictated by international law. Churchill (2002) notes that fully one third of the United States is unceded Native land and thus proposes a land base that would not disrupt the financial heart of the U.S. that could be the new Native North America. The new Native America would of course be governed under Native law, which Churchill (2002) argues is, in its pre-Columbian state, inherently environmentalist, antiracist, anticapitalist/economic inequality, anti-homophobic and anti-sexist, in short, democratic, and would therefore probably be appealing to many people from the settler-community, who, contrary to popular opinion, would not be expected to give up their homes or small businesses if located on Native land.

Aware of the erosive effect the colonizers' system of indoctrination has had on these egalitarian Native values, Churchill (2002) notes that "the extent to which these realities do not now pertain in native societies is exactly the extent to which Indians have been subordinated to the mores of the invading, dominating culture" (p. 379). Because the process of colonization has perverted traditional ways contributing to deep philosophical divisions among Native communities, where none were before, suggesting that land reclamation would result in an automatic return to traditional ways is, at best, romantic and naïve. However, this is not to suggest current arrangements are satisfactory. The fact that Native peoples, as a whole, based on every social indicator of oppression, such as poverty, are by far the most oppressed group in North America warrants serious attention and major changes, as does the suffering of many other groups in North America (and throughout the world, the focus of Chapter Four) such as African Americans, or Africans *in* America as Europeans are *in* America but not *of* America, as only those indigenous to the land can be. As this seems to be a simple "fact," deciphering who is European, who is African and who is "Indian" is not so clear-cut after five hundred years of intermingling. With these complexities in mind, as alluded to above by LaDuke, what is needed in this day and age are workable pedagogies of unity and accompanying philosophies of praxis.

While land reclamation is undoubtedly part of the solution, alone, it is not enough. A radical social education is also needed for everyone, Native and non-Native alike. Such an education, outlined in Chapter Four, following critical pedagogy and Native American–conceived and –controlled tribal education systems, should be designed to facilitate the development of critical multicultural citizens, able to not only read the word, but their world as well, and therefore endowed with a land-centered revolutionary consciousness complete with the sense of empowerment needed to put it into action, that is, the restoration of dignity, justice, self-determination, and humanization generally in North America, both philosophically and geographically, and the possibility of a utopian future. Providing a more concrete place of departure for considering what the settler-Left's role might look in this process, through summarizing what he understands is the general sentiment of Native Nations engaged in land reclamation regarding non-Native progressives and radicals, Churchill (2002) notes:

...When Indigenist movements like AIM advance slogans like "U.S. Out of North America," non-Indian radicals should not react defensively. They should cheer. They should see what they might do to help. When they respond defensively to sentiments like those expressed by AIM, what they are ultimately defending is the very government, the very order they claim to oppose so resolutely. And if they manifest this contradiction often enough, consistently enough, pathologically enough, then we have no alternative but to take them on their word: that they really are at some deep level or another aligned, all protestations to the contrary notwithstanding, with the mentality that endorses our permanent dispossession and disenfranchisement, our continuing oppression, our ultimate genocidal obliteration as self-defining and self-determining peoples. In other words, they make themselves part of the problem rather than becoming part of the solution. (p. 383)

As Churchill alludes, the heart of the antagonistic relationship between settlers and communities Native to North America is control of ancestral lands. The significance of these land issues lies within the fact that settler/colonizer populations have overwhelmingly pursued an agenda of replacing the Native philosophies with foreign conceptions of land. While aware of the complexities that emerge when entire civilizations are brought together under dubious circumstances, addressed in the second half of this chapter, we continue by considering the two poles of perception (immigrant and Native) when considering land in post-Columbian North America and the historical development of the two in context.

Before predator came and, for the Lakota, until 1877 when Crazy Horse was murdered by his own people, who had been co-opted by the U.S. government, Native societies held their ancestral lands communally, united around a common culture that situated them as a natural part of the landscape—the human element of physical place (Marshall III, 2001, 2004). From this perspective it did not make sense to disconnect a physical place, i.e., North America, from its culture—culture being the domain of humans. The people inevitably resisted and continue to resist the destruction of who they are as a people, a human group, with the goal of reconnecting the sacred hood (the people with the land, based on ancient relationships holistically conceived). Outsiders were, and still are, it seems, as suggested above by Churchill (2002) and alluded to by LaDuke (1992), welcome in, but the destruction of the sacred hoop/cycle of life, of which Native peoples are a natural part, from an Indigenist perspective, is not only wrong, but it is objectively incorrect. An attack on any part of the hoop is an attack on the whole. The extermination of the bison (documented in Chapter Two), therefore, put the whole system out of balance. Joseph M. Marshall III's telling of the Lakota creation story, demonstrates the profound sense of interconnectedness between all life and the land, and the value of sacrifice characteristic of Lakota culture, and is therefore worth quoting at length:

> A creation story describes our people coming up into the world through a hole in the Earth. One person remained behind. Those who came out liked this place of light and warmth and decided to stay. It was obviously the right decision because the people wanted for nothing. Everyone was happy until hard times came. Drought laid waste to the land and famine came thereafter; the people became weak and began to die. The one who had stayed behind saw what was happening to those who had left and was sad to see them suffering. That last one came out of the hole and became the bison, the *tatanka*, and multiplied until they covered the earth. The people hunted the bison and ate its flesh and were saved. As time went on, the people saw other ways to use the bison; from its hide they made coverings for their dwellings, from its bones they made toys and weapons, from its hair they made rope, and from its horns they made spoons and cups. Every part of the bison was put to use. The people became strong again; in fact, they grew stronger than they were before. For that they honored the sacrifice of the bison in their songs and dances. (p. 103)

Marshall's account demonstrates the importance of a bona fide homeland (not the homeland of someone else you have claimed as your own despite their objections) reflected in the pride Native people have who still occupy the land from which their creation stories and stories of migration and rebirth are based. When the Native people are gone, the land becomes vulnerable to abuse (demonstrated below in the Pacific Northwest), and without indigenous culture, it becomes dull, boring, and loses its vitality—something is missing/not right. Again, the goal of native resistance has always been to reconnect the hoop, the interpretation of what that means has been a point of contestation within the many native communities in North America, an area often targeted by outside colonizing forces seeking to divide and rule people in their efforts to "tame" (i.e., extract its inherent value as profit/capital) the land.

The "taming of the west" abolished the communal system indigenous to the land via the Native people, and replaced it with a foreign model based on the individual ownership of land that, stripped of its people and thus culture, was proclaimed by the new ruling class to be neutral or objective real estate to be chopped up, commodified, and sold in lots and policed with an equal amount of rigidity. Slaughtering was used until the less costly "pushing-to-the-side" worked. Too costly to exterminate the remaining Natives, the colonialist governments found a more cost-effective way of replacing the philosophy informing the use of the land in education where Native communities were taught the ways of "civilization," and therefore expected to accept "reforms," such as the Allotment Act, designed to break up the human commune and thus the land being used communally. Within this colonial practice *in* the world, we find the ancient Greek philosophical dichotomy between the spiritual world and the material world. Refusing to acknowledge the cultural and spiritual, the colonizer, in his own mind, and the minds of his labor force, reduces Native peoples to an objective part of nature, which is inherently corrupted, to be tamed/subdued, and ultimately, exploited or eliminated. Native people have obviously rebelled and resisted this process of colonization/predation, and have therefore either been pushed to the side, slaughtered, or accepted defeat, at least temporarily, hence the inherent hope within Native philosophy for what the world already tends towards, that is, harmony and its cyclical nature. Once subjugated and demographically reduced to next to nothing, to be absolutely sure the threat of Indigenous land claims would be gone forever, a massive campaign was undertaken led by Richard Pratt to indoctrinate Native communities with Western philosophy as "bronze" people in the Platonic sense of subordinates/wage slaves within capitalist relations of production, and therefore stripped of their Indigenous culture.

While deculturalization has been mind bogglingly detrimental to Indigenous culture and thus Native resistance, it has also negatively affected the settler Left. Within the settler-community's environmental movement, land, unfortunately, has not tended to be viewed any more spiritually than their own ruling class. While there is an emerging tendency among environmental scientists, such as marine biologists, to understand humans as connected to and thus dependent on, the natural ecology for survival, acknowledging the inherent worth within all life-forms, an ancient Native belief, its spiritual understandings stop here failing to connect specific people (Native people) with specific places (their Native land). While environmentalists tend to see ecosystems as important because they serve a needed function for all life, including humans, they too often engage in a relatively ahistorical scientific discourse void of politics (Native Americans) because politics are best dealt with by the social scientists, as if science and technology are not highly political endeavors. Similarly, Marxists tend to view land as primarily to serve the needs of people equally, but within the industrial model of the Western system, which has also proven to let the "Indian question" go un-addressed. Native philosophy, on the other hand, sees people as just one part of the ecosystem and should therefore be in balance with it, as the environmentalists do, but that the balance is best understood and directed by the Native medicine men whose powers are derived from specific geographical places (Deloria, 2006). The restoration of wild salmon runs in the Northwestern areas of the U.S. and southwestern Canada provides a telling account of the interaction between settler and Native views of land, as well as offering direction for the future.

Antagonism in the Pacific Northwest:
Mother Earth Versus a Source of Wealth

Like the great bison herds for the Lakota, the monumental salmon runs for the four tribes of the Pacific Northwest, the Nez Perce, Umatilla, Warm Springs and Yakama, including many of their bands such as the Cayuse, the Wasco, the Tillamook, and the Chinook, provided a rich source of sustenance and therefore a deep place-centered cultural tradition that served to keep the ecology in balance since time immemorial. This quantifiable ecological balance maintained by all Native peoples was/is informed by the belief that the role of the tribes is to serve as the primary "...caretakers of the earth for seven generations ahead and that they have the responsibility to ensure their future success" (Talbot & Galbreath, 2006, p. 552). Such an understanding, as demonstrated below, has resulted in holistic philosophies of practice that facilitate the development of long-term visions, usually situated within creation stories that firmly root the people to specific geographical places. Like the Lakota's creation story, the Native peoples of what are now the states of California, Oregon, and Washington, and Vancouver, British Columbia have similar stories intimately interconnected with the land and its dominant creatures. For example, the Colville Tribe tells of how

> ...Some time in the distant past—when Coyote was the really big man on earth and when there was no Columbia River—the Colville country was covered by a big lake. To the west, a long ridge of mountains prevented the waters of the lake from flowing to the ocean. Coyote was wise enough to see that if he could make a passageway trough the mountains the salmon would come up from the ocean and provide food for his people. So Coyote used his powers to dig a hole through the mountains that allowed the Columbia River to flow to the ocean as it does today. The salmon were then able to swim up the river and Coyote's people had plenty to eat ever after. (Robbins, 1999, p. 2)

This story describes the intimate relationship between the people, the salmon, and the land therefore serving as the basis for an Indigenous pedagogy for

Native citizenship firmly contextualized in its reading of the world. Careful not to deplete salmon populations the 50,000 original Native inhabitants were able to yield an annual catch of 41 million pounds by strategically spreading out fishing activities among the thousands of miles of the Columbia Basin's streams and tributaries. Very specific fishing regulations designed to protect the stocks were also firmly in place within these Native societies. Providing a clear summary of these rules of engagement, which included ceremonies of thanks, Talbot and Galbreath (2006) note that:

> The return of the first salmon runs was an anxiously awaited event each spring. Upon permission given by the headman, fishing would commence and was followed shortly thereafter by the annual salmon feast, as commanded by Coyote. Many of the Native people would then move downstream to establish camps at their traditional fishing places along the main stem of the Columbia and its tributaries. At each major fishing location, a headman was the recognized leader. The headman would determine when and for how long fishing would occur, so that fish would be caught only at their prime and exploited judiciously and equitably. The fishing season would continue off and on through the fall, coincident with surges in the return runs of the various stocks and species. Night fishing was disallowed, and fishing was intermittent over the season, with the periods of no fishing in recognition of the need to assure adequate escapement of the adults to the spawning grounds in order to renew each population. All parts of the fish were utilized, and capture of more fish than one could use and process were transgressions subject to punishment. (p. 553)

These ancient fishing practices that protected the natural balance of the land and its ecosystems when compared to the imported practices of capitalist land use represents one of the starkest examples of a dualism possibly imaginable. It has been estimated that the annual runs in the Columbia River system alone, before depletion, were upwards of 16 million. Drawing attention to the vitality and geographical significance of this naturally wealthy region, William Robbins (1999), in "The World of Columbia River Salmon: Nature, Culture and the Great River of the West," does not leave his readers in want of descriptive detail:

> Although the salmon runs peaked for only a brief number of days each season (and for each species), the heaviest and most concentrated fishing took place at certain natural obstacles on the Columbia—at Kettle Falls, Priest Rapids, Celilo Falls, and the Long Narrows—and at similar strategic points on tributaries such as Sherars Falls on the Deschutes and, for spring runs of salmon, at Willamette Falls near present-day Oregon City. In the vicinity of The Dalles, which included spectacular Celilo Falls, the proper mix of topography (which constricted the river) and dry windy climate

(which enhanced the drying of fish) combined to forge one of the most productive
freshwater fisheries anywhere in the world. (p. 5)

As the wild salmon stocks of the Northwest were gradually, and then rather
rapidly, eaten up by white encroachment and the subsequent technological
innovations of commercial fishing and canneries, so too diminished the
peoples Indigenous to this region, helped along, of course, with the usual dose
of mass murders and physical land removals and relocations, fueled by federal
policies designed to open up the remaining reserved Native lands to white
settlement and development (logging and commercial fishing). Missionaries
began their work in the 1830s bringing with them dreaded pathogens—measles,
smallpox, and typhus, for example. White settlers began trickling into the
Pacific Northwest at the turn of the nineteenth century; by the 1840s and with
the discovery of gold (that substance that has turned many of those motivated
by personal gain into blood-thirsty, ravenous lunatics), that slow trickle turned
into a river of thousands, bringing with them the colonialist view of land
informed by a culture of economics "...that viewed the natural world as capital,
that obliged humankind to use that capital for self-advancement, and a
conviction that the social order should promote the accumulation of personal
wealth" (Robbins, 1999, p. 7).

Beyond the miners and trappers, some people amongst the settlers immediately saw the potential for profit in the abundance of wild salmon in the
Northwest, as did the U.S. House of Representatives when engaged in
establishing settlements in the region (see Robbins, 1999), but were not able to
begin to fully capitalize on it until the 1860s (discussed below). Further
contributing to the influx of white settlers in Oregon Territory between 1850
and 1855 was a land grant offered by Congress where 320 acres of Indigenous
real estate were given to individual white *men* and a square mile to married
couples. By 1855 more than 2.5 million acres of Native land was already
claimed by 7,437 white settlers (Beckham, 2006). However, these Donation
Land Claims could not be made by those who already possessed it, namely the
Cayuse, the Chinook, the Klamath, among many other bands, or anyone else
of color for that matter, especially those of African descent. During the 1840s
and 1850s Africans *in* America, specifically, were barred from Oregon
residency, a sentiment written into Oregon's state constitution in 1857, and not
revoked until 1926 (Bigelow, 2001). White elites were fearful that if blacks
moved to Oregon, already indignant over their bitter relationship with slavery,
they would join the cause of Native Americans, as they had in other areas

(discussed below), therefore posing an even greater threat to the institutionalization of white supremacist hegemony. Summarizing the antagonistic relationship between Native and settler communities in his comprehensive documentation of *Oregon Indians,* Stephen Dow Beckham (2006) recounts:

> The problematic nature of relations between Native Americans and the pioneer generation gained bloody confirmation in events on the Columbia Plateau in 1847-1848. In November a few members of the Cayuse tribe, aggrieved by the wholesale deaths of their people and irked by the attitudes and actions of the missionaries at Waiilatpu, attacked the mission. The incident resulted in the deaths of more than a dozen Euro-Americans. In its wake settlers of the Willamette Valley invaded the Plateau to seek retribution, round up alleged perpetrators, and put the natives of that region on notice about the might and intention of the Americans moving into their country. (p. 5)

Contributing to Beckham's analysis, Thornton (1987) observes that American immigrants, desperate to dominate the region, brought many wars and battles to those native to the Pacific Northwest such as "...the Rogue River Wars in Oregon Territory and Northern California in the 1850s, the Yakima Wars of 1855-56 and 1858, the Round Valley Wars in California in the 1850s and 1860s, the Bannock Wars of 1877-79, the Modoc War of 1872-73, [and] the Nez Perce Wars of the late 1870s" (p. 106). In practice, the propensity for violence among the many invaders often manifested itself as groups of them attacking small, relatively defenseless Native villages "sometimes in the name of a particular war, and be virtually wiped out overnight" (p. 107). For example, between 1851 and 1856:

> A series of three "Rogue River Wars" are fought in rapid succession to subordinate the indigenous peoples of northern California and southern Oregon (Rogues, Klamaths, Shastas, Modocs, Tunis, Chinooks, Mollalas, Tillamooks, Calapooias and others). Survivors are aggregated on tiny reservations while the balance of their land is occupied by "white settlers." (Churchill, 2003c, p. 50)

Even more specifically, however, the story of the Kalapuya of Oregon's Willamette River valley is indicative of the pattern of destruction that befell those native to the Pacific Northwest, especially bands smaller in numbers. From 1780 to 1980 the population of the Kalapuya fell from 3,000 to 65 persons as a result of both disease and immigrant-induced economic collapse. Thornton's (1987) narrative describing the deleterious impacts of an imposed economy on the Kalapuya's way of life is instructive in highlighting not only the philosophical difference in settler and Native conceptions of land, but also the predatory nature of the former:

> Traditional Kalapuya subsistence patterns had been based on fishing eels, salmon, trout, and steelhead; hunting elk, deer and various small animals and insects; harvesting wild plants, nuts, berries, and especially camas; and raising tobacco... After 1828, however, serious American farming and husbandry began where the Kalapuya lived, and fields of wheat and pastures for cattle, horses, and hogs soon reduced their traditional natural resources. After 1841, Euro-American settlement became even more intensive, and eventually the Kalapuya simply became unable to feed their population. Hunger and starvation resulted; the inevitable depopulation occurred. (p. 125)

Severely disempowered by the ravages of disease and foreign violence, Native peoples were continually marginalized, stripped of their lands, and pushed to the side throughout the mid- and late eighteen hundreds by the cultural/economic practices of an increasing settler population. For example, in a period of seven months, between 1854 and 1855, the U.S. government was able to sign nine treaties with more than seventeen thousand Native peoples relinquishing them of more than sixty four million acres, which now comprise most of the states of the Pacific Northwest (Blumm & Bodi, 1999). Intent on securing hegemony in the region, Isaac Ingalls Stevens, first governor and Superintendent of Indian Affairs for Washington Territory, re-organized the political structure of the communities native to the Northwest into small bands of tribes appointing those most receptive to white encroachment to the position of "chief." This imposed political organization has persisted and continues to exist in the present era—representing yet another dark alliance between oppressed and oppressors. However, despite these manipulations, the tribes had the foresight to write into the treaties statements guaranteeing traditional fishing rights (Talbot & Galbreath, 2006), which have become increasingly important as white encroachment, not respectful of Native conceptions of land and how it is to be managed, began to deplete fish stocks and destroy their natural habitat.

While the commercial fishing practices of the eastern seaboard were put to use in the Pacific Northwest, such pursuits were largely a sideshow to the more lucrative logging and trapping industries until the size of the working class in Great Britain and the eastern United States exploded, which required an inexpensive source of protein to fuel the wealth-generating potential of this highly exploited and over-worked source of human labor power. To profit from the creation of this new industrial market, commercial fishing technology was developed in three primary areas: extraction, packaging, and shipment. With an intercontinental railroad stretching from the East Coast to the Columbia River realized, and therefore the availability of an efficient and reliable shipping method, and the development of a technique for sealing fish in airtight cans, the first salmon cannery was opened on the Columbia River in 1866 by Hapgood, Hume and Company (New England capitalists that were already involved in the Northwest timber industry). Technology was also developed for extracting the fish from the rivers. Initially, a variety of netting methods adapted from Native fishers were used such as gillnets, traps, and seines, but much larger in capacity due to the use of teams of workhorses employed to literally drag the massive hauls of fish from the waters. However, a uniquely industrial capitalist device was developed, the fish wheel, and thus completely foreign to Native Northwestern America, that worked to literally pump salmon from their runs faster than previously thought possible. Painting a picture of what this contraption looked like in full swing, Robbins (1999) describes it as:

> ...An elaborate Ferris wheel-like structure powered by the current that scooped fish from the water. First used on the Columbia in 1879, the highly productive wheels (both stationary and mounted on scows) literally pumped salmon from the river; the giant Phelps wheel at The Dalles took 227,000 pounds of salmon from the river from May to July, 1894. And on a single spring day in 1913 the Suffer brothers' wheel no. 5 turned a record catch of 70,000 pounds. (p. 11)

At the height of operation it has been estimated that there were canneries on virtually every Oregon, and northwestern, coastal stream. By the late 1800s and early 1900s fish stocks had been noticeably diminished. Removing massive quantities of fish from streams and rivers was only one source of wild salmon depletion. The development of residential areas, continued logging practices, and the damming of major waterways had a tremendously detrimental impact on salmon habitat and ecosystems rendering recovery in some areas impossible (Lackey, Lach, & Duncan, 2006a). For example, with the construction of the hydroelectric Grand Coulee Dam, one of many massive undertakings on the main stem of the Columbia River designed to meet the propaganda-induced and thus manufactured, electricity needs of an increasing settler population; over 1,100 miles of salmon spawning grounds were eliminated forever. What is more, increasing urban sprawl has meant not only encroachment on salmon habitat, but the increasing pollution from sewage, lumber mills, and factories has left the oxygen levels in many waterways so low as to render them lifeless (Robbins, 1999). As a result, every species of salmon fish stocks, at one time thought to be limitless, are now severely endangered. For example, in the Columbia Basin current salmon runs are approximately only 1.7% of their pre-Euro-American size. For Washington, Oregon, California, and Idaho, combined, the number is 5.2% of its original salmon population. In British Columbia, however, the numbers, while far from acceptable, are substantially better than those within the contiguous forty eight states, with salmon populations at 36.2% of their pre-contact numbers (Lackey, Lach, & Duncan, 2006b, p. 24).

The reductionist wealth-extracting conception of land that fueled this destruction has inevitably led to the area's tribal governments, on more than one occasion, taking the state to court based on articles written into treaties guaranteeing traditional fishing rights forever. For example, in the Treaty of Medicine Creek of 1854, Article III states that "the right of taking fish, at all usual and accustomed grounds and stations, is further secured by said Indians..." (quoted in Blumm & Bodi, 1999, p. 178). While it has been argued that Native fishing rights have been illegally limited since the signing of treaties, such as Medicine Creek, it was not until fish stocks in the Pacific Northwest began to be dramatically reduced that we see major efforts to prevent Native peoples from fishing while simultaneously protecting the fishing practices of white settlers. In 1889, for example, after Washington achieved statehood, numerous laws were passed limiting Native fishing activities in western Washington rivers in the name of conservation while ignoring white commercial fishing in the ocean and Puget Sound (Blumm & Bodi, 1999).

However, because of the forethought of the Native elders involved in the construction of treaties, making sure eternal fishing rights were firmly established, northwest Natives have been relatively successful in the courtroom. In 1905 the U.S. Supreme Court ruled that Native fishing rights could not be taken away by state licenses (or federal grants), such as those held by the operators of fishing wheels who unsuccessfully attempted to prevent Native fishing when stocks began to diminish. However, the rights of Native peoples have always been tenable as far as the settler-state governments of the U.S. and Canada are concerned. Triggering the emergence of the American Indian Movement (AIM), during the 1950s and 1960s, the U.S. government engaged in a policy aimed at terminating Native sovereignty resulting in the termination of over 100 tribes affecting over 12,000 individuals, and more than 2 million acres of land. Affected in the firestorm of terminations were the Klamath of southern Oregon, who, as a result of officially ceasing to exist, no longer had fishing rights. Gains from the Native pushback included Judge George Boldt, federal judge for the western district of Washington State, ruling in 1974 that the governments of Indigenous tribes had the right, as implied within the Stevens treaties, to regulate the harvest of up to 50% of salmon runs (Blumm & Bodi, 1999). Summarizing the magnitude of Boldt's ruling, while situating it in the context of Native sovereignty, Charles Wilkinson (2005), a white man from the settler-community, an esteemed law professor at the University of Colorado and former attorney for the Native American Rights Fund between 1971 and 1975, comments,

> An initial spark for reasserting tribal authority over land and natural resources came from Judge George Boldt's landmark decision upholding tribal treaty rights to harvest Pacific salmon. Judge Boldt, who ruled that the treaties guaranteed to the tribes the opportunity to harvest 50 percent of the salmon runs, also addressed tribal government authority. Opposition to such tribal powers was formidable. Washington, like other states, insisted upon an exclusive right to regulate the Salmon harvest, but Boldt upheld a significant role for tribal regulation...The tribes soon moved beyond regulating fishing to improving the salmon runs by hiring staffs of fisheries scientists. (p. 310)

This ongoing battle to improve the salmon runs provides a brilliant example of Indigenous philosophy informing the contemporary concrete context—that is, the protection of the habitat that is necessary for the survival of wild salmon, without which traditional Native fishing could not occur. In 1980, similar to Boldt's ruling, federal judge William Orrick ruled in the Ninth Circuit Court in the western district of Washington State that fish habitats were protected by the Stevens treaties, which was later overturned. However, it was also ruled that the tribes have a right to protect the necessary habitat for fish to survive (Blumm & Bodi, 1999). While these are ongoing issues and struggles, Native peoples, it seems, have steadily moved forward protecting and strengthening natural habitat wherever they can. For example, within a year of Boldt's ruling "the Puget Sound tribes together invented a new kind of institution, the professional intertribal natural resources organization" (Wilkinson, 2005, p. 310), where the 23 regional tribes united under the banner of the Northwest Indian Fisheries Commission (NIFC) to collaborate on both the science of fish and politics. Following the formation of NIFC, the four tribes of the Northwest—the Nez Perce, Umatilla, Warm Springs, and Yakama—formed the Columbia River Intertribal Fish Commission (CRIFC). In their operations CRIFC and NIFC utilize both Western and Indigenous epistemologies in the production of knowledge such as the work of fisheries scientists operating state-of-the-art laboratories specializing in fish health and genetics *and* "...interviewing elders to obtain the traditional knowledge that enriches tribal resource management" (Wilkinson, 2005, p. 311), which then informs their work in the concrete context of streambeds and tributaries. In other words, their work reflects a keen awareness of the dialectic relationship between the theoretical and concrete contexts where each informs the other in a never-ending process of reflection and action (Freire, 2005).

As a result of these actions and the role the Northwest tribes are perform-ing as co-managers of the salmon "resource," wherever traditional fishing rights have been secured, as guaranteed by federal law, Native communities have wholeheartedly begun the arduous task of rebuilding fish stocks and their natural habitat. The Warm Springs Indian Reservation stands as par excel-lence in their salmon recovery strategies, drawing the attention of environ-mental scientists and marine biologists from Oregon State University (OSU) culminating in OSU/Warm Springs salmon-recovery collaborations—proving that even PhDs can learn a thing or two from Native traditionalists. Advocating for these types of collaborations on a global scale, Semali and Kincheloe (1999b) note that "engaging Western science and indigenous knowledge in a dialogue with one another grants indigeneity a level of respect it has tradition-ally not received in Western education. This itself is a profoundly transforma-tive act" (p. 47).

The approach taken by the tribes, and recently adopted by Western scien-tists, does not romantically evacuate the present, paraphrasing Vizenor (1990), that is, it does not tend to focus on going back to the pre-dam era, but seeking viable solutions in the world that exists now as it is, such as working with the Bonneville Power Administration to decrease passage mortality and increasing main-stem spawning areas by regulating flow rates and spills with the ultimate objective of maintaining as natural a river system as possible. Other initiatives have included rebuilding watershed areas damaged by logging practices, especially clear-cutting, as well as fencing out livestock, which has inflicted considerable damage to spawning areas when left to roam freely among mountain streams. Aware of the continuing decline of wild salmon popula-tions, which are already critically low, and in many cases teetering on the brink of extinction, the tribes have been strong advocates of hatchery supplementa-tion. In addition to bringing areas on the brink of extinction back to stable levels, along with rebuilding and protecting fragile habitat, tribes are working to see hatchery supplementation used to bring fish back to extirpated areas, bring fish stocks up to healthy levels while the effects of measures, such as habitat restoration, can manifest their beneficial effects, and to bring stocks up to support moderate tribal livelihoods according to treaty-mandated harvest rights (Talbot & Galbreath, 2006).

Reflecting on the fishery management practices and initiatives for policy and habitat restoration of the tribes of the Northwest, conservation scientists André Talbot and Peter Galbreath (2006) comment that "...we have grown to appreciate, adopt, and advocate the very special perspective that the tribes have regarding the importance of salmon in the ecosystem, including the ecosystem's human component. Additionally, we have found their views on the goals for salmon restoration, and on the methodologies they advocate to achieve these goals, to be scientifically sound, as well as socially and economically pragmatic" (p. 551). Offering an even larger lens from which to understand the sentiments of Talbot and Galbreath, Wilkinson (2005) summarily notes that "if the far-flung effort to preserve the endangered wild Pacific salmon succeeds, the work of the tribes will have been a central reason" (p. 311).

We have yet to see, however, if the settler-community's environmentalists, conservationists, environmental engineers, fishery biologists, limnologists, marine biologists, interdisciplinary environmental specialists, and other such scientists, en masse, suggest returning unceded Native lands to Native communities as a solution to recovering wild salmon runs, which seems obvious because Natives have scientifically proven without reasonable doubt to have the best record at maintaining the health and spiritual integrity, holistically conceived, of the natural environment, that is, of the land, our common mother. This Native perspective of land as the mother of all that lives represents the epitome of relational thinking. In other words, viewing everything that exists as having, in the end, a common origin demonstrates that the survival of one part of the web is dependent on every other part of the web. Put another way, the interests of Native peoples, the interests of settlers, the interests of wild salmon, the interests of the spotted owl, the interests of the humpback whale, the interests of the Amazon rainforests, the interests of all life, at not only the end of the day, but at the beginning and middle of the day, as well, are all the same.

The view of land held by the majority of the settler-community, on the other hand, has not historically seen that the earth has a sacred Mother to be revered, but a value-laden and wild planet, an amalgam of *natural* resources, to be exploited and tamed. As Black Elk (Neihardt, 1932/2004) observed in

1932, those who view the world as the Wasichus do "...have forgotten that the earth is their mother" (p. 167). The Western scientific reductionist, that is, idealist, view of land that fails to acknowledge the sacred in life continues to hold political and intellectual sway within all of the settler-state's institutions, such as schools. However, as suggested above, all hope is not now, or ever will be, completely lost, and the hope in today for tomorrow simultaneously exists in the past—it is still with us, it did not go anywhere: the ugly *and* the good. Stories of our collective counter-hegemonic past are instructive in terms of envisioning not only "alliances" but bona fide collaborations and communities of resistance as well—relationships born in courtrooms, nourished in stream-beds, and lived in practice. When engaging in the next section, consider the philosophical implications for educating in the context of the call for unity in the spirit of today's Native North American renaissance.

Solidarity in Native America: Transgressing Antagonism

As the preceding section only briefly touched on issues of collaboration and unity dealing primarily with the antagonistic relationship between Western and Native philosophical traditions focusing on land as the primary source of contestation, this section takes as its primary foci instances of collaboration and solidarity against predation. In other words, what follows are examples of the complex nature of human sociability, and the manifestation of human resistance coming from within Native, enslaved, and settler-communities to an utterly inhumane process—the process of predation/colonization/domination/occupation. Put another way, the result of the peoples of Europe, Africa, and those native to North America coming together in the Americas has not always resulted in antagonistic relationships, as some Europeans brought to American shores, against their investors' will, saw a more promising future within Native societies as did many Africans brought as chattel slavery. In the next several pages you will read about the primarily African and Native American Seminoles and the "tri-racial" Croatans. These hybrid communities, forged out of an instinctive democratic impulse, offer compelling lessons and possibilities for radical education for a future without human suffering. Again, when engaged in the following narratives consider how the examples of these brave and committed people might inform our own individual and collective philosophies of education for the twenty-first century. However, before exploring these stories and their pedagogical implications, we begin by briefly outlining the historical process that led to these different peoples coming to occupy the same physical space, that is, the same landbase.

African and European Labor

Because of both the vast loss of life in the newly exploited Native North American land and the relative success of indigenous resistance to enslavement on the mainland (outlined in Chapter Two), new sources of labor were needed to create value. Unlike the Arawak encountered by Columbus who were not people of warfare and thus easily enslaved, the Pequot peoples of present-day southern Connecticut and Rhode Island, for example, were better able to defend themselves and resist enslavement. From the beginning, English colonizers therefore brought both African and European laborers with them. However, the first English settlers lacked the technology and knowledge to survive in North America, and therefore relied on the support and assistance of those indigenous to the region. Like Columbus, English occupiers were also driven by the pursuit of wealth. Summarizing this era—an era marked by the beginning stages of capitalist accumulation that would violently develop into what we know today as globalization, or global capitalism, explored a bit further in Chapters Four and Nine—Zinn (1995) writes:

> It seems there was a frenzy in the early capitalist states of Europe for gold, for slaves, for products of the soil, to pay the bondholders and stockholders of the expeditions, to finance the monarchical bureaucracies rising in Western Europe, to spur the growth of the new money economy rising out of feudalism, to participate in what Karl Marx would later call "the primitive accumulation of capital." These were the violent beginnings of an intricate system of technology, business, politics, and culture that would dominate the world for the next five centuries. (p. 12)

This quest for wealth drove early colonialists to acts of barbaric fanaticism (a trend that is as strong and intense today as it was in 1492). First in the Caribbean Basin, then in North America, one of the primary sources of replacement labor were the peoples of Africa. Africans constituted one of the first major transplanted populations in the Americas, along with Europeans. It has been estimated that nearly one million Africans were captured and brought to the Americas against their will in the 1500s. In the 1600s that number rose to 2.75 million, and continued to increase until the nineteenth century, at which time 4 million people from Africa were brought as cargo/human commodities to be bought and sold by the American plantocracy. At the height of America's human slave trade, during the 1700s, a staggering 7 million Africans were forced onto ships and made to suffer the most wretched of conditions and brought to America. In total, at least 15 million African people were forced into American slavery. It has been estimated that for every African who stepped foot onto American shores, five corpses were left behind in either Africa or en route. That means that somewhere in the neighborhood of 60 million Africans lost their lives in the process of putting 15 million living Africans on American soil (Anderson, 1995). While Chapter Two documents the genocide suffered by Native North Americans, what has just been presented represents the African holocaust/genocide. From the outset Africans fled forced labor and the barbarism of predator joining Native societies when they could. Within Native cultures Africans found similarities to their own holistically conceived indigenous philosophical traditions. The life-affirming philosophy of Native Americans attracted many people imported to the Americas for labor from not only Africa but Europe as well. Many of these people sought refuge from the life-denying barbarism of colonialist wealth extraction. This aspect of Indigenous philosophy (oneness with nature) has also been used by Western European colonial interests as "evidence" of the former's "primitiveness," paving the way for a continuous genocidal war and land grab. It seems as though we have come full circle, as highlighted above.

To reiterate, many contemporary scientists are embracing a native view of the world that sees everything as interconnected and therefore interdependent, as well as possessing inherent worth beyond the accumulation of wealth/capital/surplus value (see Chapter Four for a more comprehensive discussion of Marx's critique of capitalism and it has recently informed some genres of critical pedagogy). However, still tending to be missing from the scientific environmentalist perspective are Native cultures and peoples. Nature is still viewed as a thing outside of human culture. Humans might be understood as part of the ecosystem, but only in terms of animalistic functions. Arguing that a Native view of culture is intimately connected to the environment (place) contrasted with a Western immigrant view of culture that is focused on a chronologically ordered list of events (Deloria, 1994). Again, this despiritualized ontology and accompanying Western scientific epistemology were rejected by many Africans and Europeans whose sole function from the colonialist perspective was to create value for an emerging ruling class.

What philosophical tradition condones stripping people from their ancestral lands and simultaneously stripping the land from their human ancestors? It is the same philosophy that attempted to sever the connection between land

and people in Europe with the privatization of the commons and closing in time and the calendar with the end of the festival, which was a huge chunk of each planetary cycle of life, that is, a year (Ryan, 2006). It is a philosophy that does not respect the interconnectedness of all things and that only respects the accumulation of highly centralized wealth and power. It is a philosophy against life—all life—it not only is vampirish, paraphrasing Marx, but cannibalistic as well.

The concentration of wealth does not respect democratic decision making because it gives a small number of voices an extremely large amount of weight compared to the majority of voices. Such situations make mass movements a democratic necessity. The only way the masses can assert their voice and advance their interests is to become organized through a process of unity formation. This is an increasingly difficult task, as the power elite continuously devise new methods of division. A movement informed by indigenous and critical philosophy can provide a powerful tool against the divide and rule tactics employed by predator, that is, the ruling class of the settler-community.

Again, not all Euro-Afro-Native engagements have been marked by antagonism and conflict. European, African, and Native North American philosophies have not only been altered as a result of colonization, oppression, and resistance, but by solidarity as well. There are a number of documented examples of European laborers, enslaved Africans, and Native American survivors of genocide who, out of the necessity to survive with their humanity intact, came together united by a common human thread and built new cultural formations and lifeways out of a hybrid amalgamation of what they originally brought to the table. I will highlight two such examples in the following section. First, I discuss the "disappearance" of the first settlement of English immigrants off the coast of the Carolinas. Then, because of the magnitude of the massive resistance they staged against settler-state encroachment, I highlight the Seminoles, who had flourished in present-day Florida.

Gone to Croatan

In "Caliban's Masque: Spiritual Anarchy & The Wild Man in Colonial America" (1993), Peter Lamborn Wilson revisits what came of those early settlers off the coast of North Carolina on Roanoke Island who mysteriously disappeared during the late 1500s. In 1585 Richard Grenville, under the authority of Englishman Sir Walter Raleigh, sailed to the Americas with the intent of securing "heathen and barbarian lands" (Thornton, 1987, p. 66). In

order to fulfill their mission, under a charter inherited from Raleigh's half
brother, Sir Humphrey Gilbert, the men founded one of the first English
colonies in the Americas on Roanoke Island, Virginia, part of present-day
North Carolina. After establishing the colony, Grenville left 108 colonists on
Roanoke and returned to England with plant samples and perhaps some
Native peoples to present to his investors as evidence of the potential wealth to
be generated and extracted from this "new" land. Sir Francis Drake returned
the following spring of 1586 finding the colonists in such poor health they
were returned to England ending the first English colony in North America.
As a result of their stay an epidemic was spread amongst the surrounding
Indigenous communities, probably typhus, resulting in many deaths. However,
a small contingent of enslaved Africans and Native Americans and a few
English were left behind. Intent on securing his investment, Grenville soon
returned only to find the colony abandoned, and therefore left a few new
colonists with some provisions. In 1587 Raleigh then sent more than 100 fresh
colonialists—men, women, and children—under the governorship of John
White. White did not stay long, returning to England for supplies. Finding
himself in the middle of the war with Spain when he returned to England,
White was not able to return to Roanoke until 1590 only to find the colony
once again deserted (Thornton, 1987).

The missing colonists, consisting of 85 men, 17 women, and 11 children,
having been left by their state-sponsored investors and nobility to work the
land, left no evidence of their whereabouts other than an engraving on a tree
reading "Gone to Croatan," or just "Croatan" (Thornton, 1987; Wilson,
1993). The Croatans were a local community of Indigenous Americans. The
English investors, after returning to the place of their investment and having
realized there would be no returns/profits, claimed their laborers were brutally
slaughtered by the "savage Indians" yet providing no evidence of human
remains or struggle. These stories have found their way into U.S. history
textbooks, providing a convenient justification for the "tragic" and "unfortunate" genocide committed against those native to North America. It was
known that the Croatans were a friendly tribe who occupied an island south of
Roanoke, but this "clue," for whatever reason, was not followed up on. Years
passed before another ship made its way past Croatan only to find it deserted
as well. Their fate:

> Clearly fed up with slaving for a bunch of absentee London gentlemen, the lower
> classes of Roanoke had simply dropped out and gone native. They moved to Croatan

and joined the tribe, then moved again to the mainland near the Great Dismal Swamp, where they avoided discovery for a long time (despite elusive rumors of "gray-eyed Indians"). Later they absorbed runaway slaves into their population, and survived as a "tri-racial isolate community" for centuries. (Wilson, 1993, p. 97)

The settlers, it turns out, most likely having merged with the Croatans as well as Africans, unhappy with the oppressiveness of colonial rule, created a "tri-racial" community living deep in North Carolina's swamplands for centuries, and therefore undetected by mainstream colonialist society. Today, the people of this community, the Lumbee Indians, numbering more than 28,000 as of 1980, know who they are, claiming that the blood of the colonialists continues to run in their veins (Thornton, 1987), some of whom continue to possess the names of their English ancestors who carved those famous words on that tree, "Gone to Croatan." This story is consistent with the traditional adoption practices of Native American societies. Summarizing such practices and unofficial policies, Churchill (2002) comments:

Indians habitually intermarried between groups and frequently adopted both children and adults from other groups. This occurred in precontact times between Indians, and the practice was broadened to include those of African and European origin, and ultimately Asian origin as well, once contact occurred. Those who were naturalized by marriage or adoption were considered members of the group, pure and simple. This was always the native view. (p. 380)

This practice allowed oppressed peoples brought to the Americas an alternative to the dehumanizing conditions they faced within European colonies. The penalty for colonizers "going native," as it were, was severe, sometimes death. The colonizers depended on the labor of their colonial subjects to generate wealth, and could therefore not tolerate dissension. What the story of Croatan highlights is the fact that not only can humanity exist without the presence of a small ruling elite but our survival perhaps depends on it (Malott, 2006). What is more, the survival of the Lumbee demonstrates that we still have alternatives. Contributing to the strength of our argument here is the fact that the cast of the lost colony of Roanoke does not stand alone. Let us now turn to another example of a "mixed-racial" community forged out of the suffering of occupation, slavery, and dehumanization that, again, defies the "inevitability" of African-European-Native American conflict.

While the story of the Croatans and Lumbee is one of hope and solidarity, one of the strongest alliances forged against settler-state oppression in

North America manifested itself in present-day Florida. This African–Native American unity was created amongst the chaos of slavery and expropriation—Africans fleeing enslavement and predominantly Creek Native Americans (although many other oppressed tribes merged) fleeing the barbarism of forced removal at the hands of "white" people and others who had given in to coddling the aggressor. These people came to be known as Seminoles, a Creek word that can be roughly translated as those who secede or break away—in short, fugitives, rebels, or renegades. What these Africans and First Americans created was something new out of the old—that is, new forms of indigeneity forged out of the necessity of survival and refusing to give up the natural freedom to use ones creative capacities (labor power) to create balance with the earth through humanizing the world from an indigenous perspective. As we will see below, it has been argued that the strength of the Seminoles, forged out of lessons bitterly learned, constitute the only indigenous community in North America that never completely surrendered to the government of either Canada or the United States.

The Seminoles

> The entire Afro-Native American cultural exchange and contact experience is a fascinating and significant subject, but one largely obscured by a focus upon European activity and European colonial relations with 'peripheral' subject peoples. (Forbes, 1993, p. 1)

For example, there is substantial evidence pointing to the long history of pre-Columbian contact between Africans and Native Americans. Commenting on this phenomena that "never makes it into history textbooks" James Loewen (1995) notes that around 750 B.C., voyages, launched from Egypt, reached the Atlantic coast of Mexico, where giant basalt stone portraits of West African heads can be found to the present day, which have been dated to 750 B.C. However, despite the relevance of this untold history, we will focus our attention here on the specific post-Columbian exchanges that gave way to the dynamic emergence of the Seminoles (Forbes, 1993; Katz, 1986; Porter, 1996), which can be understood as an extension of the long history of solidarity and unity among people who, most recently, came together around the need to defend themselves from a common enemy of a European source. Despite the rich history of the close relationship between Africans and Native Americans throughout the Americas resulting in as much as one third of the U.S. African American population possessing Native American ancestry, these stories are rarely told in mainstream history textbooks. According to William Loren Katz (1986) in *Black Indians: A Hidden Heritage*, whitestream U.S. history books obscure and distort this rich history by inventing stereotypical "differences" between Africans and Native Americans portraying Africans as passive and willing slaves and Native Americans, as noble savages whose time has tragically, yet unavoidably, come and gone. Ultimately, what is ignored and attacked is the humanity and dignity of Afro-Native American peoples, as well as the deep friendship and political alliance between those who share a common oppressor. As a result, the invaluable lessons that could be learned from this powerful alliance, a merger if you will, between Africans and Native Americans tends not to be learned in whitestream schools. In Florida, as we will see below, this alliance posed a real threat to colonialist hegemony. This threat was so great that some historians point to the policy of genocide by European colonizers (see Chapter Two) as not only part of the process of depopulating and then repopulating Indigenous land, but also a way to "prevent their alliance with Africans" (Katz, 1986, p. 7).

Among the European powers (the French, Dutch, Spanish, and English in particular) operating within the North American context, the English were arguably the most overtly genocidal bent on creating as many "Indian free zones" as possible, regardless of the human cost, with the ultimate goal of repopulating Native land with European stock and transforming the "wild" land into the accumulation of highly concentrated wealth (Churchill, 1997). The Seminoles were born out of English trickery, slavery, and genocide. The English, in their colonization of the eastern seaboard, the Carolinas in particular, from the beginning, that is, once they acquired the necessary knowledge of the land and how to survive on it from the Indigenous communities they were immersed in, began pitting tribe against tribe, always in the interests of the emerging bosses. By 1733 the Yamasee, the Guale, the Apalachee, the Cofitachiqui, the Timucuan, a portion of the lower Creeks and a significant number of formerly enslaved Africans, fed up with being divided and ruled, many of whom were on the brink of extinction, eventually migrated south to Florida becoming, and remaining, Seminoles (Churchill, 1997; Katz, 1986; Porter, 1996). The term "Seminole" is a Creek word that means runaway or rebel. Accepting Africans into their society was natural for the Seminoles, as they themselves were multi-ethnic and came from communities that frequently adopted "outsiders." As it turns out the relationship between Africans and Native Americans in Florida was based on mutual aid.

The original inhabitants of Florida had been all but exterminated, and the region was "controlled" by Spain. The community and people that would come to call themselves Seminoles began in present-day Florida with Africans fleeing the cruelty of Anglo slavery. These Africans survived employing a method of cultivating rice originating from Senegambia and Sierra Leone (Katz, 1986). When Native American Seminoles arrived in Florida, they learned how to sustain themselves and build a flourishing establishment from ex-slaves. The dense swamp lands and tropical jungles of Florida with their deadly reptiles and alligators provided a temporary barrier between escaped Africans and white enslavers unwilling to risk the dangers of the wilderness to retrieve "runaways." Excursions into the wilderness by enslavers to capture Africans began once the marooned villages became large enough to pose a threat to plantocracy hegemony by being a future destination in the back of free-thinking enslaved Africans' minds in the South. As the Native Americans in the swamp relied on Africans for agricultural knowledge, Africans depended on the military protection from their Seminole friends. The U.S. was unable to defeat the Seminoles, who were fast becoming a nation of one— composed predominantly of Africans, Native Americans, and their "mixed blood" offspring.

The colonialist, enslaving aggressor understood that breaking this unity was the key that would destroy what was becoming a "red-black Nation" within the United States, which, from the colonialist enslaving perspective, was absolutely not acceptable. In an attempt to break up this unity, Native Americans were encouraged to own slaves, that is, to enslave those they had befriended. To appease their white neighbors, the Seminole Indians responded by saying that the Africans were now their slaves. However, aware of the egalitarian relationship between Africans and Native Americans in Florida, the Seminoles continued to attract Africans from brutal white plantations. Realizing that dissension could not be externally sown within Seminole society, the white plantocracy organized their militias, armies, and Native American allies and set out to crush "red-black" independence. However, it wasn't until the Spanish left Florida that the U.S. was able to more aggressively attack Seminole villages.

In Florida the Seminoles were able to relatively peacefully thrive and develop culturally and numerically for nearly one hundred years serving as Spain's primary defensive force against English encroachment. For Africans enslaved by English cruelty, Florida represented the promised land, a real utopia in a land of un-freedom. In an effort to strengthen their position against an increasingly invasive English military Spain offered a safe haven for Africans seeking emancipation, which, it should be noted, was a tactical decision, not a moral one. Within Seminole communities one would find African villages, Native American settlements, and hybrid arrangements giving way to the "Black Indians."

When Florida fell to the United States in 1819, the Spanish army simply left, leaving the Seminoles to their own devices. Once again, the Seminoles were faced with English barbarism at their doorstep. What ensued was a series of wars and relocations inflicting damage to the Seminoles in genocidal proportions. For example, they lost as much as 50% of their population during the mid to late 1800s (Thornton, 1987) fighting what had become the U.S. (the former emerging ruling class of the English, now the new ruling class of the Americas) and its war to conquer the Seminoles in order to force them to relocate to "Indian Territory," Okalahoma and Arkansas, for example, and begin importing new labor power putting them to work extracting wealth out of the land of Florida.

Offering a portrait of Seminole solidarity and unity was the Creek leader Wild Cat (Coacoochee) and the African chief John Horse (Cohia) who together led their Seminole Nation from Florida to Indian Territory, to Mexico and then to the United States, twenty years after slavery ended, to work as Scouts. Summarizing the relationship between these two figures, William Katz (1986) notes that "their friendship would last for twenty years and revolve around their agreement that red and black Seminoles were blood sisters and brothers whom no foe could part" (p. 64). What this critical pedagogy of solidarity looked like in practice for Wild Cat after being relocated from Florida to "Indian Territory" Katz (1986) comments, "Wild cat hoped to establish a military colony for oppressed Indian and black people. He wanted to recruit from the Five Civilized Nations, from Texas and Arkansas plantations, and perhaps elsewhere once his movement gained momentum" (p. 70). After having fled the slavery and hostility dominating "Indian Territory" in the United States and finding temporary refuge in Mexico serving the Mexican government as border guards, John Horse's deep sense of solidarity continued to inform his practice. Katz (1986) provides one such example in the following passage:

> In 1856 the issue of Seminole refusal to take sides in Mexican politics came up sharply. The ruler of Coahuila ordered John Horse's troops into combat against a political rival. Horse refused. Rosa Fay remembered his position: "'Here we are,'

> John Horse would say, 'all living as in one house. How can I take up a gun and kill
> you, who are my brother, or how can I take up a gun for you and kill that other man,
> who is also my brother.'" (p. 74)

While their Mexican hosts were at first upset for the Seminoles' consistent unruliness, their stance was made clear and ultimately accepted as a result of Horse's advanced diplomatic skills. The Seminoles eventually returned to the United States, and what was remarkable about their return was the fact that "a Black Nation negotiated its entrance into the United States by formal treaty" (p. 76). When it was all said and done the Seminoles managed to resist European and then United States subjugation fighting for their right to be free and sovereign people for over a century, an achievement unrivaled in the Americas. Generations of Seminole warriors were born and died in their community's just war for self-determination that spanned from the swampy marshlands of Florida to the deserts of Texas and eventually Mexico.

Today, "Red-Black Seminole Indians," still with no land of their own, despite being promised a reservation by the United States in a treaty that somehow "disappeared," for their service as Scouts in the Southwest, are scattered throughout the South; a sizable community, for example, lives in abject poverty on both sides of the Rio Grande near Eagle Pass, forgotten and unseen as the Zapatistas were before they "covered" their "face to have a face" and forgot their "names" so they could "be named" (see Chapter Nine). Because of the long period of time the Seminoles militarily resisted the United States and the consciousness that generations of Seminoles were raised with as a result of growing up in struggle against the aggressor, at some level, I think we can trace contemporary African American militancy back to the Seminoles. Huey P. Newton, co-founder of the Black Panther Party (BPP), himself came from the South, as did many Panther leaders such as Assata Shakur, who, after being captured in a military engagement with New Jersey State Troopers, escaped from behind enemy lines and currently lives in Cuba having been granted political asylum. The United States government has recently placed a one million dollar bounty on Shakur's head, signaling the intensification of the U.S.'s efforts to destroy Cuba's independence (Malott, 2007). Similarly, by 1837 the encroachment on Seminole lands was intensifying, making it increasingly risky for African Seminoles to be captured by "slave hunters." As a result, many African Seminoles fled to the Caribbean because slavery had been abolished there since 1834 (Katz, 1986). What is more, like much of the Seminole Nation, Shakur and her Black Liberation Army, the "underground" military arm of the Black Panther Party, have never officially surrendered to United States' hegemony.

* * *

What these examples demonstrate is that humans are dangerously susceptible to manipulation and deception. Almost without exception, when native peoples had their land, their livelihood and sense of self, ripped out from underneath them, they became increasingly susceptible to the deception of believing the aggressor is a suitable ally. However, what the European colonizer, or those informed by the European model of colonization, has proven time and time again is that once put to work in the service of the colonizer, that is, your task is complete, you become the next target, you are disposable—under this system we are all disposable. Even the whites themselves have been proven to be expendable from the boss' point of view.

For example, in present-day western New York the white working class violently pushed the Six Nations from their lands into Canada after the U.S.' Revolutionary War. After "clearing the way," the settler-population, which has absorbed many Indigenous people, were then put to work transforming the region into an industrial wasteland rendering the local elite truly ruling class wealthy. However, the settler-community in western New York, for all intents and purposes, has since been left to rot with the closing down of the industrial machinery, symbolized in the 1983 closing of Bethlehem Steel in Buffalo, New York. With the region's economic base torn asunder rendering the local population destitute, even after centuries of loyal service subjugating not only native North Americans, but the people the world over, in a series of wars, interventions and covert coups (Blum, 1995; Chomsky, 2001), the people have been left in poverty and susceptible to discursive, ideological manipulation. The ruling class has proven that they have no more concern about the people who are supposed to come from the same "racial stock" as their own mothers and fathers than they do for anyone else. Their motivation is profit. Morals and values are not part of the equation because that would challenge them to consider the human and environmental costs of plundering, which would encroach on margins, and that is simply not acceptable. Our only option is therefore to unite.

It seems apparent that the settler and Native communities of the present era are far less prepared to cope effectively and resist economic warfare than the pre-indoctrination-era peoples were of the past five hundred years. They had a different philosophical perspective than the oppressor. While such disparate worldviews caused much confusion, as noted above, it offered Native Americans a unique lens that immediately unveiled the absurdity of the entire colonization and wealth extraction process because such pursuits are informed by a distorted view of the world. Those indoctrinated within the settler-community therefore have a more difficult time recognizing the insanity of the system. To avoid manipulation and being taken advantage of by the bosses, we need to learn how to actively engage with our world to unlearn the hegemony of oppression—that is, to become critically conscious. This requires a non-indoctrinating, non-dogmatic critical education, an approach that we have come to know as critical pedagogy made official by the late, world-renowned, critical-revolutionary, Brazilian educator Paulo Freire. We now turn to Chapter Four, which begins with a brief discussion of the pedagogy of the Lakota leader Crazy Horse as a segue into Paulo Freire, critical pedagogy, and education generally.

Chapter 4

Critical Pedagogy in Native North America: Western and Indigenous Philosophy in the Schooling Context

Western Hegemonic Philosophy in North American Settler-Education

I begin this chapter with an analysis of Western hegemonic philosophy because it represents the approach that has dominated the entire history of what we can call formal schooling in North America since the 1600s and has been applied to all peoples of all ethnic/cultural/language/regional backgrounds. The goal of education has always been twofold: first, to train community "leaders" (including teachers) in the application of "law" (as it pertains to every aspect of colonialist society) to serve the interests, even if by default, of the rich and powerful, and simultaneously, to mold those who are being colonized on their own land, and those brought in as imported labor, into accepting the "law" of the settler-state as legitimate, as just, as inevitable, and at times, divine (i.e., "in God we trust"). This is achieved by institutionalizing a one answer and one approach formula to knowledge production, rendering the occupying force the only legitimate possessor of truth and knowledge. The framework from which this approach to the social structure is based on is hierarchical and is therefore represented in unequal educational practices, giving way to the normalization of social class.

In Chapter One we were introduced to Plato's myth of metals where gold metal people, the elite few, were deemed intellectually and morally superior and thus most fit for leadership positions, and on the other end of the spectrum were the brass metal people, the vast majority, who, because of their assumed low moral and intellectual fiber, were fit to do no more than take the directive of their natural superiors. Not only was this idea alive and well in

Columbus' predatory pedagogy he called Christianity, but it was thriving in colonialist education as well, and continues to serve as the dominant philosophy in settler-state schooling. In the following discussion we explore the multiple functions education has played within and between different groups of people.

Education, especially higher education, has been touted within the settler-community as evidence of the existence of meritocracy, that is, if you work hard, are a "good" (i.e., obedient) citizen, and (have access to the material and cultural capital needed to) go to college, then it is expected that you will be rewarded with "success" within the capitalist system that exists. Education has therefore been held up in the West as a key to full democratic participation (within the limitations of capitalism). Because of the social power and privilege afforded those with a formal education in Western societies, it has been used as a tool of oppression by denying it to certain people such as African Americans. Much of the civil rights movement of the 1960s and 1970s in the United States was focused on achieving equal access to educational opportunities for historically oppressed peoples. Demanding the right to an education has not only been implicated in accommodating the system that exists, that is, attempting to "succeed" within it, but it has also been advocated for as a means of becoming critically conscious and politically active, that is, transformative.

For example, African American emancipatory scholar W.E.B. DuBois, who Joe Kincheloe (2004) positions as an influential figure of central importance in critical pedagogy, argued that education should serve the interests of the students, and therefore work to subvert the basic structures of power within capitalist, white supremacist society. Much of DuBois' work can be seen as part of the long legacy of ancient African dialectics discussed in Chapter Two. Within the context of DuBois' dialectics, formal education is highly desirable to the extent that it is presented as an indispensable tool in the project of humanization. In other words, humanity's struggle to free itself from all forms of oppression is portrayed as not possible without a revolutionary form of mass education. To deny people a transformative education is therefore an act of oppression or subjugation.

At the same time, education has been used by the United States and Canadian governments to exterminate what it is about Native Americans, beyond genetic composition, that is characteristically Native American and that is, in one word, culture. Children, as young as four years old, were physically removed from their communities, from the love and nurturance of their mothers and grandmothers by "coercing" (violently if needed) families into allowing their children to be taken away to schools far from their communities and for years on end. Roughly between the late 1800s and the mid-1900s more than half of all Native American children had been removed from their homes to be forced to act and think like white children (Churchill, 2004) and therefore become something other than what they formerly were through the boarding school project. This compulsory assimilation was put into practice in the classroom by beating Native children over the head with ideas like the U.S. and Canadian governments and white society in general represented every-thing good and civilized and that "Indian" ways were shameful and savage. The "unhappy history" (colonization and genocide) of Indigenous peoples was rarely discussed, and if it was, it was to be contrasted with the superior future that is now within their grasp thanks to the generous gift of "Western civiliza-tion."

In addition to manipulating the curriculum, Native American children were *whitestreamed* by severely controlling their actions and very closely monitoring their behavior. The "teachers" accomplished their objectives through a number of means: changing the children's dress and hairstyles from their individualized traditional tribal attire to institutionalized military-style uniforms; destroying all of the cultural materials they brought with them from their home communities; banning all cultural practices and severely punishing "students" for engaging in their Indigenous cultures such as speaking their native tongues, even outside of "class"; and by only allowing English to be spoken while spending the majority of one's time toiling in boarding school factories.

In 2001 the Truth Commission on Genocide in Canada found that main-stream churches and government were directly responsible for the deaths of at least fifty thousand children as a result of this process of compulsory assimila-tion. The list of crimes these institutions were found to be guilty of includes murder through beating, poisoning, hanging, starvation, strangulation, medical experimentation, and forced sterilization (T. Smith, 2005). The report also found that "...clergy, police and business and government officials were involved in maintaining pedophile rings using children from residential schools" (T. Smith, 2005, p. 40). Indigenous children were so thoroughly dehumanized and commodified through the predatory process of value production that they became frequent victims of sexual predators, who flocked to boarding schools under the false titles of "priest" and "teacher." In other words, while cultural genocide both damages the soul and deters the mind from reaching enlightenment, physical and sexual abuse provide the final attack on one's sense of self, giving way to the creation of a slave.

It was an openly expressed policy among Indian boarding schools that the students would contribute to the funding of their own cultural destruction through their collective labor power expended at "school." Some girls toiled in sweatshops sewing linens and garments while others worked in laundries or bakeries producing an abundance of food sold to the surrounding white communities while they themselves were malnourished. The labor power of boys was put to the task of turning out commercial items in wood, metal, and leather shops. Churchill (2004) cited a 1928 U.S. investigating commission that determined that most of what went on at Indian boarding schools would be illegal in most settler-communities because of child labor laws. Native American children were forced to work long hours often for no wages at all, but in some instances were "paid" between one and three cents an hour as an "incentive." These "wages" were often put in a fund and then typically mismanaged and squandered by the BIA (Bureau of Indian Affairs).

As a result, many Native American children, when they returned to their communities, were not only traumatized from years of abuse, but in many ways they were cultural outsiders, that is, for all intents and purposes, non-"Indian," and haters-of-self. Many Indigenous boarding school "students" were therefore not only lonely, scared, and preyed upon at "school," but they found themselves with dangerously damaged self-esteems in whatever context they found themselves in, giving way to an epidemic of suicide and drug and alcohol abuse. In response, the Boarding School Healing Project (BSHP) was established in 2000 informed by a multi-pronged approach to activism. First and foremost the BSHP provides an invaluable source of support for the victims of abuse while simultaneously documenting abuses and educating the general public. The BSHP is also dedicated to holding those responsible accountable through national and international courts (T. Smith, 2005).

As should be expected, and alluded to by the BSHP, amid the atmosphere of boarding school repression emerged a culture of resistance because our humanity, while it can be limited, it can never be fully destroyed. Regardless of how harmful our conditioning has been, we always retain the ability to become conscious of our own consciousness (Freire, 1998, 2005). Put another way, despite how hopeless a situation appears, there is always hope, it is an ontological need of the human condition (Freire, 1999). Summarizing the frequency and ways Native American children fought back, Churchill (2004) notes:

...Native children were not merely the passive victims of all that was being done to them. Virtually without exception, survivor narratives include accounts of subversion, both individual and collective, most commonly involving such activities as 'stealing' and/or foraging food, possessing other 'contraband,' persistence in the speaking of native languages and running away. In many—perhaps most—residential schools, such activities were so common and sustained as to comprise outright 'cultures of resistance.' (p. 51)

The primary goal of replacing the Indigenous culture with the foreign settler-culture was to transform the peoples' relationship to the land, making them willing accomplices in their own subjugation and rendering the process of colonization that much easier for the oppressor. Native children were to internalize the same white supremacy and support for the system that other people slated to be workers in the settler-communities were to incorporate into their consciousnesses. The implication for white people is to hate the other, while the implication for people of color, such as Native Americans, as we have seen, is to hate the self. Consumed by their own guilt, however, many white people wind up hating themselves too (see Chapter One). While white supremacy is obviously more harmful to people of color, white people would also be better served by a system based on positivism rather than the very negative order that exists. Once again, this is one of those intersections for radical solidarity against whiteness.

The educational goal for Native children and the majority of Europeans and Africans brought to North America to be put to work for the investors was to instill a fear of God, that is, the ruling authority, and a commitment to sacrifice and hard work because it would appease the fearful God and lead to salvation. While the schoolhouse was often used for Europeans and Native Americans, the classroom for Africans was more often the plantation. While white laborers, often flogged or whipped for falling victim to Satan, that is, showing any signs of free thinking, they were nevertheless born into the Western world and therefore tended not to possess worldviews that challenged the occupier's use and control of the land. This, in part, helps to explain the harsher measures the U.S. and Canadian governments have taken against Native children, reaching genocidal proportions. In other words, those raised in the settler-communities were born and bred to be wage earners, to be externally controlled, which essentially, is to be a slave. Native American communities with an independent existence from the settler-states socialize themselves to be free and not externally commanded. The true goal of boarding schools was therefore to colonize the mind and enslave the body.

The goal of education for those deemed most suitable for manual labor (Native and African Americans and the vast majority of whites) was designed to replace any previous conception of self with "worker"—that is, to define oneself as a slave, a worker. If the only thing your identity is based on is being a worker, then you will feel incomplete if not working, or taking orders. This sense of dependency was and continues to be reinforced in the schools through a banking model of education, where the teacher and/or the creators of curriculum are deemed to be the sole possessors of valuable knowledge and the students therefore as void of useful information and understandings. In this model education is something that is done to you—you go to school to *be* educated. In this context the students' success is measured by how well he or she can follow directions and regurgitate prepackaged knowledge—often referred to as *the* "right" answer (Freire, 1998).

In response to this alienating education and oppressive mode of work, which should not be confused with a community employing their collective labor power to actively engage *with* the world and not merely *in* or *on* the world, that is, passively, many Native American communities have taken control of their schools and embarked on a campaign of cultural rejuvenation with an emphasis on traditional value systems, customs, and language.

Indigenous Philosophy in North American Settler-Education

> Deloria's essays are not primarily about raising standards or improving test scores; rather they constitute a reasonable call to consider the advantages of building an educational practice on a foundation of American Indian metaphysics that "is a unified worldview acknowledging a complex totality in the world both physical and spiritual." This undertaking will not be easy, and we do need allies. (Wildcat, 2001a, p. 9)

Again, the focus of tribally conceived and controlled education has been on countering the deleterious effects of the boarding school experience. However, the ideological damage inflicted by boarding schools has, at times, impeded the process of putting formal education in the hands of tribal communities as advocated for in the federal government's Great Society programs of the 1960s. For example, in 1969 Gerald Vizenor (1990) reported that Commissioner Bennett of the Bureau of Indian Affairs, himself a Native American graduate of federal boarding school, defended the BIA arguing that all the decisions of the past were the best that could be made at the time and in so doing apologized for every imaginable atrocity committed by the federal settler-state government, including genocide. Bennett was put under fire for not taking a more active role in fulfilling U.S. President Johnson's mandate that Native communities establish "Indian school boards" thereby partially relieving the BIA from administrative control of their local schools. By May of 1969, despite the BIA's foot-dragging, 174 of the BIA's 222 schools had Native American elected school boards (Tippeconnic III, 1999). The first fully tribally controlled school was the highly acclaimed Arizona-based Rough Rock, which was turned over to the Navajo in 1966 just prior to its opening (Vizenor, 1990). Rough Rock was the first school to have elected a completely Native American school board.

From its inception Rough Rock placed special emphasis on their bilingual program, providing students with instruction in both English and Navajo. Many of the teachers at Rough Rock are Navajo, and there has been special care taken to ensure a culturally appropriate curriculum with Navajo mothers in every classroom weaving on traditional Navajo looms while telling the children stories in the customary oral tradition. The Navajo administration has stressed the importance of having philosophy taught by medicine men. These efforts have resulted in greater community and parental involvement, which has been challenging given the bad reputation of education in Indian country, due primarily to the horrors of the boarding school era. Rather than experiencing punishment and discipline for being "Indian," students at Rough Rock are rewarded and encouraged to explore their indigeneity and develop culturally as Indigenous people. U.S. President Kennedy pointed to Rough Rock as a model for other reservation schools to follow. However, driving the push for tribally controlled schools has not been the benevolence of Congress or Parliament or any particular presidency or prime minister, but a movement of dedicated and persistent Native American educators, institutions, organizations, tribes, and other community-based power blocs. The legislation this pushback has been responsible for includes:

1972—*Indian Education Act*—Committed funds to making Native American education culturally relevant. (Tippeconnic III, 1999)

1975—*Indian Self-Determination and Education Assistance Act*—Enabled the U.S. federal government to create 638 contracts between the BIA and tribes for tribal control of schools and health services. (Tippeconnic III, 1999)

1988—*Tribally Controlled School Act*—Allowed tribal boards to move from "contracting" to "direct granting," which was intended to institutional-ize tribal control of schools, contributing to the sense of permanency. (Tippeconnic III, 1999)

1990-present—*The Vanishing Money Situation*—Since the 1990s and the ascendancy of neo-liberal policies in the capitalist world, we have seen an attack on the public sphere marked by sharp cuts in funding for public programs such as education. While tribes control more "Indian" schools than ever before, more than half as of 1994-1995, the resources and fed-eral support for such programs seems to be drying up, despite the efforts of the grassroots pushback. (Tippeconnic III, 1999)

Despite the fading support for Native American education by the federal government of the United States, the hopeful spirit of determination seems to be alive and well within many Native American communities—these neglected communities, which some Native Americans have alluded to are essentially refugee camps (Neihardt, 1932/2004), suffer from the highest unemployment, poverty, and alcoholism rates in North America. Summarizing the spirit of this movement for tribal sovereignty, John W. Tippeconnic III (1999) notes,

> In the midst of this educational reform and improvement across the United States, a movement toward self-determination is taking place among American Indians and Alaska Natives... Mainstream schools interested in exploring alternative ways of teach-ing and learning will have new opportunities to establish mutually beneficial connec-tions with tribally controlled schools that emphasize Indigenous knowledge and "Native ways of Knowing." (p. 33)

The teacher training texts developed in the interest of facilitating the manifesta-tion of such culturally relevant educational practices and collaborations tends to focus on challenging prospective teachers to develop cultural competence within themselves, which is especially relevant because it is mostly white teachers who teach Native American youth, both on and off the reservation. On reservations white teachers continue to work in both tribally controlled schools and even more so in BIA-controlled facilities. What is more, 90% of all Indigenous youth within the United States attend public state-controlled and-run schools, and 90% of the teachers within these institutions throughout North America are white. It is therefore not surprising that in texts such as *Collected Wisdom: American Indian Education* by Linda Miller Cleary and Thomas D. Peacock (1998), which is essentially a teacher-training manual for future and current teachers of Native American students, white teachers are highlighted who have developed sophisticated levels of cultural competence and are therefore successful in their work with Native American students. One such "white" teacher of Native American students highlighted in *Collected Wisdom* (1998), "Ketron," stressed the importance of listening because of all the cultural knowledge he had to learn to become a teacher respected in the community. Such examples provide future white teachers with role models they can learn from in their struggles to become antiracist educators who are part of the solution and not part of the problem. Also instructive to their approach to Indian education are their "profiles" on Native American teachers.

These Indigenous teachers are presented in *Collected Wisdom* as role models or examples alluding to what the authors believe are positive manifestations of culturally appropriate and *practical* Indian education. In Chapter Four, "Creating a Two-Way Bridge: Being Indian in a Non-Indian World," Wayne Newell is "profiled" and in the process described as "...a successful individual who has found balance between his Passamaquoddy culture and the school in which he is a teacher" (p. 100). Cleary and Peacock (1998) go on to praise Newell for being a respected traditional person in his Indigenous community, an accomplished Passamaquoddy language teacher at Indian Township School in northern Maine, as well as having "lived successfully in the non-Indian work and academic environment" (p. 100) having earned a master's degree from Harvard University.

The vision for Indian education that emerges from *Collected Wisdom* is similar to that put forth by the progressive educator collective Rethinking Schools. For example, in the Introduction to the second volume of *Rethinking Our Classrooms,* Bill Bigelow, Brenda Harvey, Stan Karp, and Larry Miller (2001), making the case for how schools should be "laboratories for a more just society" (p. 1), argue that educators have two primary responsibilities to their students—to help them survive within the world that exists and to transform it—and if either of the two are neglected, the teacher has not fulfilled her or his obligations.

Cleary and Peacock's (1998) example of Wayne Newell, the Native American teacher, is presented as an example of someone who has survived within the world that exists and simultaneously is engaged in transforming it as a Passamaquoddy language teacher assisting his predominantly Passama-quoddy students in following a similar path to higher education, and thus to surviving within the world that exists. Newell's work as a language teacher, in the context of the United States with its long history of cultural genocide, is in itself transformative. In other words, teaching Native children their Indigenous culture, if successful, is to change the world that exists because it would be a beginning in countering the many generations of cultural loss. Reflecting on the transformative nature of his work as a teacher of native language, Newell is quoted by Cleary and Peacock (1998) passionately arguing,

> What people didn't understand is that those boarding school terrorists thought that culture could disappear in a generation, and they would have white-thinking children. They couldn't erase it, and therein lies the hope...And when that spirit is reawakened, and it's within our own language, you've become a whole new person; you're alive again. (p. 102)

While acknowledging the harmful impact of the boarding schools noting that "we became like the conquerors" and "the biggest helpers" of cultural geno-cide, Newell simultaneously satisfies our ontological needs in the profound sense of hope he expresses when reflecting on his endeavors as a Native American cultural worker/teacher. Cleary and Peacock (1998) situate Newell's hope in the context of the ability to "successfully" live in two worlds, in an "Indian" world and in a "white" world. One of the struggles highlighted by Cleary and Peacock in teaching Native American students about their culture is developing programs that successfully engage their interests—interests that tend to be heavily influenced by the dominant society's consumer culture. As evidence for their position that many Native students are not interested in their culture, Cleary and Peacock (1998) cite a teacher of Native American students, Kay Lasagna. Consider her words:

> I gave a pretest on Sioux culture to my students, and 94 percent of them failed it; they knew little or nothing about their culture. I was given some federal money to start a culture center, and I couldn't get any of them interested in a culture center or partici-pating in it. They were interested in the same things other kids were interested in; they were interested in cars, in dating, in the school dance that was coming up, in the bas-ketball game on Friday night. And their background just wasn't that important to them. (p. 107)

While the deleterious effects of cultural genocide and cultural imposition are obvious, all hope is not lost as previously alluded to in the discussion on Newell, the Native American teacher from present-day Maine. Perhaps Lasagna's failure to engage her Lakota students in cultural work is because her "culture center" romantically situated Lakota culture in the past, and was therefore viewed as irrelevant by her students who live in the concrete context of the present moment. In other words, maybe this educator's approach did not demonstrate the relevance of traditional values for negotiating the challenges and struggles of the here-and-now. Lasagna clearly has an idea about her students' interests—cars, dating, the school dance, and basketball—the question is, how could she draw on their interests to spark a passion within them to know and own their Lakota culture (i.e., Lakota philosophy and language)? That is the challenge of the critical educator—to be in a perpetual state of self-reflection as part of the process of continually bettering one's practice. Similarly, in the following discussion centered on the text *The Seventh Generation,* we see that the conclusion the authors come to is that the ways in which Native students draw on their traditional values to inform their lives is not something that can be dictated from above, or externally controlled, especially in the context of the dominant society that is marked by deception and trickery.

After publishing *Collected Wisdom,* Cleary and Peacock realized that they "should have included the voices of young people" because students are the best equipped to "tell us about education" due to the fact that they are "experiencing it at the moment" (p. 3). To fill this void Cleary and Peacock joined forces with Amy Bergstrum, "a young Ojibwe teacher" and wrote *The Seventh Generation* after interviewing 120 Native American students, some in the author's own communities in the northern Midwest of the United States and others they traveled to interview whose Indigenous identities include Abenaki, Aleut, Choctaw, Cree, Dakota, Hoopa, Inuit, Karuk, Lakota, Mohawk, Navajo, Oneida, Penobscot, Seneca, Ute, Wampanoag, and Yurok. Collectively, the students in their sample attended public, tribal, federal, and alternative schools off reservations in cities, on reservations, and near reservations.

The Seventh Generation: Native Students Speak About Finding the Good Path by Amy Bergstrom, Linda Miller Cleary, and Thomas D. Peacock (2003) is written for not only Native American students, but teachers of Native American students as well. For students *The Seventh Generation* is a source of self-affirmation, and therefore a potentially empowering inspiration, while simultaneously providing advice from one's peers on matters of central importance such as how to successfully negotiate life in two worlds. A re-emerging theme throughout the beautifully illustrated and laid out volume, *The Seventh Generation,* is the racism Native students have to contend with in mainstream schools dominated by Eurocentric curriculum and teachers that subsequently do not understand that students who come from "more tradi-tional homes" have to "accommodate" their "learning style to...the ways in which the teachers and curriculum expect [them] to learn," which is difficult, frustrating, and oppressive because it tends to take Native American students out of their "natural ways of being and learning" (p. 40).

The authors of *The Seventh Generation* privilege these voices of Native youth because they offer current and future Indigenous students insights on resisting being transformed into something other than Native American while simultaneously succeeding within the world that exists. While the implications of *The Seventh Generation* tend to point to the goal of surviving in two worlds clearly articulated in *Collected Wisdom,* there is more of an emphasis on students' ability to find "the good path" on their own, which is left open for the students and therefore not necessarily defined for them as negotiating two worlds. The good path is defined in *The Seventh Generation* as "a set of traditional values" that "are universal to Indigenous people, indeed, to all humankind," which are given special attention because "the solutions to many of the problems in Native communities, including education, lie within the values of our tribal cultures, or ways of being" (pp. 129-130). This perspective is instructive for not only Native American students, but for teachers of Native American students as well.

For educators, *The Seventh Generation* (2003) provides considerable in-sight into the worldviews, hopes, fears and desires of these 120 Native Ameri-can students, and is therefore a valuable tool for non-Native and Native educators alike in developing geographical and generational-specific cultural competence. Towards these ends in many such curricula preservice teachers are introduced to relevant cultural differences such as the different ways "...majority and minority students interact linguistically and cognitively" (Yazzie, 1999, p. 87) because misunderstandings due to interaction styles can lead to distrust and therefore hinder teaching and learning. Such work contributes to what tribally controlled schools tend to be good at: that is, fostering a sense of self-respect within Native students. As a result, some of these schools have drastically reduced push out rates from 70%-80% down to

20%-30% (Tippeconnic, 1999). These trends serve as an affirmation of the prophecy of the seventh Indigenous generation of the current post-freedom (see the discussion of Crazy Horse below) stage of colonialism, which was predicted by many Native peoples that a long period of cultural loss and hardship followed by a resurgence in Native languages, culture, and traditional values by the seventh generation. For example, after the massacre at Wounded Knee in 1889 where the Minneconjou Lakota leader Big Foot (Mohawk, 2000) and other teachers of ancient philosophy were lost, a number of Lakota medicine men had visions and made such predictions of great loss and rebirth. Bergstrom, Cleary and Peacock's (2003) *The Seventh Generation* stands as a powerful source of hope for the seventh generation, offering valuable contributions towards healing the deep wounds that have been, and continue to be, inflicted over the past five hundred years of intense, persistent, and extremely deadly predation.

However, despite the many benefits of this important work in Native American education, from a critical pedagogical perspective, these efforts could be enhanced by a critical engagement with critical pedagogy. That is, while Native approaches to education have been praised for their efforts at cultural rejuvenation, they have simultaneously been criticized for neglecting to consciously develop within their Native students a critical vision for dealing with the global encroachment of capitalist hegemony. Contrary to Native philosophy that understands everything to be interrelated, much of the collaborative work Native and non-Native teacher educators are developing for teachers of Native Americans dichotomizes individual cultural development and the skills needed to survive in the world that exists as if there is no relationship between the two, that they are mutually exclusive. What this false dichotomy seems to be intended to hide is the contradiction between advancing an educational program designed to strengthen students' Indigeneity and therefore their existence as land-based peoples while uncritically gaining the skills to be employable within the very system responsible for genocide, exploitation, and the destruction of land. In other words, presenting this false dichotomy covers up the fact that, while Native American education is much better today than it was just thirty years ago, it has not yet completely been relieved of coddling the aggressor. Until the project of cultural rejuvenation is connected to transforming the basic structures of power within dominant society, Native education will have room for improvement. Critical pedagogy provides invaluable insight here.

What follows is a careful consideration of what that might look like for us, as future and current educators, in practice. At the heart of this discussion are the many insights offered by critical pedagogy that have been scattered throughout this book. Critical pedagogy is an approach to education designed to preserve the *wildness* of the human creative spirit, that is, the very essence of human nature—freedom and democracy. A truly contextualized, and thus "wild," education begins with the very ground underneath one's feet. What is the indigenous philosophy under your feet? That is our place of departure. How have those Indigenous knowledges been suppressed and defended, and how are they connected to other indigenous cultures? In this spirit of critical contextualization we begin our discussion of critical pedagogy with Crazy Horse, one of the last great "wild" Lakota leaders. Within this discussion we begin to see how the values of an ancient Indigenous ontology combined with critical pedagogy can offer ways to approach cultural rejuvenation that are revolutionary, that is, that are transformative because they challenge us to consider the need for real system-wide change, not just tinkering, but complete *de*struction and total *re*construction.

Critical Pedagogy in Native North America

Before we continue, this sub-section warrants another brief pause. In *Recovering the Sacred: The Power of Naming and Claiming,* Winona LaDuke (2005) beautifully documents, and in the process celebrates, Native North Americans' recent strides in recovering and revitalizing the intimate relationship between land and culture that has been so severely degraded in the process of predation. In her book LaDuke (2005) dedicates a chapter to Native Americans, efforts at challenging the settlers' unjust practice of "naming that which he has no right to own" (p. 149). Not only does LaDuke retell the stories of a few of the many successful campaigns against the white supremacist "Indian" mascots of colleges and universities, but she also documents one of the victories opposing the corporate, for-profit use of names such as Crazy Horse to sell beer. For example, Stroh Brewing Company released Crazy Horse Malt Liquor in 1992 resulting in the Lakota Tribal Court filing a legal defamation complaint that resulted in a formal apology from the manufacturer and the discontinuation of the offensive labeling (the beer was renamed Crazy Stallion). The Lakota's statement makes perfectly clear the historical and cultural insensitivity embedded within the product Stroh Brewing Company was setting out to profit from:

The purposeful use and appropriation of another ascertainable person's name or likeness in an insulting and disparaging manner, without consent or permission of the lawful owner of said name or his heirs and especially in the commercial exploitation for financial gain in association with a product that has proved so deadly to Indian people, are despicable and disparaging invasions of privacy and are egregious violations of Lakota customary law protecting the spiritual, personal, social and cultural importance of an individual's name to an individual and his family during his life and his spirit and reputation, along with those of his relations, after his life so as to amount to disparagement and defamation of both the individual and the group. (Lakota Tribal Court complaint against Crazy Horse Malt Liquor quoted in LaDuke, 2005, p. 145)

It has been my intention in the following sub-section to draw on the legacy of Crazy Horse not disrespectfully or disparagingly, as settlers have done in the past in their quest to commodify and exploit everything "Native," but as a way of honoring his commitment and dedication to social justice, which continues to hold great contemporary relevance. In this way I hope to contribute to the proper education of the settler-community about the history of Native North American resistance and the colonialist attempt to destroy it and its peoples. In other words, this is my effort to not contribute to maintaining, but rather contribute to, in however small a way, ending the process of predation. That is, by saying "no" to predation and searching for ways to connect that commitment to my practice, as an educator, I invite students, as future teachers, to also say "no" to predation and to find creative ways to live that choice both individually and collectively. LaDuke's (2005) *Recovering the Sacred* offers invaluable insight here by providing many examples of the roles some settlers have been playing in returning ancestral lands to Native peoples as conscious acts against predation—that is, in one word, solidarity, which has always been humanity's most powerful weapon against oppression and injustice. With this spirit of solidarity in mind let us return to our discussion of Crazy Horse, considering the many ways his story can inform our critical pedagogies.

We therefore begin this section by considering the critical pedagogy embodied within *The Journey of Crazy Horse* (Marshall, 2004) as told by the community from which the legendary Lakota leader came. Within this story is embedded Lakota philosophy and how it informed their struggle against settler-state oppression, and thus to remain free, that is, not colonized. Crazy Horse is represented by Marshall (2004) as the epitome of the traditional Lakota way, because he uncompromisingly defended it through resisting the subjugation of his people, which meant holding onto the ability to humanize the world informed by Lakota culture. This meant not surrendering the natural right of all life to be self-determined and self-sufficient and not de-pendent on external power for survival such as government annuities, which was an enslaving pacification and therefore represented war on the people. This war on the people had to be resisted, which proved difficult for Crazy Horse and his people because the U.S., using deceit, divisiveness, and genocide as military tactics, did not prove to be an honorable enemy unlike their traditional rivals the Crow and the Snake (Shoshone) people. The colonial enemy against humanity during Crazy Horse's day is still with us today, that is, the spirit of Columbus (outlined in Chapter Two). There is therefore much to be learned from his example. The purpose here is not to romantically long for the days of old, but rather to consider what might be learned from yesterday, to help us better understand and fight today and therefore more effectively organize for the future. As suggested above, this requires a revolutionary approach to cultural rejuvenation for all people.

Putting this general sentiment forward in "MindFuck," The Coup, in a verse reflecting on the state's deadly war on political dissidents from the perspective of an African American woman searching for the strength and guidance to resist the oppressive present in the leaders of the past, such as Malcolm X and Dr. Huey P. Newton, lead vocalist Boots Riley notes, "she wish the great leaders wasn't always dead. She could resurrect 'em inside of her instead." It is readily apparent from Marshall's (2004) account that, for the Lakota, contrary to Eurocentric historians, Crazy Horse is considered one of these "great leaders" and one of the last great "wild" Lakota leaders with lessons that remain relevant in the contemporary context of global capitalism. "Wild" because he was part of a widespread refusal, along with Sitting Bull's contingency, longer than any of the other Lakota bands, to give up their freedom and relocate to one of the "soldier forts" built against the will of the Lakota on Lakota territory. Also "wild" because he was educated to be a warrior and hunter in the traditional Lakota way, that is, he was raised by the women of the community for the first four to five years of his life and then weaned into the world of the men and mentored in a one-on-one relationship for ten to twelve years resulting in a very sophisticated knowledge of self situated in community and geography.

Crazy Horse witnessed, with much frustration and heartache, other Lakota leaders, such as Red Cloud and Spotted Tail, and their bands, slowly giving in to settler-state oppression and thus the occupation of their lands, despite the Lakota outnumbering white soldiers. What Crazy Horse observed was the Lakota trickling down to live on U.S. agencies by the soldier forts, thereby giving up their freedom for "white things" such as the power over their people divisively *given* to them by the U.S., which represented the status they were not able to obtain within their own societies. With hegemony and therefore the manipulation of ideas it is not always necessary to have greater numbers, a lesson most bitterly learned (and still learning). As more and more bands gave into the U.S., therefore weakening their ability to militarily resist, and consequently suffering many horrific atrocities at the hands of the U.S. military, such as the butchering of women and children, Crazy Horse and the other Lakota headmen and their councils struggled to know what was best for the future of their people: should they continue to resist and face extermination, or give up their freedom and the ability to fully live as free sovereign people on reservations? Commenting on these difficulties and the necessary qualities it demands in a leader, Marshall (2004) explains:

> Facing the overall problems of life...especially as the one to whom the people looked for answers—was far more difficult [than making quick, effective decisions leading his warriors in the heat of battle]. People were constantly coming to his home to talk and the old men called him frequently to the council lodge.... He [therefore] sought out the solitude of the prairies or the mountain slopes.... In such places, he could gather his thoughts and pile them up like stones and examine them, one by one. His friends and relatives thought he shouldn't wander off alone as much as he did.... A leader's place was with the people.... When a man belonged to the people, he no longer belonged to himself. (Marshall, 2004, pp. 175–176)

From Marshall's (2004) account, what this required, more than anything else, was discipline—it was, and remains, an indispensable quality of a true servant of the people because a true leader teaches by example as she or he leads. Similarly, Freire (2005) argues that because we are teachers and therefore have the responsibility to serve the best interests of our students against oppression and dehumanization, we are political militants, which demands a well-developed, theoretically sophisticated discipline—needed, for example, because it is a lifelong struggle to put aside personal desires for the larger benefit of one's community, most radically defined as "all that exists." As long as the need to resist exists, this discipline will be necessary because it is human to look inward, which is important, but we have to safeguard against allowing our self-reflections to be dominated by our ego and personal desires. For example, after successful raids on the enemy, rather than build up his own wealth and status, Crazy Horse is said to have distributed captured horses to those most in need, such as "the old ones." In so doing Crazy Horse demonstrated his commitment to Lakota values such as generosity and community, which earned him a place of high regard within his society. As leaders are teachers and therefore not only responsible for making wise decisions while leading, they educate the people by demonstrating what values support critical participation and therefore the best interests of the whole. Teachers, as leaders, thus forfeit the right to squander their lives away with bad decisions that detract from the work of revolution. At the same time, our lives (our labor power) are not ours to allow to be externally controlled by ruling elite inter-ests—it would be irresponsible for us to coddle the aggressor in any way—our labor power belongs to the humanization and therefore liberation of ourselves and the world in which we are situated. This demands that, as the first line of defense, we be extremely conscious of our own weaknesses. While these internal struggles remain the same today as they did in Crazy Horse's day, the external concrete context of resistance is in a perpetual state of flux/transformation therefore requiring constant reflection on and revision of the tactics of insurrection. Marx, in a sense, describes this as the historical development of competing interests or internal relations.

Signaling this change in context, on his deathbed, Crazy Horse told his father, Worm (the name he humbly gave to himself after giving his name, Crazy Horse, to his son, before then, known among his people as Light Hair), "tell the people they should not depend on me any longer." Crazy Horse and his Lakota community acknowledged this need for flexibility and change early on in their resistance against white encroachment as they had to readjust their military tactics because whites did not care about courage; they only cared about killing, as it was their only measurement of military success because the goal was not to demonstrate courage, but to dominate and oppress. Crazy Horse taught the importance of adjusting the theoretical context of armed resistance to the concrete context of the battlefield because if theory does not match reality, then tactics will be ineffective. While the specifics of Crazy Horse's context are relevant, I will not focus on them here. Rather, I want to draw attention to the current relevance of maintaining a dialectical relationship between theory and practice. The goal of the occupying force is essentially the same today as it was in the mid-to late 1800s, that is, to maintain total control of the productive and creative capacities of the people because it is within this capacity to labor and humanize the world that lies the greatest strength of the people, our ability to labor, without which, the oppressors have nothing. It is therefore capital's weakest link because we can resist it being externally commanded and put it, and thus ourselves, to work fighting against being externally commanded and fight against the destruction of our only home, the Earth, our common mother. Again, while the enemy of the "wild" Lakota, and humanity and all life generally, is currently the same, the concrete context is different.

Crazy Horse operated from the position of pre-defeat and pre-colonialist indoctrination. Today, unfortunately, we are all more fully engaging the world from the position of post-defeat, and therefore from being indoctrinated with the oppressor's values, ideas, and beliefs. The good thing is that there is only one model of domination, so we all share a common enemy, and therefore have no other option but to unite as one while celebrating and drawing on the strengths of our differences. Now, more than ever, we need the pedagogical example of Crazy Horse's discipline and his uncompromising selfless commitment to the people to most effectively utilize and build upon pedagogies of counter-indoctrination infamously represented in Paulo Freire's *Pedagogy of the Oppressed* (1998), to best resist the concrete context of the capitalist present. This is a revolutionary approach to cultural rejuvenation. If this theoretical marriage were represented in a movie, we might creatively write the script with Crazy Horse and Paulo Freire leaving an engagement with Marx and Gramsci on their way to Chiapas to create democratic community in dialogue with the Zapatistas (as we will see in the final chapter of this book).

Because the concrete context of the contemporary moment so thunderously demands a well disciplined, fully-committed-to-the-people critical pedagogy, we will now take a look at critical pedagogy, which, again, we have been doing throughout this entire book. While actively engaging with the following section, reflect on the case you could make for why your adoption of a critical pedagogical approach to curriculum and pedagogy would be in the best interests of the current or future students you have the responsibility of educating. Also, reflect on the relevance of Crazy Horse's example of discipline, courage, and commitment as it pertains to the struggles you might face becoming a critical pedagogue and therefore a teacher of critical consciousness.

This is intended to be a radical pedagogy of solidarity, critical solidarity—that is, a solidarity informed by not only an objective understanding of the world, but the desire to transform both the basic structures of power and what it means to be fully human. These are not mutually exclusive objects of transformation because the objects of change, widespread poverty-induced suffering and highly concentrated wealth, represent the antagonistic relationship between the bosses and those who rely on a wage to survive, the hegemony of which depends on the development of certain kinds of humans. The object of critical pedagogy is therefore the development of critical consciousness and thus a more fully humanized person—that is, revolutionary cultural rejuvenation. The philosophy native to North America that gave way to leaders such as Crazy Horse therefore warrants close examination and consideration when we produce critical pedagogies for critical consciousness and humanization. Longtime American Indian Movement activist/poet/musician John Trudell (1995) puts the discipline demanded by Crazy Horse in a contemporary context:

> The only thing I would say to anybody is think clearly. Think clearly about what you are doing. Seek coherency. It's the time to be clear and coherent, responsible. It's just that time. No matter what it is we're doing. No matter how we are participating... The only way we get on that train [toward self-destruction, even if we think we have chosen peace] is because we don't understand the path of peace. We need to think more clearly about what the path of peace means because there are many illusions on the path. Maybe in the end the only peaceful thing we would be able to accomplish to initiate change is to unite and not spend money—to not spend money in unison. Somebody would have to listen then.

Trudell offers a fine point of departure into critical pedagogy via Paulo Freire—that is, a clear and coherent understanding of the dialectical relationship between the theoretical contexts of our pedagogies and the concrete context of how we are living our lives, which is essentially the compilation and accumulative effect of the choices we make. Trudell's comments, to be sure, embody the same spirit of armed love and the discipline required by the present concrete context characteristic of Freire's work. It will take discipline to unite and then simultaneously deciding not to participate in the system of plunder. The manifestation of that choice will be evidence that we have in fact united around a genuine understanding of the common good, not a deceptive, imagined common good that conflates the common good of the rich with the common good of the poor, which represents a bold-faced lie because the common good of the rich is antagonistically related to that of the poor, they are mutually exclusive. What we have seen in the figure of Crazy Horse are qualities that seem to be exceedingly relevant and therefore demand close analysis when considering what it means to be fully human from a critical pedagogical perspective. Freire (2005) offers a natural transition point here in his discussion of what he identified as "indispensable qualities of a progressive educator." Because this book is concerned with bettering our practice as teachers, let us consider some of those qualities Freire argued were needed to best assist our students in developing their own critical consciousness in the context of our practice situated in the tension filled relationship between the theoretical and concrete contexts (for a full discussion see the "Fourth Letter" in Freire's (2005) *Teachers as Cultural Workers*).

* * *

Freire (2005) begins outlining what he considers to be the indispensable qualities of a progressive educator with humility, which is in no way intended to be interpreted as a form of masochism. That is, to be humble does not imply self-negation or a lack of courage. Humility here, from a critical pedagogical perspective, acknowledges that because the absolute truth cannot come from a single source, it is in the best interest of creating democratic community for all perspectives and voices to hold equal political and social weight. It is therefore the responsibility of the radical educator to teach how to listen by listening, and in the process we demonstrate humility. We do this by listening to those we are engaged with in the teacher/learner relationship.

However, Freire reminds us that listening is not enough. As educators we have a responsibility to teach content. Another indispensable quality is therefore decisiveness. That is, we must have the capacity to make curricular and pedagogical decisions. This requires us to be competent in our subject matter, which demands lifelong study and scholarship. Freire never ceased to remind us that all of these choices we make about content and the ways in which we teach are always political choices because all knowledge supports a particular understanding of the world. The question is therefore whose interests are supported by the curricular and pedagogical choices we make. For example, whose interests are supported when the science of electricity is taught in schools without, at some point, situating the technology within the larger social, historical, and environmental context in which it has always existed? A more obvious example: whose interests are supported when the story of Columbus as the great discoverer is presented as an objective fact constituting the one correct answer to the question "who discovered America?" Because of the power of hegemonic indoctrination, these challenges are not easy for teachers to incorporate into their practice. What we must have towards others and ourselves is therefore patience/impatience. Let me explain:

if we are too patient with ourselves as educators, for example, we will not push ourselves hard enough to improve our practice. At the same time, if we are too impatient with ourselves as educators, we run the risk of making unsound decisions that lack the proper tension between theoretical and concrete contexts.

Another related barrier many of us face is the fear of freedom, a consequence of an authoritarian society. In other words, when we live in the shadow of oppression, we often become fearful of the power of the bosses. In this context courage becomes an indispensable characteristic of the progressive educator because humanization requires an active engagement with all knowledge, including dangerous or subjugated knowledge (see Chapter One). Fighting the bosses, as it were, takes courage because it not only requires putting oneself in physical or economical danger, but it requires one to demonstrate the tenderness of love—even if it is an armed, militant love. That is, to be a critical educator, an agent of change, requires one to love oneself so one can love one's brothers and sisters, which is the foundation of solidarity and therefore the heart of creating a revolutionary movement. Without love we will witness no qualitative changes in anything. Love, for radical educators, means loving one's responsibilities as a transformer, and it means having love for the learners' inherent human right of becoming fully human and therefore in complete control of their creative capacities.

With these insights in mind, let us now turn to the heart of Freire's critical pedagogical project, which will simultaneously shed considerable light on why his work has been so incredibly influential. The late Brazilian educator Paulo Freire is known as the founder of what North Americans know as critical pedagogy, therefore situating one of the major influences of North American critical pedagogy in South America. Freire's militant, humanistic teachings have been widely influential globally. For Freire, at the heart of society are the relationships between humans, which are largely determined by the consciousness of the participants. The goal of Freire's critical pedagogy is therefore to create the conditions whereby the learner becomes conscious of her own consciousness, and in this process of humanization, in radical unison with other learners, transforms society. As demonstrated above, Freire (2005) was very aware of the fact that such a task requires of educators to possess very particular indispensable qualities.

From his most early works, Freire took as his place of departure the world as it is. Critically engaging with the world, as it currently exists, requires discipline—discipline because, our task, educating, critically conceived, is anything but easy, it is not easy to be a good critical educator, as it requires clarity and coherence, and is therefore indispensable. It then follows, and thus rendering it a requirement, that we take everything we do with the absolute utmost seriousness. That means every course we teach, every piece of scholarship we pursue, every professional presentation we deliver, and every way we live our lives, critically conceived, is designed to create critical consciousness within ourselves and in our engagements with others in, on, and with the world. Crazy Horse demonstrated that when we are political militants, as are teachers, every choice we make is inherently political in both our personal/private relationships and in our public choices because everything is related and the public and private cannot so easily be fragmented into a false dichotomous relationship. There is nothing that is not political and every aspect of our lives exists together. In this world of indoctrination every hegemonic value, idea, and belief we have internalized informs every relationship we have in every capacity of our lives—there are no "safe" zones of sociability. Lifelong internal self-reflection in unison with collective struggle is therefore an indispensable aspect of becoming an increasingly effective critical pedagogue—that requires, no, that demands, in the most committed and militant sense, discipline. If we expect to become competent at anything, we must develop an internal self-discipline, driven by passion from within. This is where we can consider the implications of combining mainstream multicultural approaches, such as current trends in Native American education, and Marxist critical pedagogy. What kind of new philosophical scaffolding can we develop when we join these forces? Consider these questions as you engage in the following discussion of Marxist critical pedagogy, which focuses on the most current developments in the field.

Marxism and Critical Pedagogy

The following section takes as its place of departure the insistence that the ongoing struggle *against* institutionalized oppression and thus *for* revolutionary change has a lot to learn from not only Indigenous knowledge but critical Marxist theory as well. Before we begin evaluating the invaluable insights offered by such counter-hegemonic work, as it pertains to our preparation as future or current teachers for social justice and against dehumanization, we outline what specifically we believe it is within the global concrete context that demands such an approach.

The Global Context:

o Every day more than thirty thousand children throughout the world die of easily preventable starvation-related diseases because in a capitalist market-driven system, food is a source of profit, not a source of nutrition (Shah, 2007)

o The global climate is changing, and scientists throughout the world agree that it is predominantly human-induced, presenting perhaps the number one threat to the future of life on the planet (Shah, 2007)

o Pollution is rampant, contributing to global warming and depletions in plant and animal biodiversity (Shah, 2007)

o The richest couple hundred people have a combined net worth that exceeds nearly half of the world's population (Shah, 2007)

o The world's indigenous populations, with very few exceptions, have been colonized by European peoples and remain in a state of subjugation and dependency to Western powers (Semali & Kincheloe, 1999a)

o Nearly one billion people, a sixth of the world's population, entered the twenty-first century without basic literacy skills (Shah, 2007)

o Twenty percent of the people in the most developed countries consume 86% of the world's commodities and services (Shah, 2007)

o 121 million children throughout the world are without education (Shah 2007)

o If the current trajectory is not substantially altered, and quickly, crises and catastrophes of every kind imaginable are in our near future:

    o As corporations continue to privatize the planet, by the year 2025, it is predicted that two thirds of the world's human population will not have access to fresh drinking water, one of the most basic rights of all living things

The harshness and severity of what has just been laid out, I am afraid, leaves us susceptible to the hopelessness and despair that deprives us of our "onto-logical need," that is hope (Freire, 1999). Given this context the analysis provided by the late revolutionary naturalist and founder of the MOVE (not an acronym) organization, John Africa, is more relevant now than when it was made more than twenty years ago. His teachings provided the basis for the construction of a revolutionary family committed to defending the inherent right of all life to exist free from exploitation and oppression:

It is past time for all poor people to release themselves from the deceptive strangulation of society, realize that society has failed you; for to attempt to ignore this system of deception *now* is to deny you the need to protest this failure *later*. The system has failed you yesterday, failed you today, and has created the conditions for failure tomorrow... (Quoted in Abu-Jamal, 1997, p. 113)

Because Marxist critical pedagogy takes as its primary place of departure the concrete context and asks what are the primary forces determining this material reality, John Africa's insights offer a valuable place of departure for the following discussion. The labor power of people is the primary force that has built every human society in history. Under the present capitalist system, that driving force, humanity's labor power, is externally controlled by a small elite ruling class. This situation, the relationship between bosses and workers, is the primary relationship that creates capitalism. Marx argued that the mode of production, that is, the form of economy, has the largest impact on the relationships between people and between people and the rest of material existence. Today this planet, our Mother from an Indigenous perspective, is completely dominated by capitalism—we live in a global capitalist world system. Even the decisions made by Castro and his sovereign socialist nation of Cuba and the tribal reservation governments in the United States and Canada are hugely affected by the capitalist world, which *is the* world. It therefore follows that Marxist critical pedagogy be focused on the pedagogical roles education has played and continues to play in accommodating (and the possibilities of transforming) the antagonistic relationship between the two primary classes in capitalist society—the capitalists themselves, who are only a small percentage, of the entire population, and the vast majority, who constitute *the rest of us*, that is, those who depend on a wage for survival.

The goal of the United States government has always been to create a state of dependency where every human population within its sphere of influence is dependent on it for jobs or welfare. That is why the U.S. has been punishing Cuba for more than fifty years, that is, because they fought for their independence and therefore to be out from under the yoke of Yankee imperialism (Malott, 2007). Similarly, the independence and sovereignty of Native American communities has never been intended to survive. The fact that Native communities still exist and that socialist Cuba has maintained the level of independence it has is nothing short of amazing. It is a testament to the will of humanity to instinctively resist dehumanization and oppression.

In other words, Marxist critical pedagogy is interested in understanding the way education is used to normalize and naturalize the act of placing our ability to labor on the market as a commodity to be purchased as a moneymaking investment. Selling ourselves to profit-seeking entities implies forfeiting control over one's labor power and handing it over to the bosses. That is, the act of buying a person's time implies that the seller must expend her labor power according to the will of the purchaser(s). In this relationship the seller is not free to humanize the world in his own vision, but is forced to create and re-create the world according to the buyer's vision, supporting the buyer's interests, which tends to be a detriment to the seller because, while profit is privatized and held in just a few hands, the social cost of production is social-ized, which means that the public pays the bill—a bill paid for in the form of exposure to hazardous materials from mining uranium, poverty, and suffering from low wages to fund highly concentrated centers of power needed to be established as an imperial superpower, such as the Untied States.

The way in which I have begun to describe capitalism here is designed to uncover the inherent injustice built into the system. Given this stark reality Marxist educators ask: how is it that humanity seems to consent and contribute to their own oppression? From this question we realize that manufacturing consent requires indoctrination as a way to tame the wild—that is, the tendency to want to be free, democratic, not oppressed or without liberties. The history of ruling class Europe in the Americas since 1492 has been the total and complete taming of the wild, and therefore the decontextualizing and discon-necting of all that is, which is naturally connected and contextualized. The goal has always been to extract as much value out of the land and people as possible, denying the intrinsic natural (wild) value inherent within everything that cannot be bought or sold. Those very real use values in land, in specific geographical locations, keep people grounded in whom and where they are.

For Marx our *wildness*—that which differentiates us from all other spe-cies—represents our creativity, our consciousness, our most essential human disposition, and therefore the fact that we are not driven by pure instinct. It is what makes us fit to take care of this world, and, at the same time, fit to destroy it. The situation becomes apparent when we consider that it is only humans that can correct human errors. Because all people have a natural common interest to be free and therefore embody the potential to be con-nected in radical solidarity and therefore untamable, we must be indoctrinated to believe we are not only *not* related, but in competition with each other for a finite source of sustenance such as food supplies and wealth. This process represents the manufacture of scarcity. Indoctrination has worked so well that most white people who were raised as U.S. citizens do not understand the land in a contextualized way and act accordingly. Even many of our white radical brothers and sisters who wholeheartedly make every conscious decision to act in the most just way possible do not have in their daily thinking process an awareness of being on a tamed land stripped of its natural Indigenous human component. An Indigenous critical pedagogy moves the development of our critical consciousness in this direction toward awareness and solidarity, and as a result, transforms our practice in the world.

In North America critical pedagogy has had a dynamic existence and can be traced to not only Paulo Freire, but, taking his work as a place of departure, to bell hooks, Peter McLaren, Henry Giroux, Stanley Aronowitz, Joe Kincheloe, Shirley Steinberg, Rudolfo Chávez, and others. In North America critical pedagogy has unfortunately gained the reputation of being an almost exclusively *white male Left thing*, and is therefore viewed as not conducive to the issues and concerns of people of color, even though it has never been just a *white* thing, and in fact started out as a *black and brown thing*, as argued above (Kincheloe, 2004). However, despite historic reality, and as a result of the campaign against critical pedagogy, people of color tend not to see critical pedagogy as conducive to solving racial issues. If critical pedagogy is going to be relevant in the struggle ahead, its reputation as a white thing must change (Kincheloe, in press). Part of the process of rejuvenating critical pedagogy must include placing strong emphasis on not only the Latin American influence on critical pedagogy, but the African influences as well. In other words, the history of critical pedagogies in North America precedes the influence of Paulo Freire. Because of critical pedagogy's diverse background (it is in fact a global phenomenon), its transformative potential is vast.

Up until this point in the book I have left the topic of critical pedagogy's transformative potential up to your imagination, as it should be. However, straying from critical pedagogy orthodoxy, I have included two ideas of how critical pedagogy has and might be put to use in the world. What follows are therefore two examples of how we can use critical pedagogy to intervene in the material world. The first example challenges us to think about how foundations courses can better foster the development of critical consciousness. The second example pushes us to employ our imaginations in conceiving of a bloodless revolution, the ultimate materialization of the utopian project of critical pedagogy. This last example might seem "out there," and you might accuse me of dreaming too much, but following Freire (2005), we in fact dream too little, and the act of conceptualizing (dreaming) is a necessary and practical step towards action. The following example is therefore intended to spark your imagination, create discussion and debate, and ultimately, serve as our place of departure.

Critical Pedagogy in Action: Two Examples

Understanding and Action: Intervention in the Foundations of Education

The foundations of education primarily deal with philosophy and theory. While it is important to understand all existing theories and philosophies that influence and have influenced education, such as idealism, Marxism, and postmodernism (see Chapter Two), this example is specifically concerned with looking at issues in education from a critical theoretical perspective. The place of departure for this particular form of education is therefore critical theory. What is critical theory and where does it come from? There are too many critical theories (from Marxism to post-structuralism to neocolonialism) coming from too many positions (from Africa, the Middle East, North America, Latin America, and the Caribbean, to Europe) to include here (see Chapter One). Because the idea of a common public education in North America has roots in Enlightenment values and ideals, this approach begins with the Enlightenment.

Critical theory represents the tradition that has emerged as the primary vehicle through which the Enlightenment's scientific promises of human progress have been and continue to be fought for. Human progress here can be read as movement toward greater equality and democratic rule, and thus internal versus external control of an individual's labor power in the interests of the common good. Considered one of the most important educators of the twentieth century, Paulo Freire argued that teachers, acting as an example of democracy in action for their students, should intervene in the world supporting the learning interests of their students and the creative interests of the teachers, and therefore the internal control of student and teacher labor power. One avenue Freire stressed the importance of was the union, and that a strike can serve as a powerful example for learners of democracy in action. The theory that best fits this agenda is critical theory, which was born out of necessity as the Enlightenment was almost immediately betrayed.

At the heart of critical theory is the idea that it is not only extremely important to understand the world, but to change it as well. Teachers' role in classes that deal with the role of education in society should not only examine the manifestation of pedagogical and curricular issues in the classroom, but should deal, in a very concrete way, with the impact policy has on curriculum and pedagogy, and how those policies can either assist or hinder a teacher's capacity to provide the education that best contributes to democratic citizenship. Democratic citizenship, according to Enlightenment reasoning, includes not only understanding but also action and therefore a philosophy of praxis. As I alluded to above, one of the most central concerns of the Enlightenment was resisting the external control of one's labor power. If teacher education programs are to stay true to this, then they need to extend students' engagement in education beyond the classroom and into policy.

Classroom intervention and observation should be saved for methods classes and student teaching. Foundations classes should include a component that engages students at the level of policy. This example, in practice, would do just that—give you as future teachers experience in the realm of policy so when you become teachers, you will be more fit to fight for your own rights as workers and your students' rights as learners. When constructing this plan of action, we would want to begin to answer the following type of question: where can teachers most effectively impact policy? We might hypothesize through observation, study, and discussion that city council meetings, PTA meetings, and union meetings represent areas where teachers already have a voice, and therefore might be good places of departure for intervention.

Because the marriage between theory and practice is of the utmost import here, this endeavor should begin with an intensive, collective study of theory. While engaged in the process of studying theory, we would use it to understand current policy and practice at the macro and local levels while doing observations at various meetings that deal with policy issues. We would then study what teacher activists and community groups are pushing for in terms of education policy that does better at staying true to Enlightenment values and ideals than what tends to currently exist. Once we have established an adequate understanding of the competing approaches to education and the interests they support, we will intervene in the world implementing a collectively constructed, theoretically and concretely informed, and educator-guided plan of action.

When we engage ourselves in this process, the connection between theory and practice cannot be overstressed. During one of my first semesters teaching Introduction to Sociology at New Mexico State University, I found myself in the middle of a university-wide free speech movement. The free speech movement, coined the "Speech Is Coming" campaign, became a central part of my sociology class because it was a convenient example of how society works that I could draw on in class discussions. In describing our activities, regularly scheduled open Speech Is Coming meetings naturally became a focus of class discussions (anyone who has ever been involved with any kind of bottom-up, democratic organizing campaign knows that a large part of one's effort includes a lot of meetings, as it is necessary to constantly be evaluating and planning movement activity). As a result of these discussions, interested students and class participants began attending meetings and getting involved in the campaign. While this experience was no doubt extremely educative for my sociology course, there was still a theoretical gap between what my students did in class and their involvement outside of class. This was partially due to the unplanned nature of their involvement, but more importantly, my inexperience and inability to fully connect theory and curriculum to the movement and student action in it.

Unlike the sociology course described above whose official purpose is understanding for the sake of understanding, teacher education classes are supposed to facilitate understanding as part of the training for a very specific task or use of one's labor power—the task/job of teaching. From an Enlightenment perspective this training should include the skill of attaining and maintaining control of one's labor power. To achieve this it is important to know what interests those in charge of creating education policy serve and support.

This activity would begin by looking at the local context. For example, in cities across the U.S. the mayor and her or his administration have the task of creating and implementing education policy as well as overseeing economic initiatives. It does not take a tremendous amount of research to uncover examples of how governments tend to view education as an economic initiative issue. When looking at city governments it is therefore necessary to not only look at their education program, but their plan for the economy as well. In Buffalo, New York Mayor Byron Brown was elected in 2005 with 60% of the vote promising to help give Buffalo a new foundation by attracting investment and creating jobs:

o   Emphasize accountability and efficiency in city hall
o   Progressive public policy initiatives
o   Economic development activities
   o   Situated in context marked by:
      ▪   1/3 of Buffalo is illiterate; one in three adults can't read
      ▪   Almost 75% of eighth graders are not reading at grade level
      ▪   A+ Education plan advocated for in campaign designed to foster proficiency in math and English in an effort to meet state standards and increase standardized test scores

What can we learn from digging deeper into these issues the Buffalo City Office raises? This research and resulting discussions would theoretically prepare us for further understanding and intervention. Ultimately, what this example is designed to do is develop critical consciousness within future educators. The criticalization of future educators is extremely important because only when we ourselves are critically conscious can we create the educational conditions where students have the opportunity to develop their own critical consciousness, and in the process, empower themselves. The next example of *critical pedagogy in action,* the *just say no* campaign, is only possible once critical consciousness has been developed. While history is chock full of examples of individuals and groups who have resisted the process of predation, and in the process, said no to participation, the complete fulfillment of the campaign is dependent on the development of critical consciousness on a global scale. In the following discussion these points are elaborated on.

"Just Say No (to external control)"

The following "just say no" campaign has been in effect since at least 1492 when the Taino Indians of present-day Haiti said "no" to Spanish enslavement and capture attempting to physically resist. The campaign developed a new layer of complexity and hope when Bartolomé de las Casas gave up his plantation, refusing to participate in the wealth extracting process, and putting his labor to use, instead, documenting the unspeakable atrocities committed against these Native Americans. This campaign manifested itself in the Indian boarding schools when Indigenous children resisted assimilation. The Seminoles, as highlighted in Chapter Two, never officially surrendered and therefore never stopped saying "no." The gray-eyed Indians of Croatan emerged out of a collective "no" by those slated to be the first English settlers off the coast of the Carolinas. The white John Brown said "no" by organizing an armed resistance against slavery by waging war on the enslaving government of the United States ultimately resulting in Brown's death, which set a precedent for resisting and contributed to the abolition of slavery. The same system of predation, with slight modifications, exists today, and our participation in it is just as self-destructive as it was five hundred years ago. To provide one example, nobody is safe when the whole planet is contaminated with the by-products of industrial manufacturing. It is therefore our right and responsibility to just say NO!

The following summary challenges you to consider a few examples of issues we would be wise to say NO to and some of the arguments for such action, which begins to shed light on the fact that anything short of collectively saying "NO," or "ya basta" (enough), as the Zapatistas put it (outlined in Chapter Nine, the conclusion), is insane. While reading the following list think of other things, from a critical pedagogical and/or Native American perspective, teachers would be insane not to say no to. Also, think of ways you could engage your current or future students in a *just say no campaign* (beyond saying no to drugs) that is academically rigorous and challenges them to *go beyond*, as it were:

o   No, I will not fall the last of the Pacific Northwest's old growth timber forests, a major source of spiritual significance for many of the region's Native American populations

o   No, I will not drill oil in Canada, Venezuela, or the Middle East, one of the primary sources of the world's pollution and cause of global warming

o   No, I will not fight that war for you in Iraq (or Iran) because your wars are always over the unjust control of land, people, and/or resources (like oil) that should be left alone in the first place, and because capitalists always use the labor power of poor people to fight their wars for them

o   In other words, no, I will not allow you to use my working class labor power to kill working class people in other parts of the world so the ruling class of my country can get richer

o   No, I will not fight any of my brothers and sisters and will harbor no ill feelings toward anybody based on who they are or what they may or may not believe because now is the time for radical solidarity and true unity o   No, I will not arrest my brother for selling and smoking marijuana because we have to stop allowing the bosses to talk us into oppressing each other

o   When we oppress each other, we are house slaves (see Chapter Nine), and when you have a nation of house slaves, you have a very hard time fighting oppression

o   No, I will not allow my labor power to be exploited or externally commanded in any way because you have consistently used it: to enrich yourself at the expense of the natural environment, our common Mother Earth; without any regard for my own safety; and to create the world in your own image, which is dehumanizing for me because it denies me my right to create, that is, to be human

o   No, I will not use your prepackaged curriculum because it is decontextualized and therefore not in the best interests of the students, and because it is our responsibility to do the best we can for our students

o   No, I will not purchase your cars or your gasoline, or any of your destructive manufactured wants because they are killing the planet just as cigarettes kill the lungs and then the body

o   Just say NO to the big stuff like having your labor power externally controlled, *and* the small stuff like purchasing prepackaged highly processed food because it is wasteful and not healthful

o   Say NO to everything because even the small things become major issues when enough people participate in not participating like the grocery store boycotts orchestrated by the United Farm Workers in California in their relatively successful efforts to improve their lives through self-empowerment and direct action against the bosses

o   This is just the very beginning of the list of things that we refuse to do because they represent a process of reactionary suicide

o   The entire social structure that exists today in the twenty-first century represents reactionary suicide

o   By saying no to our reactionary suicide, we are affirming revolutionary suicide because we are killing the house slaves within us thereby rebirthing ourselves as change agents

o   Reactionary suicide can only and has only led to widespread death, suffering, and degradation of every sort imaginable, and therefore must be wholeheartedly rejected

o   Revolutionary suicide represents a rebirth, that is, hope for a better, less oppressive future and must be affirmed and reaffirmed, over and over

again because it is constantly under attack by reactionary suicide, which
has become a behemoth giant, and as a result, has tricked many people
into believing that what is insane, participating in the system that exists, is
actually sane, and that which is the only sane thing we can do, to reject the
system en masse, is insane (see Huey P. Newton's autobiography *Revolutionary Suicide* published in 1973)

But this *just say no campaign* requires critical consciousness, and it just so
happens, as we saw above, that is what critical pedagogy is good at. In order for
us to have the sense of empowerment, we need to collectively, and in unison,
just say no, we need to understand some fundamental concepts about how the
system works and our role in reproducing it as we have seen throughout this
volume. For example, we need to know that because our labor power is in the
hands of us, the laborers, and because without it there is no profit, there is no
generation of wealth, there is no capitalism, we are capitalist's weakest link, to
paraphrase Glenn Rikowski (2004). Because we are capitalist's weakest link
(we hold the one thing they need to survive as capitalists, our labor power),
those of us who rely on a wage to survive, nearly 99% of the entire worlds'
population, are in a strategic position to transform the world and create a new
global social order based on life-affirming values—such as generosity is more
important and valuable to the life of the community than the accumulation of
personal wealth, as the Lakota, the Mayan of central Mexico, as well as many
of Native Americans have and continue to demonstrate. If every person who
relied on a wage to survive said no to participating in the system as workers
and consumers, then there would be no one to put us back in our place as
slaves. If this happened, if *we* made this happen, then *we* would experience
and participate in a bloodless revolution. For me, the manifestation of a
bloodless revolution would be the ultimate materialization of critical pedagogy's utopian vision. For this to happen, we need a very large percentage of
the human population to participate in not participating. For example, if the
police and military were not actively engaged in saying "no" to the bosses, then
the results for those who were saying "no" would most assuredly be disas-
trous—this much is certain.

Critical pedagogy therefore has its work cut out for it, and we, as critical
pedagogues, have our work cut out for us—that is, to continuously challenge
and re-challenge ourselves and the students we work with to actively engage
with the word and the world because that is how we develop critical consciousness. In other words, critical consciousness does not imply indoctrina-

tion or telling students what to think or what to believe—it implies the opposite of this. Such an approach requires that the radical educator have faith and trust in the people. It requires the confidence that if people become fully informed about the world and their role in reproducing it, and obtain the necessary sense of empowerment, they will choose freedom over slavery. As suggested above, however, this task is not easy because we are constantly being bombarded with propaganda that presents slavery (capitalism) as freedom, and freedom (some call it socialism, others call it self-determination) as slavery. Think of ways these messages are presented to the public. For example, what role does the media and schooling play in perpetuating this version of reality?

One of the tasks of critical pedagogy is therefore to make the conscious choice to advance itself informed by the many gifts of native philosophers and leaders, people I understand to be critical pedagogues. In an effort to gain a better understanding of critical pedagogy and how it sees itself in relation to the native land it exists on in North America, I asked a number of critical educators to share with me how they understand their own work in relation to native land. While the work ahead is momentous, critical pedagogy seems to be up to the task. The following commentary has led me to the conclusion that critical pedagogy is not dead: it still has a pulse. And if I am said to be wrong because critical pedagogy really is dead, then I might say, in unison with not only the punk rock band, the Stiff Little Fingers, but with the voices below to be sure, "we're still dying!" Consider the philosophical underpinnings among their responses. We might ask, what do their insights say about their own philosophies of education? Finally, what kind of educational collaborations might we, as current and future educators, engage in with scholars of Native education?

Chapter 5

The Past, Present, and Future of Critical Pedagogy With Joe Kincheloe

To say that Joe Kincheloe is a brilliant and prolific writer can only be an understatement. He has produced mountains of scholarship as dense and rich as the Appalachians from whence he came, generously giving curricular life to the educational left for over thirty years. Among his many areas of expertise, the one that ties them all together is critical pedagogy, of which Joe is a leading figure because of his ability to bring people from diverse backgrounds together in critical solidarity collaborating on projects that celebrate our rich epistemological diversity—and done for humanity and against oppression (paraphrasing the Zapatistas, see Chapter Nine). As you engage Joe in his discussion of education, Native America, whiteness, and other topics woven together in relation to one another, consider again how his perspective might inform your own future practice.

* * *

Curry: How do you, as a critical scholar within the North American education left, understand the work that you do and the undetermined future you see yourself as part of creating in relation to Native lands and peoples?

Joe: People are absolutely unaware that they are using Native land—it is not part of Western consciousness—that we are on Native land. Just the fact that we would even begin to talk about this is an amazingly revolutionary act. It is really unfortunate to have to say that because it is so damned obvious, and yet it is not something I have ever heard anyone talk about anywhere I have ever lived or taught. That is basically true for everyone in the United States and Canada—those were originally Native lands. It seems rather obvious (even though nobody seems to think about it) that a central dimension of any critical pedagogy has to deal with the subject of indigeneity, and it is something very few critical scholars are aware of or interested in.

The fact that I taught on the Rosebud Sioux Reservation in the early 1980s obviously made me very conscious of those things. Ever since then I have been working for the Rosebud Sioux Tribe (for the last 27 years). That experience has therefore made me sensitive, but it is not something that should be isolated with just a few people. The whole idea of doing critical pedagogy from an Indigenous perspective (like when I wrote *What Is Indigenous Knowledge?*) is to be sensitive to the fact that we profit every day from the lands that were once occupied by Indigenous people and were stolen from them, and that history, the thievery and the broken treaties, are absolutely phenomenal when you just look at how the land controlled by Native peoples has diminished. I studied the history of the Rosebud Sioux Reservation, and you can look at a map from 1869 with the treaties that were being signed at that time, which gave the Sioux all of the land from the Big Horn Mountains in Montana and Wyoming all the way to the Missouri River in North and South Dakota. From then on, every year that went by part of that was cut away until all that was left was a tiny spot of land in South Dakota, although still sizable. It is just overwhelming—and that is just the typical incident.

There are a whole range of issues that are important here. One important issue here is the basic social political cultural understanding of our occupation of those lands and the fact that we are privileged by that, and then coming to terms with what politically economically needs to be done to make retribution for that is one aspect. That should be a part, from just an educational perspective, of every curriculum in North America. Every single school should have a tremendously powerful part of their curriculum explaining the indigenous lands and people who occupied the lands that the school is on and serves, and then how those lands were stolen from those original occupiers. You would think that that would just be common sense.

Curry: That is right. I work in Buffalo, New York, so any serious education class should begin with the land right under our feet. Technically this region is still Six Nations land, who leased it to the state of New York for 999 years under the false premise that if they did not, the federal United States government would take it. This is a history that not many public school history teachers are aware of or attempt to include as part of their curriculum.

Joe: When I taught social studies in Tennessee I had students look at me confused when we covered the section on "Westward Expansion," which lets you know where it is coming from, when we studied what groups occupied the land on which we were standing, which seemed to me to be an obvious thing you would do in a history class. Of course nobody had any idea of the Cherokee who occupied those lands, or when it was taken or how it was taken or that entire process. Most of them remember those lessons thirty years later.

Curry: Absolutely, that is how learning becomes exciting and very real, even if it makes them mad at first.

Joe: Yes, and just given the different place and time when I was teaching nobody got mad, they thought it was really cool because it was just so different, and there had not yet developed the right wing recovery effort, the backlash. So I never had a single student have anything other than a positive feeling about this subject matter, and that was in Tennessee! Wow, what a different time.

Along those lines—the lines of curriculum—one can begin to think in terms of the political and economic gains that came from the appropriation of lands. In addition, and for me this is something that I am just obsessed with and have been for the last thirty years, is the idea of the power of Indigenous insights and Indigenous ways of being (ontologies) and Indigenous epistemologies, and that it seems to me that as long as one understands and acts upon the continuing exploitation and oppression of Indigenous people, and that has to be a prerequisite, and at the same time I would make the argument that all people in North America—white people in particular—have so goddamn much to learn from Indigenous knowledges and ways of being.

Curry: The collaborative salmon recovery strategies in the Pacific Northwest between marine biologists and tribal peoples, as discussed in Chapter Three, are a perfect example of what you are talking about. That is, the content Western scientists have to learn from Native peoples.

Joe: Not to mention the physical sciences. I am thinking of the knowledges that the Andean peoples brought to agricultural scholars about how to grow different crops in different soils at different altitudes. What the Andean people have developed is just phenomenal. Also, the insights of the shamanic traditions using hallucinogens, there is a lot to learn there too.

Curry: It seems that one of the major lessons to be learned from Indigenous knowledge is that the Idealist dichotomy between the mind and the body, between the physical and spiritual worlds are false. In other words, everything is connected and interrelated, and everything therefore has inherent worth and a natural right to exist. While these insights seem obvious, they are not.

Joe: Yes, it is so true that all of these dimensions of our lives are connected and to try to fragment them, as Western society has done, leads to catastrophe. What we have to be careful of, for obvious reasons, is to not exploit Indigenous knowledge, where the Westerner makes profits from Indigenous knowledge. The idea, rather, is to use Indigenous knowledges in all of these different domains from the physical sciences to the social sciences, to the humanities, to questions of spirituality, to epistemology, ontology, cosmology, to really be a part of a bricolage of knowledges that lead to certain forms of political change, and a change in the nature of the way we relate to ourselves and the world. To me that is not an exploitation of Indigenous knowledge. What that is, is paying homage and respect to indigenous knowledge and using it as a mechanism of changing Eurocentric destructive ways of being and seeing. That is really central to me as a response to your question. That we have this two-tiered response: one, that we commit ourselves to raising consciousness and acting to end the oppression of Indigenous people, and two, that we make use to the gifts that Indigenous people have given us in a non-exploitative way, to not make money and do the things that have traditionally been done, but to actually change ourselves because of the wisdom that we have encountered.

Curry: Ward Churchill argues that these efforts to change ourselves informed by Indigeneity should be guided and directed by Indigenous philosophers and scholars as a cautionary measure against white people running around saying that they are Native American.

Joe: Wannabe Indians, yes. If you go to a reservation, you will see that phenomena playing itself out. It was amazing to watch that phenomena unfold on the Rosebud Reservation.

Curry: In light of what you just said about drawing on Indigenous knowledge to change ourselves and being part of the process to end the process of predation, as teacher educators, how can we proceed without leading our non-Native students down the road toward "Indian hucksterism"?

Joe: Let me start by saying that it seems to me that if you are going to do whiteness studies, you always do it in a multi-racial way. The same thing applies when we write about Indigenous knowledge. For example, you do not simply do whiteness studies as a group of white people. You do it along with non-white peoples that you learn from, and that are part of the learning community that you set up. With Indigenous knowledges you are not just setting up a group of white people that are learning about Indigenous knowledges and then applying them to white people. In other words, you make sure that it is a multi-racial or multi-ethnic process where you include Indigenous people as a central part of what you are doing. It has to be multi-racial in its orientation. If you are not doing that, then it can too easily turn into exploitation.

Curry: Can you talk a little more about your work on critical pedagogy as it relates to our discussion thus far?

Joe: It has become apparent to me as I have been building the Freire Project here at McGill, which is essentially about critical pedagogy, that I wanted to frame what I was doing in not just doing critical pedagogy, but a particular take on critical pedagogy. One of the things informing this project is the fact that critical pedagogy has reached a watershed in a historical moment where it has to decide what it is going to do from here on out, and if it doesn't make some important decisions, it will become a blip in the chronicles of educational history. Critical pedagogy has the potential to become far more important than it has been.

Again, there has to be decisions made at this historical juncture about whether or not we are going to continue to allow many people in North America, especially in non-white sub-cultures—Indigenous, African America, Latino, Asian sub-cultures, and not to mention around the world—to look at what we do as basically a North American appropriation of a South American thing. In many ways the state of critical pedagogy right now in North America constitutes a few North Americans appropriating a Freirean pedagogy and taking it into a U.S. or Canadian context. At a speech at AERA (American Education Research Association) last year in a session on critical pedagogy where Apple, McLaren and myself were speaking, as I looked over the very large audience of people in attendance, I noticed that there were very few African or African American people there. I have talked to enough African American and Indigenous people to know that one of the reasons that that was the case is that they see critical pedagogy as primarily a North American white thing, and often times a white male thing.

With this insight in mind, one of the reasons why I called the project at McGill the Paulo and Nita Freire Center for International Studies of Critical Pedagogy is very much the emphasis on the international. If we cannot convince African Americans, for example, or Indigenous peoples in particular, that there is something to be gained from joining together with those of us in critical pedagogy for certain types of common ethical, political goals, then I really think we have lost the battle. We have got to make sure, and let me focus on Indigenous people for a moment, that Indigenous people see critical pedagogy as an ally. At the same time, critical pedagogy has to understand that part of its tradition and historical knowledges and theories that it draws upon, are not just from the Frankfurt School, although that is extremely important, obviously, but they also come from diverse, non-white, often Indigenous, and other cultural contexts.

For example, I will run into Pakistanis who will say, "Joe, have you read such and such? You need to read her. Her work has been around for years and it really is kind of a critical take on life in the Islamic world." Critical pedagogy therefore needs to have what she is doing as part of the canon. The same thing would be true of Indigenous scholars. And yet when you look at critical pedagogy that is typically not mentioned in the canonical aspects of what we call critical pedagogy. It is the notion of critical pedagogy as ally, and aware of the issues that shape Indigenous life, and Indigenous knowledge and indigeneity as part of the critical canon. One of the reasons I therefore find myself doing work in all of these areas is to bring together all of these different knowledges—the bricolage, if you will. In other words, the bricolage of all these different knowledges is to inform the next phase of critical pedagogy. Indigenous knowledge thus becomes a central part of that. That is, the Indigenizing of critical pedagogy, the internationalization and non-whitening of it.

Curry: Beyond the Paulo and Nita Freire project/center, what might this look like in practice?

Joe: What that would mean is that the community action that critical pedagogy people would engage in would involve the types of things that we were talking about earlier incorporating Indigenous concerns into curriculum, in the context of schools, and making sure that no matter where they are, they are aware of the Indigenous issues and have made them a part of their pedagogy/praxis/action.

Curry: In Chapter Two we discussed land reclamation actions by Native Americans, such as the Six Nations' campaign in Caledonia, Ontario (Canada), who have sent out an international call for supporters and human rights observers. What role should critical pedagogy serve in this context?

Joe: It is central to what critical pedagogy does. Critical pedagogy has to be involved in those things at a variety of levels. There are things critical pedagogy can do with that context, and there are also things that critical pedagogy should not do. Critical pedagogy is obviously not going to be the leader of the reclamation effort, obviously. But at the same time there are ways of being an ally in the context. For example, critical pedagogues might be people who contextualize the situation from an historical, cultural, political, and economic understanding. Critical pedagogues can help shape the consciousness of people about why it is that the Mohawk Tribe (for example) is engaged in a land reclamation when typically, given the politics of knowledge in the twenty-first century, most people would not have any idea of why Native peoples are involved in such endeavors. I have talked to people who had no idea why a group of Native people were taking a particular action, and then when I explained to them the situation, the treaty rights and treaty nullifications that went on, many people say they had no idea.

Many of these actions are led by Native American Clan Mothers and the fact that there are groups of people that support the grandmothers is, in itself, a huge, huge contribution. Because when that does not happen, you could have a group of people in academia trying to tell the tribes what to do. It is like saying "ok you Indians, this is what you need to do, and anybody who does not agree is sexist" or whatever happens to fit the white supremacist framework of *the white man's burden.* The attitude is "if I am not the leader, I do not want to have anything to do with it." What people involved with critical pedagogy should do is to go to cites of Indigenous land reclamations, for example, and humbly stand holding signs with statements such as "we're in solidarity with the grandmothers." The idea is to listen.

The night I left the reservation they gave me a naming ceremony— a semi-formal ceremony with the Tribal Council, the Tribal Chair, and lots of students. They made me a member of the tribe, gave me a name, and tied an eagle feather in my hair, when I had it. The tribal chair got up and as he was talking about it and said, "Joe, we love and really appreciate you being here and we're sorry you're leaving. We appreciate more than anything else that you were one of the few people that was ever on the reservation that did what you did and didn't try and save us." That is the point and that was in 1982. That idea is so central that you are not trying to save people.

Curry: Could you comment on the tensions and contradictions within Native communities as outlined in your article on Russell Means and Indian education?

Joe: I was so taken aback by Russell Means because he was on an ego trip—the ego trip of a white person in that he was trying to get famous. There was no doubt about that. All of the values of the Sioux that I had studied and lived with working in a Sioux institution and being around Sioux people were not characteristics of Means. One of the things that became so obvious to me and so sad is why it would be that on the Rosebud Sioux Reservation and on the Wounded Knee Reservation why there would be a civil war that emerged around the American Indian Movement (AIM). There were undoubtedly bad guys on every side and good guys on every side. It was one of the most complex things, it was like Iraq. You had the AIM people calling the people who worked in U.S. governmental institutions related to the BIA as "government Indians" in a disparaging way. The people working for the government would call the people working in the American Indian Movement as posers, people who had come in from the outside and were trying to tell the people living on the reservations how it was they were supposed to live. They ended up literally in gunfights with one another. It was so sad to have those divisions. They were undoubtedly the divisions that always occur in colonial situations. If you go to any African country, you will see the same thing. Colonialism works so insidiously to turn the colonized against each other in their efforts to try to deal with the colonial presence.

In my article I was really hard on Russell because he was so disrespectful of many of the people that lived on the reservation. He was so much seeking fame within the white world. There was also a patriarchal dimension where twenty, year, olds would come to him when I was interviewing him and say "can we go into Rapid City and do a load of laundry?" and he would go "not now." I could not write about this guy in some kind of heroic fashion. I really struggled about what to do because it was so non-Left wing politically correct to write a critical piece on Russell Means. He was a heroic figure on the Left. I decided to do the honest thing and write it, and of course people wrote me hate mail saying, "Why would you attack a great Indian leader?" In that case I was trying to act out a critical pedagogy and play a role as an ally and someone who was a knowledge producer who was trying to lay out some of the issues as well as I could, given my own limitations and cultural biases. In that context, thinking about the role of critical pedagogy, it is never simple. It is true that well-intentioned critical pedagogy people can disagree with each other. But when we do disagree with one another, we have to do it as members of a larger family that are trying to do good things, and avoid what typically happens around the politics of personal destruction.

Doing this work around AIM really taught me a lot about complexity and the complexity of taking a critical stance, and, nevertheless, the necessity of doing it. There is no way that we can do work in Indigenous issues and not get criticized by different groups surrounding it. There are obviously white European people who will criticize us coming from the dominant cultural perspective. We will even get criticized from fellow critical pedagogy folks, and we are going to get criticized by Indigenous people. What I am asking of critical pedagogy is a lot. That is, I am asking a lot of critical pedagogy in that to do the types of things that we need to do to be involved with these Indigenous struggles, or the struggles of minorities in general within dominant culture, requires us to get dirty, and you have to have the guts to know that you are going to get criticized. It is so easy to shy away from those things. For example, several people told me, in a critical pedagogy context, when I wrote the Indigenous Knowledge book, not to write the book, and that I was an idiot for doing it because critical pedagogy should not be doing that. I was told that I would be accused by some people of appropriating indigeneity and accused by other people of having hatred of European culture. It was true and good advice, but it was advice that I chose not to take.

Chapter 6

Critical Challenges for Becoming a Teacher in Native North America
With Lauren "Candy" Waukau-Villagomez

As you read the following interview take seriously the challenges generously posed to us by Dr. Waukau-Villagomez ("Candy") who speaks from the perspective of a veteran Menominee teacher, principal, and professor. In particular, think about the case Candy makes for why teachers should engage in a never-ending process of self-reflection. Through this discussion chapter Candy extends our understanding of what it means to be a teacher in Native North America by providing rich example after example from her experiences working in the education system on her home reservation in Wisconsin. Consider her insights:

* * *

Candy: I had an interesting but irritating conversation with my husband's nephew the other day. He was born and raised in south Buffalo, and works at the casino. One of his friends he works with has a wife who is a school teacher here in Buffalo. She recently retired, and he was talking to me and my daughter Samantha. He asked, "What do you think about schools? Don't you think kids are horrible?" And, "Don't you think it's kind of horrible that we can't punish kids anymore? Don't you think you have black kids, doing whatever, and they just get away with anything, and you can't discipline them? They have these people on welfare, why can't they get off welfare? You have to go to work, and you have to take whatever job you can get."

As we were having this discussion, I attempted to make the point about how tough it is when you are poor, and how poverty renders life more difficult. In so doing I noted that it is not as simple as just going to McDonald's and getting a job because they pay below subsistence wages. It doesn't work that way. And so he said. "We made it! My grandfather made it, he was from Mexico. My mother is a nurse practitioner." He needed to know that his mother benefited a great deal from the 1960s and 1970s War on Poverty. I said, "Well your mother has all kinds of advantages. She didn't get out of poverty because she was more hard working than anybody else, she's very fortunate." His response was that that was then and this is now.

I was frustrated not only because of his attitude, but also because of his ignorance, which the schools are partly to blame because they send culturally unprepared teachers into a social context marked by changing demographics in schools manifesting itself in many more children from different cultural backgrounds in classrooms. In other words, you still have white middle class teachers who have a very difficult time relating to what's happening in these children's lives. With my nephew we tried to talk about the importance of Head Start and other state-sponsored social programs for traditionally oppressed people because these children need them. The community should provide funding for whatever the health and well-being of the children demands—that is social responsibility. He responded by proclaiming that he was not interested in paying for such programs, which simply reflects the conservative nature of the current times. The schooling that he had received clearly had not provided him with a critical lens to evaluate and analyze his world.

I think it makes it very difficult for children when their teacher does not understand them. Do not get me wrong: I am not a bleeding heart. I firmly believe that there needs to be standards and structure, and that students need to do certain things. I think that that is important. But also in reality, poverty makes it incredibly difficult if you're poor. It takes an exceptional person to make it out of poverty, and a lot of luck in addition to that. It is difficult for teachers who do not have the personal experience to truly understand the difficulties of children who come from poverty, who come from dysfunctional families, who come from the inner cities, or reservations. I can think of a person my sister works with who she tries to support on the reservation. She graduated from high school despite the fact that she has had a tremendously difficult life. She suffers from depression due to a chemical imbalance.

She has a son who is beautiful—a beautiful handsome Indian-looking young man. He has type-one diabetes. He was diagnosed when he was about ten. He therefore struggles with his condition a great deal. She takes pride in his being successful in school. However, she drinks to excess, and if you are on medication that is not a good thing. She lives paycheck to paycheck. She's just living on the edge of losing her job because she's drinking and staying out and not taking care of her son. She's kind of homeless in a way because she can't afford to rent an apartment. She cannot take care of those kinds of expenses, so she moves from family member to family member or friend to friend. They live out of boxes, and my aunt gets very frustrated. They have a difficult life. She's made poor choices time after time after time.

I do not think she is a bad person. However, if I have to make a prediction about her son, I would say that he will probably start drinking if he hasn't already, despite the fact that he is very successful in school. If he starts drinking, it will be devastating to his health because he has diabetes. I had a student years ago when I was a principal, when I was in Wisconsin who had type-one diabetes. She became an alcoholic. She died by the time she was twenty five. She was a beautiful young person, but died when she was twenty five, and that's what I predict will happen to this young man because he does not have a family structure or a social structure to really support him. I know he reached out to one of his teachers to help him. He asked the teacher if he could live with her because he couldn't take his mother's lifestyle anymore. He just wanted to leave badly. He's a good kid. But I think other people looking at that situation might say, "Well, if she would just straighten herself out, then life would be better." Yes, but it is very difficult for things to change once you're in that cycle. It is heartbreaking and it is difficult.

It is hard for a person from a middle class background to understand these types of situations. How do you help them to understand it, and then further, how do you explain to them the kinds of things that they can do as a teacher to be supportive in these situations? I have made a lot of mistakes in my career doing this because I didn't have a full understanding of what was happening because of my own goals. It is frustrating. For example, my daughter is having an interesting experience this summer. She is taking multiculturalism and often comes home frustrated because many of the students do not seem to want to be in the class because they do not think it is an important class. That is, they feel issues related to diversity will not be a problem for them.

They do not think a lot of the things discussed are problems where they come from, and therefore think such discussions are a waste of their time. They want what they consider to be more "practical" experiences. I tell Samantha that many of these future teachers are going to be in for an awakening because the demographics are rapidly changing. They will be dealing with children from all different types of cultures and backgrounds. It is going to be difficult for them to understand where their students are coming from or relate to their families. Hopefully, as a result of taking the course they will gain an appreciation of what multiculturalism really means and the importance of it.

I come from a well-respected and thus very powerful political family on the reservation. During the 1970s my family became politically active creating an interesting backlash. One of the things that we began talking more about and proposed was that the Menominee preference law should be strengthened. One of the reasons why we decided to form our own school district on the reservation was that we wanted Menominee teachers to educate Menominee students because we thought that was important. My mother and my older sister were very active in the development of the school district.

Again, that was in the 1970s. That had always been one of our dreams. However, you have a lot of politics on the reservation. Part of it has to do with things the U.S. government has done over the years. Their policies and practices have been very divisive. As a result, the internalized oppression of self-hatred is common because they have the idea that Menominee people do not need to know the Menominee language, arguing it is a dead language. Rather than a focus on culture and traditional knowledge coupled with mainstream skills, some people on the reservation argue that students only need to know how to read English and do math.

During this time one of my former students that I had worked with from the time she was in the third grade who went on and finished college, became upset during this process and she told my sister, "Why are you making such a deal about the Menominee first and Menominee teachers. I got my education, and I don't want people giving me an opportunity just because I'm Menominee. I want to get the opportunity because I'm good at what I do." My sister said that that is all well and good, but that is not how the real world works. If we are going to have our people get ahead in the world, we have to do this. I think years later she has come to appreciate what we were trying to do at that point. It was a painful process. She applied for a job at the school district and she was not hired. She is a wonderful teacher. She worked for me when I was a principal and superintendent at several different schools. There is therefore no question that she has wonderful credentials and that she is a very well-qualified and hard-working teacher.

She did not get the job for political reasons. They said they would hire her but she would have to be a Menominee language teacher. She said, "No, I'm a kindergarten teacher." She therefore learned a very painful lesson about the way things operate in the world. Those are things that young people who come from white middle class backgrounds that are more privileged do not understand. They just do not understand how the world works and that money and power makes a difference. My analysis here may seem very cynical. I wish it was not that way. I wish I did not know that that is the way it works, but it does. The more money you have, the more powerful you are, and the more influence you have. I think middle class teachers have to understand that this is the way the world works. I think that they kid themselves when they think that the system is fair and treats everybody equally. It is dangerous when they do not think it makes a difference where their students come from and who their families are.

Curry: For teachers who do embrace what we are advocating for, how might their understandings translate into their practice? In other words, what should these students do with their understanding, how do they translate it into practice?

Candy: I will use one of my sisters as an example here. My sister Lisa is the Tribal Chairman right now. She's a social studies teacher, and she's been a social studies teacher for almost thirty years. I think she's a good example of someone who lives what she believes. She tries to empower her students. She teaches all the different courses in social studies, world history, economics, Menominee history, and Native American history. What she tries to do is to give her students an understanding of history and she tries to teach them what their responsibilities are as young Menominee people. What kinds of things do they need to know? What kinds of things do they need to do to be good Menominee people? Why is it important to understand history? She tries to help them to understand the Menominee history. What has happened throughout hundreds of years? How does the government treat us, and what does it mean? Why do we love Richard Nixon? Why does the rest of the world hate Richard Nixon? Richard Nixon was one of the best presidents to Menominee people. Better than JFK. Richard Nixon made it possible for us to continue our existence.

Curry: How did he do that?

Candy: We were one of the tribes that were terminated by the Eisenhower experiment, which JFK did not attempt to stop. We went from being one of the richest tribes in the Unites States to one of the poorest tribes. We had our own hospital and our own electrical company, for example. We therefore produced our own electricity. We provided for the education of students off the reservation. We paid for lunches for the kids. When we were in school the tribes paid for our lunches so we could have food to eat. All the Menominee children had hot lunch every day because the tribe provided it for them. We had medical care. We had universal health care before Canada had it. We were born in the Indian hospital, and we were well taken care of then. After termination all of that just fell apart, we lost everything. Richard Nixon restored us to reservation status and we were able to save our ancestral lands, and thus began to pick up the pieces.

This occurred because we were activists, and there was thus a push from the community. We were also at the right place at the right time. This happened during the 1970s when a lot of people were involved in activism and mass mobilizations from the ground up. The movement against termination became a cause for many people, and we were able to benefit from that. However, Nixon, as the president, was the one who made it possible. My sister therefore teaches our students about this history so they understand, and when people say bad things about Richard Nixon, they will be able to offer another perspective—what he did for us.

Other things have also occurred throughout the years in various places both on and off the reservation at various institutions where our students go to school. At the University of Wisconsin at Stevens' Point one of my sister's former students was taking a sociology class during a time rampant with anti-Indian sentiment because of the different movements within Indian country such as the struggle to enforce treaty-specified fishing rights in northern Wisconsin, which was at its peak. During this struggle we learned of the dangers of getting in the way of white fishermen and "their" fish. If you do, you are risking your life. Indian people were therefore asserting their rights, their hunting and fishing rights, and that created a lot of controversy because the fishermen were resentful because of the loss of their ability to fish. Surrounding and contributing to this tension was a lot of discussion about sovereignty, which is very important to Indian people.

Within this context of anti-Indian sentiment my sister's former student who had taken Native American history classes before going to university was able to say "wait a minute, you people are wrong. You do not understand your history. You do not understand that Native people, because of treaty rights agreed upon by the U.S. government and the Menominee and other tribes, Native people have these rights. We are sovereign nations. We are not the same as white fishermen or anybody else. You need to understand this" she was therefore able to stand up and say this in a very difficult situation without the support of her professor. That was because my sister has such a dedication and commitment to her teaching, and providing her students with the kinds of things that they will need.

Through the years she has done different things based on the context of the time. Her empowering pedagogy, however, does not mean that she is a bleeding heart, which is someone who would say "oh, you poor thing, you have had such a hard life, and things are so terrible for you, and I am going to do just whatever it is you need," and if you are shoplifting, it is probably just because you needed whatever it was you were stealing. As a result, the bleeding heart sends the message that if you are poor, it is ok to be irresponsible and do whatever you want because "you've had such a terrible life." Unfortunately, this bleeding heart mentality was common in a lot of the programs of the 1970s such as Upward Bound. They would take kids off the reservation or out of the innercity and take them on trips to museums and other dominant society activities and many of the kids would shoplift, and there would too frequently be no consequences for it. This bleeding heart approach is not helpful. There has to be standards and high expectations for all students. Some people may disagree with me, but as a teacher, you have to be a moral compass. You have to be able to help children distinguish right from wrong. This is not as easy as it may seem because of differences in culture, but I think there are universal things that are right and wrong. Teachers are role models, and we have to recognize that so we can act responsibly. That is, as teachers, we have to conduct ourselves as such. Students know if you are being true; if you are being honest; if you are walking your talk.

My sister, for example, will do things for her students. Some of her students have ended up in jail, and she has bailed them out, or she has made sure they have gotten the class work that they needed while they were in jail. She has made arrangements for them to go to work, through the Huber Law, which says that if you are in jail and have a job, they will let you get out of jail and go to your job if someone picks you up and brings you back. She has picked up her students from jail, taken them to work, and then brought them back, and she is not a bleeding heart, she is tough, but that is the kind of thing that she would do. Sometimes you have to be able to determine if the student's treatment by the authorities is unfair due to discrimination and if you are able to help them or not. These are tough decisions to make because you are making a difference in someone's life.

I remember when I started out, I was very young, I was a bleeding heart, I'll admit. I had this one kid who was very tough; it was one of my first cases. I was what they called a home school coordinator. It was a way to get people of color in schools but not necessarily give you a teaching position. I therefore dealt with all the kids who were having trouble. I had this one young man, he was troubled, and he told me that he wanted to learn how to play the piano. I therefore arranged for him to get piano lessons from a lady in the community after school. Would I do that today? Probably not, I think I was unrealistic about what his needs were, and what needed to happen for him. Years later, however, I ran into him. He came up to me, introduced himself, and asked me if I remembered him. I said "oh sure." He told me all about his life, and he hadn't had an easy life. It was during the 1960s and 1970s when it was easy for kids to get into drugs, it is still easy today, and he had a stint in jail. He said, "You know? The nicest thing anybody has ever done for me was when you got me piano lessons, I'll never forget that." I laughed. Did I change his life? I do not think so. Did I show him some kindness? Yes. What he really needed, as many Native students need today, is family intervention, but I was probably too young at the time to really understand how to make that intervention for him and give him that support.

Teachers do, however, have to have a good heart. Those that are in the profession must truly love and care about children. Do teachers, especially young teachers, make mistakes? Yes. The challenge is therefore to learn from those mistakes and become better teachers. A good teacher is one who walks her talk. You cannot ask students to behave a certain way, and then not behave that way yourself. When I was a young teacher, we used to party and have a good time, but I soon realized that alcohol was such a problem for my students and their families, that even though it was not a personal problem for me, I could not do that as their teacher because they knew what I was doing due to the fact that we lived in such a small community. If I drank, they knew I was drinking.

Because we have so much to consider as teachers, we should be as skilled and competent as possible especially if we are working with students who come from poverty. They need the best that money can buy because many of them are coming in without the skills that they need. The young man I referred to earlier would probably have been better served by me had I been a literacy teacher so I could have taught him the academic skills he needed to be successful.

One of the things my sister does in her teaching that she is very good at is changing the way she teaches depending on the needs of her class. She does not hesitate to make contact with her students' parents. She is always striving to help her students become more responsible, independent, and disciplined, so they can set their own goals and standards. While pushing her students to be good people, she actively helps them develop the skills they need, such as reading, which is not always easy for many reasons such as vocabulary.

My sister has also worked with many student teachers over the years. She has them do lesson plans. She doesn't just have Native teachers; she also has had white and African American teachers as well. She said sometimes when they are presenting their lessons, they mispronounce words, which is very frustrating for her because the students at her school, who are already "at risk" for falling victim to the predatory nature of the system, need the very best, most qualified teachers. That is, teachers who know the "correct" Standard English terminology because vocabulary is an issue with these students. There is a primary focus at her school to push the students to learn the correct technical terms that they need to know, and also to think abstractly, so that they are not just concrete thinkers. The teachers therefore need to be able to constantly analyze their students in order to know and track the development of their thinking. For example, students who are more concrete thinkers are challenged and pushed to develop the skills they need to think more abstractly—that is, to expand their thought processes.

These are the skills that my sister tries to teach her students. She goes to work at six o'clock in the morning so that she can prepare—she preps every single day. She constantly changes how she teaches the material. These are things that all teachers should do. Her test scores are therefore the better test scores in the school because she constantly pushes and challenges her students to be better. It is therefore not surprising that she will advocate for her students. If she has a student who is struggling with reading, for example, she will go into the guidance office and demand that the student be given some sort of help. Or, she will work with them herself. She also keeps snacks in her room, so students who are shy and not comfortable can come into her room during lunch and eat to give them that extra support. Lunch, sometimes, is *painful* for shy students, students who do not fit in or are having problems. She therefore lets them come in and sit in her classroom, and she will visit and talk with them. Is that being a bleeding heart? I do not think so. It is looking at Maslow and trying to meet the needs of your students in whatever way you can. These are the things she does, which contribute to why she is successful. Some of the background for why she is the kind of teacher she is came from how we were raised. Our culture has always been important to us in our family. My mother was a Head Start director. She got into it when it first started. She was one of the first Head Start directors in the country. Our Head Start is one of the oldest Indian Head Starts in the United States.

My mother always believed that it was important for Menominee people to be in control of whatever was going on in the community. White people would therefore call her racist. There was a lot of teacher training money in Head Start, and she would rarely train a non-Native person. She would say "it's for Menominee people first. Whatever it was, whatever was needed, Menominee people would get it first." She would be adamant about it. We have to run our own schools, our own programs. We can have non-Menominee people there to support us, and help if we do not have the knowledge, but Menominee people are the ones who should be doing it, and always in control.

Curry: And some people interpret that as racist?

Candy: Absolutely, absolutely, absolutely! My mother's feeling was that there is only so much money, and when we hire a non-Menominee person to do a job, they should already be trained to do that job, and we should only be hiring the best. Their role is to provide support. She was always pushing her staff to be better, and she was very strict. She set very high standards because they were dealing with all kinds of babies and children. When Head Start first began, they had infant programs that went all the way up to four years old. It has changed a great deal since then. Back then, she was adamant that these children receive the best care possible. She believed that because this was on the Menominee Reservation, and it was the Menominee Head Start, the resources and the money should go to support Menominee people. She said that if this were in some other place, Menominee people would not be given a chance or an opportunity for this training. She was therefore adamant about it.

I think if you go back and look at Bandura's social cognitive theory, you will realize the importance of role models, which holds true for not only Indian children, but for all children, such as African American children, and Hispanic children. That is, they need to see their own people in positions of power and authority. It is incredibly important. If children do not see that, it diminishes them. It contributes to internalized oppression—that is, a negative self-concept based on the internalization of white supremacy. It is related to the experiments that have been done where black children consistently picked white-looking dolls over black-looking dolls as embodying ideal characteristics such as beauty and intelligence.

An example is my sister who is well respected in the community so she is asked to do many things. Sometimes toward the end of class when her students are doing independent work, she might take a phone call and conduct her business in the classroom in front of her students. For example, as Senior Class Advisor she would have to deal with a lot of issues, and her students would listen. She knew that her students would listen to every conversation she had, and if it was a difficult conversation where she was dealing with a problem, they listened to exactly how she dealt with it. I would imagine that they learned how to conduct themselves and interact with others as a leader from her. It was a lesson.

Here is an interesting little story. It represents the feelings that a people have about their culture. It helps students understand the feelings Menominee children might have about themselves and their identities as such. Even though my sister sets high standards, is well respected, and is an excellent teacher, as Senior Class Advisor she was responsible for helping her students raise money. In this day and age you cannot do a lot of things in schools anymore like sell soda because of the high rates of diabetes and obesity among the Menominee. The seniors used to have a candy store that funded their class trip to Green Bay or Milwaukee, which was closed down as a part of this health initiative.

In response, the seniors urged my sister to take their candy store underground because, they convincingly argued, it was one of the primary ways they made money for their trip. As a result, the Senior Class Advisor and the seniors began running an underground candy store, that they were not suppose to have. The unwritten rules for this non-existent store state: freshmen are not allowed to buy. Only sophomores, juniors, and seniors can buy at the underground candy store. Most importantly, no one can know that it exists. This has been in existence for at least eight years. No one tells. They might be in the middle of a sale when the principal walks in, and everyone does whatever they have to do to conceal it. The principal will walk out and they will all laugh and then go on with their business. I told my sister that first I would be scared to do it; then I would feel guilty. I asked her if she thought it sends the wrong message to the students. She said, "I don't know. I think it is a way to get over on the white man because the principal is white. That is how strong their feelings of oppression are: they have an underground candy store, they are proud of it, and they will not tell. Again, that is how oppressed and powerless they feel. This is one thing that is theirs and they will not tell.

Would I recommend this to other teachers, to one of our teachers? No, I would not. My sister is a veteran teacher who has worked with these kids for years and years. She is part of the community. This story of the underground candy store also represents the long legacy of our culture and how we have maintained it on our ancestral lands for at least the past five thousand years, which, in Indian country, is exceptional. My sister talks to her students about this history all the time, and about the pride they should have for being who they are, and how we have been able to survive, what has enabled us to survive for as long as we have, when the odds have been against us. How we have made it, what skills have been most important and instrumental in helping us.

There is an old story that my sister tells her students, which happened in about 1850 during what we call the treaty period of our history. The government wanted the Menominee to push to Minnesota. The Menominee are a unique tribe in that we are not and were not a very war-like tribe unlike the Sioux (Lakota) or some of the Iroquois people. We had already lost part of Wisconsin and our reservation land was shrinking. Chief Oshkosh and some of the other chiefs talked about it because they were concerned. They decided they would go and look at the land in Minnesota that the U.S. wanted us to move to before agreeing to anything. When they got there, they realized it was not very good land, which is usually what happened to Native people. They also knew that the Sioux and Chippewa were there, and they did not get along. When the leaders got back they told the people that they did not think that moving was a good idea. They were concerned that there would be violence with the Sioux and Chippewa, and that they were not used to the land. They then told the U.S. government that they did not want to move, and that they were not going to move. The U.S. responded by saying that they had to move, that they did not have a choice, and that they would be given a certain amount of money and acres of land. The leaders again said "no, we aren't going to do that." They then made a trip to Washington to talk to the president, or whoever was available, and said that they didn't want to move. The U.S. government then sent in what they called the Long Knives (the soldiers). The elders, chiefs, and people then got together and talked about what they would do. They decided that they would not move no matter what. The chiefs then told the people to put on their death robes and lay down their guns. The Long Knives came and the leaders told them you'll have to kill us, we are not moving. Their was a lawyer and a Catholic priest who got involved and said no we can't do this, we can't kill these people. They therefore started negotiating again, and that is how we ended up on the land that we are located on today. The government backed down and didn't move us. That is a story that is shared with our children. It occurred right on the banks of the Wolf River. When my sister tells the story, she points to different students in the class saying, "you, that was your great, great grandfather. You, that was your great, great grandmother. She was there. All of our grandmothers and grandfathers were there because they stood up and were willing to die for what they believed in. That is why we are here."

While these things are important for Menominee teachers to teach, non-Menominee teachers can also teach them. All teachers need to find their voice and teach based on what their strengths are. All teachers can make a difference in a child's life if they care, are committed and dedicated, and know their craft. Our students and new teachers in general have to take a hard look at themselves, and know what they are capable of. This is very hard to do because of our egos. We all want to think we are the absolute best at everything, which is the American way, or the way of Western culture. This desire to be the best at everything is not realistic because some people are not cut out to teach children from poverty or those from different cultures from themselves. Teachers should therefore be very honest with themselves and not take a job just for the paycheck, which, when that happens, is a disservice to the profession. Being a good teacher takes a life commitment, which is not always easy. It is especially difficult in communities with a lot of poverty because with being poor too often comes low self-esteem, and with low self-esteem comes dysfunction. As public school teachers we are mandated reporters, and in these kinds of contexts you will come across a lot to report, that is, children being abused or neglected. Teachers must therefore have the courage to report instances of child abuse. There are people on the reservation to this day that will not speak to me because I had to report the ways in which they harmed their children. Reporting is therefore not always an easy thing to do.

We teach the three hours of safe schools and the two hours of child neglect and child abuse, and we say, "That was easy, what is the big deal?" What's the big deal? It is hard. If a student walks into your class with a mark on his face, you need to say, "hey Jonny, where'd you get that black eye?" If he said that he fell out of a tree, you have to decide if he really fell out of a tree. If you suspect something else happened, then you have to report it.

Curry: What do these insights mean in the context of the whiteness of the teaching force, and Malcolm X's assertion that if white people want to be a part of the solution against racism, then they should work to end white supremacy among other white people? Is it relevant?

Candy: I think so. Students need to be aware of social justice issues. They need to be prepared to deal with what is right in the world. We need to teach students what is right, what is good, what is evil, and we need to help students take a look at issues that they may not otherwise deal with or be concerned about. It is really easy in a middle-class environment to forget the rest of the world, and the impact our lifestyle and the lifestyle of our families has on other people.

Curry: Some of the future students of our current students may even wind up in positions of significant institutionalized power, having an impact on the social policy that affects everybody.

Candy: Absolutely, all we have to do is look at the Supreme Court today. Those five people on the Supreme Court scare me to death. Roberts and that whole crew are just incredible with the havoc they are wrecking on society and poor people. There is not going to be a chance for poor people to improve their communities. The poor are just going to get poorer, and the rich will continue to become richer. Those are expressions that I remember as a young child.

This is important to think about for our students who will not work in poor communities. Some middle-class people are just not suited to work with highly oppressed student populations. You have to be incredibly strong to work in an "at risk" school. Just because you walk in the door does not mean that your students are going to love you and treat you well. Students who come from poverty can be extremely cruel and difficult to deal with. Students will tell you to fuck off in two minutes if they do not like what you are saying. If you are not emotionally strong, you will not be able to deal with it. For some people, therefore, to become a good teacher, they have to work in middle-class schools.

These teachers should therefore know about social justice issues so they can engage their students in these discussions about what is right and what is wrong. However, these teachers may find themselves in difficult situations because their critical pedagogy might effectively step on the toes of those in positions of power who are making decisions that affect poor people and people of color. This kind of teaching in middle-class schools also takes courage, and it is difficult to be courageous. It is difficult to do what is right. Sometimes it is easier to do what is wrong. For all of these complexities, it is very important for students in teacher education programs to take a hard look at themselves and determine what they are and are not able to handle. It is important to note here that there is nothing wrong with not being able to handle "at risk" children. There is a place for everybody. If people have a good heart, are committed and dedicated, then there is a place for them.

I can remember my first job as a principal. I was hired at a school where the previous principal had been there for twenty or thirty years. He used to come into work one minute before classes began and left one minute after they ended. It was a very dysfunctional school with an incredible number of problems. During my first year I really had to evaluate the staff as part of my effort to get the school back on track. There were teachers I therefore did not renew. One of the teachers who I did not renew, a first year teacher, had a very difficult second grade class. There was a young boy in the class who was very smart, but he had terrible temper tantrums. We had a system where the teachers had a bell to the front office that signaled, when rung, they needed assistance. This teacher had rung the bell, and when we got to her room she was in tears crying and the little boy is having a temper tantrum in the classroom, and the other students are wondering what is going on. The students were taken out of the classroom. Someone dealt with the crying teacher, and I dealt with the boy having the temper tantrum. Again, I ended up non-renewing her. She was very upset with me, along with half of the staff. But I told her at the hearing that I was doing her a favor even though she did not know it. I gave her two reasons for why I believed I was doing her a favor. First, I told her that this was not an easy school to teach at, and that not everybody is suited to work here, and there is nothing wrong with that, but my job is finding the people who are the best at meeting the needs of the students. I acknowledged that she was working hard, and that was appreciated, but I did not believe she was meeting the needs of the students. The second thing was that she cried in front of her students, and they would not forget that that little boy had that kind of power over her—that is, she would never live that down there. I therefore told her, "I'm giving you the opportunity to go someplace else, and do not cry in front of your students. You cannot do that. When things get tough, you have to get tough." That is one of the lessons that teachers have to learn, and it is really hard. I'm sure she hates me to this day, but I had to make my decision based on what is best for the students. There is no crying. There were days I felt like crying, bit I didn't.

Curry: You mentioned a number of times the importance of teachers knowing themselves. How might we begin to engage in this process?

Candy: One of the things that I have noticed—and I think we are all guilty of this—is that we tend to have a hard time really opening our minds and hearing what other people have to say. One of the things we often do, and I am as guilty as other people are, when someone starts to say something that we do not agree with, we close down. We need to stress this much more with teacher education students, that is, we need to open our minds and we need to listen to other ideas and thoughts, and we need to keep them around and work with them. Even if we do not agree with what we encounter, we at least need to work on thinking outside the box, that is, outside ourselves. I think that is so incredibly important.

I think for people of color, like myself, it can be very painful functioning off the reservation and on the reservation when you have been gone for so long. I have always had to be able to step back and analyze my reactions, and say, "ok, why am I reacting this way? Which part of me is reacting this way? Is this my Native experiences? Where is this coming from? Is this the way white people do things? Do I have to look at it that way?"

When you come from the dominant culture, it hasn't been necessary for you to do that, but that is what we have to ask our students to do—to reflect and step back and say, "What's going on? What's happening? Why do I think this way? Why do I feel this way?" I think if a professor says something that upsets you, you have to be able to step back and ask yourself, "Ok, why is this upsetting me?" This is difficult, but important, for students to do. As professors it is our job to challenge the ideas that our students have, and to push them to constantly think about why they are the way they are, and to analyze the way things happen the way they do. In the long run this will help them be able to appreciate and understand people who are different from themselves, and it will therefore help them help their future students. These challenges are made more difficult in programs where the majority of the students come from a similar middle class background and tend to think the same. In such contexts professors need to be even more acutely aware of the challenges they are posing to their students. Diversity of backgrounds and ideas are always extremely helpful here. Students need to be exposed to radical thought. You were talking about Malcolm X, and it breaks my heart that he died at such a young age because he had different ideas, and a different way of looking at things, and I do not think it was wrong, and I think it would have been important for the American people to hear and see it. Maybe he was saying things that America did not want to hear, but maybe America should have heard it more clearly and openly. It is therefore important for students to have interactions with people who think differently from the way they do, so they can appreciate it.

Sometimes for myself, as a professor of color, my students do not always appreciate where I came from or how I think. They have difficulties understanding some of the stories that I tell in the sense of applying it to their future work as teachers. I do not just tell stories for the sake of telling stories. I want them to take the stories, the essence of the stories, and apply it to their own lives and teaching experiences, situated in their own contexts, which tends not to be on reservations or with Indian children. However, some of my experiences are the same kinds of experiences had in the inner city. Students have a hard time making such connections because they tend to have a difficult time looking at things in a different way. That is, stepping back from their culture and beliefs.

Curry: Thinking about the importance of looking at things from a different perspective, some of our readers might need a bit more explanation on the specific manifestation of the termination policies you mentioned earlier even though it was not the central point you were making.

Candy: The government has always experimented on Native people. There was always some kind of ongoing cultural experiment whether it was boarding schools or something else. Native peoples have always been considered a problem. In reality I think the government would have preferred to just have annihilated us, but the social conscious of the country would not allow it. I think Grant was particularly hated by the American people. I think we were only saved by *The Legend of Hiawatha* by Longfellow written years and years ago in the 1800s. He made many people fall in love with the ideal Native American and saved many from being killed. This romanticizing of Native people therefore made it more difficult for the government to do some of the things they would have preferred to do.

Nevertheless, we have always been subjected to various experiments and ways of dealing with the "Native problem." There was the Dawes Act that divided reservations into allotments. After that there was something called "relocation," where Native people were offered the chance to leave the reservation for money and the promise of well-paying jobs in urban areas. Then came what was called "termination." The government said, "Maybe the problem is that these Indians are on reservations and the reservations are the problem, so we'll terminate them." They said, "We will not recognize them as Indians anymore, as wards of the government. We will not recognize this as government land anymore. We will give them the land. After this, they will be successful." We were one of the tribes marked for termination. The Menominee fought with the government for many years not to do the termination, which was delayed time and again. Finally at the end of Eisenhower's term the termination was signed into law.

As a result, the whole structure of the reservation was changed. The reservation was no longer federal land. It became county land. One of the fears of Native people has always been the loss of the land because that is what has occurred throughout all of our history. We always believed that if we lose our land, we will lose our identity and who we are because we are so connected with Mother Earth. When the reservation became county land, we lost federal support and there was no tax base to support our infrastructure, so the hospital, for example, was shut down because we no longer had the funding to meet the states' codes. Because governments are supported by taxable land and 98% of our land was forest, and therefore not taxable, we had no means to support our infrastructure, and we went from one of the wealthiest tribes to one of the poorest. Taxable land includes things like businesses and homes. After termination with no tax base, we were left quite destitute and forced to sell land. We had all these pristine forest lakes that we made bigger and began to sell lakefront plots for homes as an effort to create a taxbase. This has been our struggle, which tends to be hard for white people to understand because it requires the ability to step back and view things from another perspective.

Chapter 7

Beyond Essentialist Education in Native North America
With Shirley Steinberg, Rudolfo Chávez Chávez, Haroon Kharem, and Rich Gibson

Shirley Steinberg is nothing short of a powerhouse of assertive agency, not to mention a brilliant cultural critique and multicultural educator—a monumental scholar in her own right indeed. Shirley's ability to command a departmental meeting in full critical pedagogical formation is a sight to behold. As a new professor at Brooklyn College in 2004, Shirley's example gave me an idea of what it might look like in practice to be a radical professor in a teacher education program. Shirley's practice at Brooklyn College has served as my example as I have become more vocal and active in departmental meetings. Her example is the example of the activist professor not afraid to provide a biting analysis even if it challenges the bosses (and perhaps *especially* if it challenges the bosses). This short story is relevant here because you too will soon find yourselves looking for role models in a new profession. Who will you choose to emulate and learn from? Who will you side with? Where will you stand? What complexities might you be faced with when making these choices? When reflecting on the following discussion think of the insights Shirley offers us in terms of answering these questions for ourselves. After the following discussion with Shirley, reproduced are a few brief exchanges conducted via e-mail with other critical teacher educators. As you read their responses, think of what common threads you can identify that run through all of their comments.

* * *

Curry: How do you, as a critical scholar within the North American education left, understand the work that you do and the undetermined future you see yourself as part of creating in relation to Native lands and peoples?

Shirley: One thing I would like to talk about that is not in your question is how those who are indigenous to where I am want to interact with my work, and that becomes a real problem because as invaders, as the colonists that we are, we have so alienated Native peoples that there is this incredible loathing and fear of being around us. For instance, teaching at McGill, which is an incredible large university, there are only about 250 Native students, and that includes law school and med school, it is an incredibly huge institution. The problem is that when Native Americans do get involved, they get fucked over. For example, at McGill we only have fifty students in the department of education, which is probably one of the largest faculties. They are invisible. They do choose to be, but I think there is a subtle, or not so subtle, racism that makes them invisible. For instance, we have an office of First Nations in our faculty, and we have a First Nations director who in fact is a First Nations person. He is the only First Nations professor in the faculty of education. So it looks like we have this crappy little amount, but at least we have fifty, but in reality even the fifty are scarce because they are thrust into what is such a white man's school—McGill is a white man's school. It is an Anglophone white man's school to the point that many of the French feel alienated from it. The question is therefore: how do you feel comfortable working with indigeneity when we have such a history of fucking them over? So that becomes a really important point of it.

I therefore have to say that yes I have all these ideas, I write grants and do applications with hope that I can work and make a difference within an Indigenous society, but I do not know that I can. My university does have an extension program. We teach teacher education students on the reserves. They can therefore get teaching degrees on their own reservation with their own people. At this point I think that is one of the best ways to do that. When we bring them down to where we are, out of their own comfort zone, it becomes very difficult, they have not even been protected in their own comfort zone, so when we take them out of their communities, it is very scary.

Our little language arts classes can teach Native stories and fables. Like why the Indian got his feathers or something stupid like that or some little eagle story, but the reality is I do not know if we are making a difference, and I find it really frustrating.

Both my husband (Joe Kincheloe, see Chapter Five) and I worked on a reservation. We worked with Native peoples. I worked in Canada and he worked in South Dakota. You try to make a difference but you still come off like a colonist. Even if you are called a good white man, and a person who is a friend to the Indians, you are not an Indian, you are not indigenous, and you have therefore not suffered and felt what they have felt. For us to come to the reservations and try to work with them, it is really difficult.

In my work, in my writing, I try to incorporate Indigeneity within all of it, but I wonder sometimes if I am still tokenizing it. How authentic can I be? To give one example, I had an Indigenous artist do a book cover for me. Of course, I love the book and the artwork, and I am very happy about how the whole project turned out, but is my use of that book cover still exploiting Indigenous talent? Is it fetishizing it? Where can we as white invader colonists step back and not be fetishizing or tokenizing indigeneity in our attempts at engaging in critical solidarity? I know we are beyond making fry bread, dancing around in a powwow circle, and giving kids Indian feathers. At least I wish we were, we are probably not, but I am hoping we are. So we are past that. We are more in the liberal multicultural concept of let's talk about Trail of Tears and feel sorry. However, when I try to incorporate Indigeneity, or ask an Indigenous writer to write with me, how does it still sometimes become fetishized because it does? Then there is the issue of how do I teach Indigeneity without being Indigenous myself? Not that I can't teach Black students or Italian students, I am not Black nor am I Italian. I do not agree with the idea that we can only teach those who are most like ourselves. But then again, with Indigenous people especially, there is such a need to exoticize that anything that is somewhat good gets destroyed by the exoticizing of the person. In films, for instance, when you see something like *Dances with Wolves* that has a kind look toward Indigenous people, but then you see them all being saved by white men. As a teacher, how do I therefore not be a white man saving? For example, I can do Indigenous literacy, and I do it better with white people than I do with indigenous people. I can show *Peter Pan*, which has just been released again, and there is a song in that movie "What Made the Red Man Red?" and use it to talk about media literacy and sensitivity. What do I turn out? Media literate, sensitive liberal teachers, but I am still not having pre-service teachers incorporate indigeneity. I can also go live on a reservation and do the sweet lodges and all of that, which I have done, and it is still me invading, in a sense. The reality in North America, at least, in my opinion, is that when any First Nations Native Americans work with white people, they are just doing it to save themselves, for salvation. I think the ideal choice, from an Indigenous perspective, is not to do that.

The best way I can be a part of the solution is to fight racism and the colonialist mentality in my own community with my own people. I love working with different Indigenous groups, and I certainly taught in different countries with the Indigenous people of the area, but what do I have to tell them? Your philosophy and knowledge is brilliant, it is wonderful, which then becomes tokenized and exoticized when it comes from me. I respect you, I want to learn from you, but this is how shitty power works, and this is how white men suck. What do I have to say to Indigenous people that they do not already know? Teaching in Brooklyn I used to see that all the time, I saw it everywhere. How do you talk to oppressed and non-oppressed groups in the same classroom? You end up with one group that says "yes, yes, hallelujah sister" and the other group that is not agreeing with you, but I do not fit in either group. So I become some sort of messenger, and once again, I become a white savior. It so often comes down to being a savior of stuff.

I am very interested in Indigenous herbs and medicine, and not just Indigenous to the United States and Canada, but Indigenous to other countries. I am very interested in alternative medicines. I still feel that if I go sit in an ashram somewhere in India, I have this overwhelming feeling of appropriating and exoticizing someone else's culture. It doesn't mean I can't use Ayurvedic cures and still enjoy and thrive from the health involved in Indian medicine. But I do not think it is a bad thing to feel like an invader, an interloper, I just like to name it. I know that I am here, and I am not trying to become you, I just want to learn from you. But even saying "I want to learn from you" can be pejorative. It is very complicated.

Curry: Thinking about working with our teacher education students who are going to be playing a role in socializing the next generation of the occupiers, how might we get beyond the savior mentality?

Shirley: You have to start out slow. Hitting them over the head has never worked. I think what is too often lost in this conversation is a discussion of the pedagogy of poverty. It is sad, but we cannot talk about Indigenous groups without talking about poverty. Show me an Indigenous group, and I will show you an impoverished group. What we do not do when we talk about multiculturalism is talk about social class and poverty. Multiculturalism has a tendency to remove itself from discussions of class and economic exploitation. I would, first and foremost, reintroduce a discussion of what indeed is poverty in a phenomenological viewpoint of what it is like to not have. I would then combine that in my discussion of dominant culture, that is, teaching what dominant culture is, and showing that what it means to not be from the dominant group is, in part, to come from a deprived socioeconomic background—to be in poverty from having one's labor power exploited, from being excluded from the dominant group's economic apparatus, or, and most importantly, to be separated from the land base needed to create an independent economic foundation.

The idea in this discussion is not to forget or exclude race, but beginning with the politics of economics, which includes how poverty is dealt with in the United States and Canada, which is a wrinkled nose approach. For example, the dominant attitude is that we can reach out to the little Black, Brown and Red people and love them and use them for their art and their music, but we do not like it that they are poor because there is this obsession with the *pulling themselves up by the bootstraps they can get out of it* mentality. It is therefore not surprising that there is not an understanding that in many Indigenous communities being poor is absolutely part of the culture, it just is. The dominant society has made it that way. They were not poor when they could live off of the land and do what they want, but once they were reserved (put on reservations), of course they become poor and unable to create a living. There is no understanding of that.

With our students we therefore talk about poverty and rethinking our own understandings of it. If you are here at a university in the school of education, I don't care if your mom was on welfare, and you come from a single parent family, and you didn't have new Nikes for school, you do not know what poor is. I think it is really important to understand what poverty means. After talking about poverty, I talk about deconstructing their own identities of who they are, they need to learn to name themselves in relation to the students who they teach without embarrassment. Brown, and Red, and Black people are not embarrassed to say that they are who they are, but what people are embarrassed to name color?

I had a student in Brooklyn who came back to me who said she was really uncomfortable. She told the class that she read this book that I had given them to read about different colors of skin, it was a little kid class, and one little kid came up to her and put his arm next to hers and said look you are not white either, you are tan," and said "look at her" and he went running around looking at everyone's hands, and she said, 'I felt so uncomfortable I didn't know what to say, I was scared to talk about it.' Why are you scared that the kids' skin color is different than yours? It is the weak liberal notion of political correctness that has no place in the classroom. If you are Brown, then you are Brown, get over it. It is not embarrassing. There is this constant whisper of skin color because it is so embarrassing to a middle-class student. The challenge is therefore how to articulate your own positionality.

I just finished an article that is going to be in a book with Priya Parmar (Brooklyn College/CUNY assistant professor) on antiracist education. One of the things that Priya and I have always done when we go into a Black classroom, which we do a lot, is say "guess you noticed that we're not Black?" That blows the kids' minds away because they never had some white person say that they were not Black. Of course when I walk in they all say "oh, she's white" and I can say "I identify myself as Jewish," but they don't see me that way, they see me as a white person because I am white. When I name it, when I say "guess you're wondering why a red-headed white woman is standing here in front of you going to talk about hip hop, it totally disarms them, and makes them feel comfortable. It is like "oh-my-God, a white person who knows that she is white." It really blows people away. Naming therefore becomes an important part of my pedagogy right off. That is, naming whiteness as another color, another group. Poverty and positionality are therefore two of the most important things I talk about.

I would tell students that the idea is not to go read all the Indian myths you can get your hands on, or all the Mexican stories. Do not go learn about Anansi from West Africa so you can tell spider stories too. That is not working with indigenous people. It is almost more about therapy with us than with the people because they are pretty centered; they know who they are; they know that they are poor and Indigenous. The question is, "what do we have to do?" I challenge the students in my classes to engage the people they work with, and think about how to play both codes. It really is about code switching. I am not a total Lisa Delpit fanatic, but I do believe in code switching. We have a responsibility as teachers who are not Indigenous, if we work with indigenous people, that we teach them to code switch so they can prioritize which language they are using and code switch between their Indigenous way of seeing the world and the dominant culture way of seeing the world and be able to be comfortable in both.

The idea is not to attack the Indigenous culture and way of seeing by beating it out of the students like what was done in the residential schools where kids were beaten until they speak English and never speak their native tongue again. I am not trying to take the Cree out of the Cree. I am just trying to give two kinds of agendas, so the kid has a Cree agenda and a white agenda, so the kid knows how to negotiate in both worlds. There are not too many people who can do that. That's where the frustration, the nihilism, and the high rates of suicide and substance abuse come from because they are not comfortable in either world. Again, it is very hard. If you go to Australia and see the Indigenous people there, it is like "oh-my-God!" The only thing an aboriginal person has to do there is walk into a supermarket, a restaurant, or a bar, and the whole affect of the place changes.

* * *

The following exchange with Rudolfo Chávez Chávez offers a slightly different perspective from Steinberg's analysis by focusing on the complex and contradictory struggles of the dual positionality of the colonizer and the colonized embodied within Chicanismo—that is, Spanish European ancestry combined with an Indigenous background. Chávez Chávez is Regents Professor in the Department of Curriculum and Instruction in the College of Education at New Mexico State University. His books and articles have advanced the conceptualization and practice of critical multicultural teacher education. When engaging with Chávez Chávez consider the implications of his self-reflective practice—a practice he has taken as a lifelong commitment to perpetual improvement.

Curry: How do you, as a critical scholar within the North American education left, understand the work that you do and the undetermined future you see yourself as part of creating in relation to Native lands and peoples?

Rudolfo: I as a Chicano carry as well as a colonizing memory even though I too have been colonized. My work as a transformative intellectual is to critically name how I have been colonized but also how I have colonized, in this case my Indigenous brothers and sisters!

I am still in process of transformation; that is, of naming and making visible my historical amnesias as well as histories that have been thoroughly and systematically erased via white supremacist hegemony. I am in process of not wanting to resolve my contradiction but rather to transform them, since contradictions are part of the human condition...

Simultaneously, I must understand the difference between my oppression and colonization and Native people's oppression from systematic genocide and make it part of my concrete world rather than leaving it as an abstraction. This forces me as a Chicano to rethink my historical role as a colonizer and, sometimes but rarely, nationalistic thoughts.

Lastly, I must struggle to erase and transform the images I have within me via years of media and textbook brainwashing of what an "Indian" should be, act like, etc., as well, with my person and with all ethnically concretized persons, this includes all peoples.

Curry: How does this translate into your practice as an educator of future teachers and teacher educators who, at some level or another, depending on if they are to be teachers or teacher educators, will have an impact on socializing the next generation of the settler community?

Rudolfo: Simple, it means that I must problematize taken-for-granted reality, abstractions that have been concretized via hegemonic supremacy and operationalized into racism, sexism, and heterosexism, classism, ableism, etc....

* * *

While the following statement by Haroon Kharem is by far the shortest excerpt, it extends our definition and thus understanding of the notion "settler-community" by including those who have been involuntarily incorporated into the colonization process as a result of the slave trade—that is, Africans. Haroon is not only a social studies professor at Brooklyn College/CUNY, he is also a history teacher at Jefferson High School in East New York. As a leading figure in Afrocentric social studies education, Haroon (Kharem, 2006) has advanced our understanding of not only Africans in America, but Africa's influence on what is commonly known as Western civilization (see Chapter Two).

Curry: How do you, as a critical scholar within the North American education left, understand the work that you do and the undetermined future you see yourself as part of creating in relation to Native lands and peoples?

Haroon: My answer is very simple: We as "invaders," some voluntary and others forced, live and work on stolen land! The next generation of teachers need to understand that the Thanksgiving Story presented in schools is very offensive to the indigenous people, that we (the U.S.) have tried to exterminate a whole race of people (if we want to use the term race) by using God to justify their perceived right to take away land from someone.

* * *

Rich Gibson, co-founder of the radical, antiwar, anticapitalist education group, The Rouge Forum, has been a leading figure in the social studies Left for many years. Rich was raised in, and is therefore a product of, Detroit's autoworkers' unionized daycare centers and subsequently grew up to become a militant union organizer himself. His lifelong commitment and passionate dedication to the struggle against the bosses and "smashing the state," as he frequently reminds his friends and allies, sets the bar high for those of us similarly motivated. As you engage Rich, consider the larger context that he describes, and how we can put it to work to better understand the contributions of Steinberg, Chávez Chávez, and Kharem.

Curry: How do you, as a critical scholar within the North American education left, understand the work that you do and the undetermined future you see yourself as part of creating in relation to Native lands and peoples?

Rich: I try to teach people how to think critically, i.e., quasi-Marxistically, and to overthrow the government via a organization of nice people in good cheer.

Masses of people have made pretty good decisions about how to live (mainly) equitably and (secondarily) democratically, as in the Chinese Red Army in the thirties and forties, when it still had a veneer of red on it.

We are such a long way from a world where people can care about one another, live freely and creatively; I am not sure how to answer your question as we try to bridge the gap between what is and what ought to be.

The land that has been turned over to the Indian tribes around here [San Diego, California] is mostly worthless, or so it appears now, but the arm of capital reached in, inveigled the tribal bosses with casinos, and now the tribes are disintegrating into the predictable pyramid of haves and have-nots that (I suppose the tribal leaders would claim) is proof they are just like everyone else.

In other areas, as in Arizona and New Mexico, the tribes are on some of the most beautiful land in the world, like Monument Valley, and there is a big fight going on in regard to whether or not MV should be a casino—or just a movie location and relatively capital-free land for tribal members. I am working with some of the latter.

The flat of it is, I am not sure, but I am sure we need to get beyond capitalism.

Chapter 8

An Engagement with Critical Theory in Native North America With Marc Pruyn

Marc Pruyn has been an innovative figure in the social studies Left. Together with colleagues Marc has developed a Critical Multicultural Social Studies (CMSS) that is proving to be a useful tool within the radical social studies community, as it provides a much needed clear connection to critical theory in a discipline dominated by blind patriotism and coddling analysis. Although just as important as his social studies contributions, his work on the Mexico/U.S. border is less known. For the last ten years Marc has been a proud border professor who has consistently engaged in projects of solidarity that bring together community organizers, health workers, social workers, professors, and students from three cities within the three states of Las Cruces, New Mexico; El Paso, Texas; and Juarez, Chihuahua, in discussions on social justice related issues within their communities. Marc's ability to construct discursive bridges across vast subject areas and theoretical perspectives is showcased below. As you read, think of how important it is for teachers to be able to create connections between ideas and issues. How could this ability improve your effectiveness as an educator?

* * *

Curry: How do you, as a critical scholar within the North American education left, understand the work that you do and the undetermined future you see yourself as part of creating in relation to Native lands and peoples?

Marc: This morning I was at a teacher training in Los Angeles on mathematics chatting with some teachers, and they want to know about the Southwest where I live, the El Paso, Las Cruces, Juarez area, the place where the states of New Mexico, Texas, and Chihuahua come together. As often happens, one of the women said "gross, I don't like El Paso." I said, "It's not the world's prettiest city, but the people are very friendly and interesting." It is the place where the U.S. and Mexico come together on occupied Indigenous lands. I did not say that, but that is the way I feel. I did say that El Paso was a Mexican city until it was stolen, and I said that it was like the whole Southwest and western part of the U.S. stolen from Mexico/Spain. In response, she said, "well I don't know about that." This was a European American appearing woman teacher of the fourth grade. I said, "the treaty of Guadalupe Hidalgo, that Santa Ana was forced to sign at the barrel of a gun, said that the U.S. provoked Mexico into a war, invaded, went all the way to Mexico City, and sign it, otherwise you die. Santa Ana signed it, and then the U.S. stole this whole part of Mexico. Language rights, land rights, and dual citizenship were guaranteed Mexican citizens when they abrogated the treaty that ended that war. She then said, "All wars are that way, that's the way it is." I said, "yes, but that is not the way that it has to be. That doesn't make it right." Her response was, "we all stole it from the Indians." I came back arguing, "That is true. It was Indigenous land first. Then the Spaniards stole it, and then the US stole it from the Spaniards/Mexicans. But I don't think it should have been stolen from the Indigenous in the first place or from the Mexicans/Spaniards. That doesn't make it right."

I found it very interesting that this teacher went to the supposed defense of Indigenous rights as a way to negate the stealing of these lands later from Mexicans/Spaniards. Adding to our conversation I then said, "I think we should return to the Indigenous way of seeing it. The Native peoples never claimed to own it. They claimed it was something that couldn't be owned, and that we should share. I would like to skip all the notions of owning and stealing and say that we should all share it." By that time I had lost her and she was glazed over and scared and ran away.

Curry: Could you expand on that notion of sharing and what that might look like in practice?

Marc: Absolutely. I personally consider myself a libertarian socialist. One of the lens that helps me understand and see my world as a person, as a man, as a white person, as an academic is through the lens of Marxism and Marxist analysis. I think Marx was one of the first to identify social class and identifying how we produce wealth in our society and how we share or do not share, or steal that wealth, and how we are connected to our labor power or alienated from it on purpose. That helps me understand my world on multiple levels—Marxism. I have taken that and in recent years been gravitating toward a more libertarian socialism, which others have called anarchism, which is a struggle against all forms of abusive/coercive authority and illegitimate authority in all of its incarnations. It also embraces the dismantling of capitalism as one of those current abusive forms, and its re-creation, democratically, without authoritarianism, for the common good. That helps me understand and see my world. For myself I use that lens while understanding that I am a European-American-appearing, upper-middle-class, male professor living and working on occupied land—occupied in a number of ways: certainly occupied by the Europeans, the northern white Europeans, such as the British and Germans, who defined their path via manifest destiny with the goal of occupying all of North America and subsuming and oppressing under their thumb Native peoples and using the labor of African peoples and working class white people as they went from coast to coast. Also, as previously mentioned, I see myself as being on occupied lands as a result of them being stolen from Mexico and before that Native Americans.

Again, the notion of stealing something that is and should be shared is paradoxical in itself.

Curry: It assumes a pre-Columbian relationship to the land based on ownership that did not exist (as discussed in Chapter Three).

Marc: That is right, a dichotomous relationship that we do not necessarily have to buy into. However, I was going somewhere else with that. Will you restate your question?

Curry: How might the settler-Left go from where we are at to somewhere better without continuing to not respect Indigenous land rights, and other rights, such as language rights?

Marc: It depends who is at the head of the revolution: Native peoples (i.e., the Zapatistas), anarchists, Marxists or Leninist-Marxists are at the head of the revolution. But I have an idea of how I would answer your question:

I have moved away from being a snooty ultra-leftist that I used to associate myself with. Frankly, I have my own vision of how I think things should look like, which is, like I said before, situated within an anarchist-Marxist approach. As I have matured as an academic and as a person, I am a little less snooty about that in terms of anything we can get that is closer to social justice for all people, but speaking here specifically about Native peoples along the way is an improvement. I will abashedly admit that occasionally I will vote for a democrat, one of the parties of capital. I will support social democracy, or what some call a Euro-communism, even though that is not what I think we need to get to. Anything along those lines I think is good.

Answering your question, we should strive for more justice and less suffering under the current capitalist system we live under, but conceived as just a step towards a more utopian future without capitalism, or any form of exploitation or coercive authority of any kind. Under our current capitalist system we need two things at the very least. We need three apologies. We need to apologize to African people for enslaving them, an official governmental apology, and for having stolen about 333 trillion dollars in free labor from Africans brought to what is not the United States, and for the at least 60 million people who lost their lives en route. We not only need an official apology for those folks, but we also need economic reparations for African nations and for the ancestors of enslaved Africans throughout the world. We also need an official apology for the genocide against Native peoples and for the signing and then breaking of treaties that were part of the process of empire building in the Americas, as well as economic reparations from the United States government.

Also needed is an official acknowledgment and apology for the stealing of Mexican land that folks within the nationalistic Chicana/o community call the land of Aztlán, which are the lands of the current southwestern United States. I say that as someone who ultimately believes that identity politics and even nationhood is a lost cause, or rather it will lead us down a direction we do not need to go in terms of the pursuit of social justice. I think the pursuit of the re-establishment of a set of Native Nations, or a Chicano Nation, or an African Nation I think is not an effective use of our time and resources. But I certainly think it would be helpful in ideological struggles or other political struggles to make those three apologies, to at least provide reparations for Native peoples and Africans that were stolen and sold into slavery. That is under our current capitalist system, and could actually even be in the realm of possible political outcomes given sufficient struggle within our current context.

However, I think there should be a concurrent struggle that seeks to undo the whole notion of nationhood and borders. There are no nations, there are only corporations. Nations are figments of our imagination. Certainly there are armies and there are border guards, and there are taxes and there is highway building, there is postal delivery service, but beyond that I don't believe we even really have countries. I think we have these artificial things we call borders, and scholars such as Chomsky, Herman, and others have eloquently argued that we create this false notion of a country and a patriotism that should surround that country while really the only thing these quote unquote countries do is support the powerful (i.e., the ruling class) within them, especially the bourgeoisie, and then other privileged subgroups such as white folks, straight folks, et cetera.

I therefore think (getting back to the original inquiry) that, ultimately, defending the rights of native people, will best be guaranteed if we all collectively struggled in a Gramscian sense, not in a top-down patriarchal way, but where we all fit, regardless of what we call our ideologies, as long as they are similar, for example, Indigenous ways of seeing, Zapatista ways of seeing, anarchist ways of seeing, social democratic ways of seeing, and feminist ways of seeing. I do not think it matters what we call our perspectives and I don't think we should get caught up on these labels. For those so inclined, we also need to assist one another and facilitate the development of more folks who are able to see past the hegemony of this false shroud of nationhood and borders. In critical pedagogy we call this critical consciousness, the capacity to not only read the word, but the world as well. The quicker we can create widespread critical consciousness, and therefore work in solidarity and for mutual aid, I think the closer we can get to getting back to the support and defense of Native peoples, and our own collective, economic well-being. Again, let me summarize my two-pronged approach: to work within the system that exists for social justice while simultaneously struggling against nationhood and capitalism. For this work to happen our imaginations need to be put to the task of inspiring and motivating us with visions of how the world could be if it was informed by healthier alternatives.

Curry: Joe Kincheloe has commented extensively on the missionary approach to social justice where the white do-gooder goes to the reservation, for example, and does not listen to the community because they see themselves as there to save the "poor Indians" from themselves.

Marc: That to me sounds similar to the approach of several different ideologies. It is certainly a liberal missionary approach, which is just as bad as a vanguardist Marxist-Leninist approach. People do not need for us to tell them what the fuck to do. I certainly agree in that way with the Zapatista/Indigenous approach, which is also very similar to a Freirean approach. We certainly all possess unique cultural and ideological capital, and we can share that with one another and in sharing that capital, we can all gain and benefit in different political struggles and situations. Freire talks about the notion of Western radically trained teachers and intellectuals are authorities in what they possess, but need not be and should not be authoritarians. He took that notion to the context of the African/Indigenous communities where he worked. He would go in with teams of university radically trained folks, but they went there offering their labor, their intellectual and physical labor in creating higher levels of literacy, but they went there wanting to work with the community asking "what is it that you want to come out of this?" almost like a participatory action research agenda. Certainly we want to help you create your formal and informal levels of literacy and reading the word and the world in creative ways, but what is it that you want to study as content that will be a part of this, and what other kinds of struggles would you like to engage in, and what struggles would you like us to engage in with you"

This Freirean method is also very similar to a Zapatista approach, which is primarily composed of Mayans of central Mexico, and therefore based on a Mayan Indigenous philosophy, but it also has Mestizo members, that is, La Raza, which is European, African, and Indigenous blood, that is, Mexican. The leadership of the Zapatistas, certainly Marcos, a Mestizo, but a more European looking member of the Zapatistas, is held up as a leader. However, when Marcos and other Mestizos came to the Mayan communities from which the Zapatistas are based, actually, as I understand it, asked, "what do you want to do," not "this is what we can do for you." I agree with that, and therefore, in that way, I am a bit of a relativist. However, I still believe that my Western radical training in Marxism and anarchism and its critique of capitalism can certainly be helpful, but it is just one of many knowledges that can be gained from. That is why I find your work very interesting *and* helpful in that it is time for us Western intellectuals to go back and learn from Indigenous folks, and not just go back, but go here, go now. It is an important challenge for us to open ourselves up to learn from Indigenous knowledge and approaches.

Curry: How does solidarity manifest itself within the complexity of all peoples and all communities within the aggressors' sphere of influence, which, in North America, is all but total, being indoctrinated with the bosses' ideology? In other words, how do those from the settler-Left, who come from divided settler-communities, engage with Indigenous peoples, who also come from divided communities—divided Native American communities?

Marc: That is really important and interesting. In answering your question, there is a term that I am trying to resurrect and turn it around in a positive way—cracker—and as a cracker, as a white trash dude that proudly came from the working class whites and does not want to be part of the white exploitation of people of color, we need to be cognizant of not being righteous.

For example, thinking of Malcolm X and the struggle for African American liberation that he was a part of, if I had been there (I was

less than 10 years old in the 1960s) with my current ideological orientation, I would have happily and proudly marched with both Malcolm
X and Martin Luther King Junior, although I believe that Malcolm
X's analysis was more accurate, even though I do not think it was
where it needed to be at the time, but it developed and became even
more sophisticated. The tension here lies between the liberal position,
which tends to be described as rearranging the deck chairs on the Ti-
tanic, and a radical position, which can be understood as completely
restructuring the system. As both King and X were becoming more
and more critically conscious and therefore radical, their ability to
challenge the basic structures of power within the system intensified as
a result. It is therefore not surprising that they both wound up assassinated. That is, King was murdered when we began to include into his
praxis the analysis that the abuses and oppression of African Americans was part of a larger system of exploitation including the entire
working class. Additionally, when Malcolm X began advocating for
coalition building across religious and ethnic groups, he too was "terminated." Back to my original point, if, at the time, I would have
stood up as a proud little cracker hippy and said "King is a liberal re-
formist, and we should march with X only," I do not think that would
have been ok. If I would have physically taken myself to a march with
King or X, or both, and showed my solidarity and orientation in that
way, that would have been ok.

The same thing I suppose, if we are therefore talking Native
Americans and the American Indian Movement, which I understand
was more radical at the time, versus a more accommodationist Native
perspective in the 1970s, I do not think it is for me to say, especially as
a white man, to necessarily critique those two perspectives publicly,
but with my actual participation, intellectual or physical, putting myself
with and working with groups who I think are probably going to be
more effective in the short and long term, that would have been better.

Again, it is so important to always remember that we have all been
indoctrinated into the hegemony of this capitalist, white supremacist
system, and thus none of us are perfect, which requires us to safeguard against self-righteousness. It was Lenin, who earlier in our discussion I critiqued, but who talked about unequal and combined
development, and it is true for all of us. In fact, it was in a song that

you wrote, that we used to play together, which talked about being forward thinking in one area and reactionary in another. For example, being a fighter against homophobia, but at the same time being a sexist, or a person who understood class struggle while being a homophobe. We all have those contradictions, and I think we need to recognize that. Gramsci and the neo-Marxists have addressed that pretty well—that is, the ways in which those different oppressions and liberations are encoded in all of us.

Also, in this capitalist country, there is only one political party, the party of capital, and it has two faces—a slightly more hawkish face and a slightly more dovish face, although the distinctions in the past thirty years have been very hard to tell—that is, between the Democratic and Republican parties. So I know that—it is very, very clear to me. Yet at the same time, I register to vote, and I vote for one or the other of the parties for capital. For example, my choices have reflected this in the latest go around in the last several years, including this current cycle. Frankly, Birney Sanders, a social democrat who is a senator now, within the current system, I support him best even though I am more left than a social democrat. I remember this took shape during the last presidential election with a series of rotating bumper stickers on my car, depending on where we were in the election cycle and what my specific goal was, and so if I am going to try to appeal to other voters within the slightly more left progressive scope of these two disgusting parties of capital, then that is a political strategy. None of us, therefore, have a place, building on Lenin's notion of unequal and combined development, being snooty and superior. These are times that we should focus on principal ideological positions as intellectuals and as activists and social change agents. I use one of the many great words of Gramsci, organic intellectuals because it is important to have those well thought out positions, at the same time, these are times to be in coalition, and working collectively, and that is what is currently drawing me toward socialist libertarianism because I need to find people who are involved in interesting and engaging struggles, and that is where I place my work, and not to the exclusion of others' work.

I like how the alcoholics put it. Even after they have stopped drinking for years, they introduce themselves as alcoholics. It is like the film/documentary *The Color of Fear*, which is liberal yet still very helpful, where this group of men of different ethnicities are coming together to discuss race, power, oppression, and liberation. This one white man introduces himself as a racist, but through the film it is clear that he has been on a path to combat racism for some time. I think what he meant is that he is a recovering racist. I think the sooner we all realize the incredible power and resiliency of hegemony and the discursive messages hegemony tries to encode on us through culture and other ways, the sooner we will all realize that we are all recovering racists, homophobes, misogynists, et cetera. The sooner we come to this critical consciousness, the healthier we will be in terms of having a center from which to struggle. However, to assume one of those struggles (racism, sexism, etc.) is more important than the others, or that we have all dealt with our internalized oppressions from the dominant society and are ready to move on, is not being honest about the ongoing power of hegemony—and a hegemony at this current moment serves neoliberal global capitalism. Gramsci does make the point that there is always a hegemony, and if the current hegemony does not best serve the interests of equity and social justice, then we have to create a counter hegemony, and if that counter-hegemonic struggle is successful, then we have a new hegemony. Again, the current hegemony is in support of neoliberal globalization, which has intensified the brutal separation and alienation of people from their labor power in extraordinarily hard physical materialist conditions that you and others such as McLaren, Hill, Rikowski, and Allman have written very well about. But where we are doing ourselves a disservice is we do not recognize the insidious different ways that hegemony is playing in all of us in an attempt to divide us and keep us from the larger common struggle for social justice. Personally I find the struggle for economic justice at the heart of things, but I don't have time or interest arguing with critical race theorists or other folks that think race is more important, the struggle against racism, or the struggle against sexism or homophobia, they are all important. My time and interests just happens to be with economic justice. In summary, I have little time for snootiness or prioritizing one thing over another because that seems to feed into the hands of global capital and oppression.

Curry: Given your comments thus far, could you reflect on the future of critical pedagogy? Joe Kincheloe has argued that critical pedagogy has a reputation for being a white thing, and for it to be relevant, its reputation needs to change.

Marc: I think my approach to some of these issues might be slightly different than Kincheloe's, although I understand and respect where he is coming from. I do not think it is very fruitful for us to self-flagellate or to beat one another up in our scholarship or at our conferences. If we get to the work of work at a conference instead of spending the majority of our time saying "woe is us, aren't we awful," which is not terribly productive, then we can really focus on addressing issues and developing tactics. What too often gets in the way of the work is what I have called the "comma wars." That is, we all have a list of things we think need to be changed, and that we are opposed to such as racism, sexism, homophobia, or economic exploitation. These are all legitimate things to struggle against because they are all forms of oppression. But when we spend our time arguing about the order of that list, I become bored and frustrated and would rather engage my labor power in intellectual work and more fruitful endeavors.

There is also the issue of nomenclature. Frankly, I do care what people call what it is they are doing as long as it is part of the struggle against oppression and in the service of social justice—any form of social justice such as promoting more equitable gender relations, economic relations, whatever. In other words, whether someone calls themselves a critical pedagogue, a Marxist, an anarchist, a feminist, a critical race theorist, a Zapatista, whatever it might be, I know those are all important struggles, what they are all trying to do are good things. I am not interested in recruiting more people to this thing we call critical pedagogy because that is just a name for what guides me and is connected to a set of literature like Freire, Kincheloe, Steinberg, McLaren, Macedo, DuBois, and many others. I do not think it is terribly important that we call it one thing or another. McLaren has even argued that critical pedagogy has been neutered and associated with critical thinking so he started calling it revolutionary pedagogy. I therefore think we do not need to spend our time on things that are not helpful, especially now, these days, living under the yoke of neo-liberal global capitalism and the resulting barbarism of economic conditions and gender slavery, sexual slavery, white su-

premacy, and the mutilation of our environment, which is threatening
our long term and short term viability as a species.

Curry: What might that look like in practice, that is, getting to the
work of work, as you put it, so as to make what we do more relevant
and effective?

Marc: In teacher education, as a radical, as a critical pedagogue, as a
Marxist-anarchist, and whatever else I could call myself. As that man
working with people in their early twenties who are going to become
teachers, for me what has been helpful is discussing notions of hegemony and socialization and uncovering those and critiquing them,
such as the so-called normalcy of capitalism or patriarchy, or hetero-
normativity. Doing things that are playful and fun, but hopefully in
ways that draw from the cultural capital of the young folks that I work
with, and drawing on disciplines that Kincheloe, Steinberg, and others
have promoted so well, such as cultural studies that helps us understand that popular culture helps inform and shape our hegemonic
views of the world and at the same time it has been used counter-
hegemonically. By doing that with teacher education students I feel
that I can help, along with them, creating a cognitive dissonance that
might look like students saying, "what, what's going on with the fact
that so many people in the world live in poverty today?" and then exploring those inquires, and as a result, creating intellectual tools they
can later use as teachers. Particularly useful here over the years have
been the alternative, radical historians such as Howard Zinn and
James Loewen, and the work of radical teacher activist groups such as
Rethinking Schools. Drawing on these folks and others I have been
striving to more methodically analyze capital employing the core dialectical tools developed by Marx with the students I work with because
it plays such a central role in all of our lives, globally.

   In providing students with a set of tools to help them get through
hegemony we also have to provide them with examples of how others
and ourselves have worked as community change agents both inside
and outside of the classroom. These examples are not meant to be
guides or methods to follow but examples of people who have tried to
create change and how that has worked for them. The people at Rethinking Schools really help in that regard because they provide ex-

amples of teachers who have tried to implement critical pedagogy, for a lack of a better word, in their classrooms. These examples are fundamental in helping students begin to envision how critical theory might inform their own teaching, that is, what it could look like in practice. It is a huge struggle, but within my classroom, with the future teachers I work with, that is what I try to do. But I would like to do more, and I draw inspiration from people like you, Dave Hill, Peter McLaren, and others who really seem to be able to push it in ways that even up the ante of cognitive dissonance even more. That is how I see the rubber hitting the road for me as a professor.

In other aspects of my life I try to get out and support other kinds of struggles that are not in seminar rooms. Therefore, when there are protests against the racist Minutemen along the border, I go to those. Also, when the workers, the least protected set of workers on my campus, the custodians and other "blue collar" workers, began to unionize, I went to their meetings, I passed out their petitions, I spoke at their rallies. I am not trying to build myself up, but we need to go to protests and assist in organizing unions and do concrete things in those ways, which, again, are outside the seminar room.

Curry: Thinking about the fact that 90% of teachers are white, and that the teacher education students we work with will be playing some role in socializing the next generation of the settler-community, how might we specifically challenge the perpetuation of what we might call the occupier mentality of manifest destiny?

Marc: I think this is where the critical race theorists and the folks doing multicultural education are extremely valuable and insightful. These folks challenge us to begin our work with our own consciousness, so we have to be aware of the thinking of our students. Many of the preservice students we work with are not in the place in terms of their thinking that I would want them to be. I would like them to question, more directly, issues of power and inequities. I also think we need to put more emphasis on how we economically value our teachers. If we valued teacher labor power more and showed it in wages, then we could create more of a demand for people wanting to be teachers, then we could impose stricter requirements in terms of being

critically conscious, and therefore expect a whole lot more from them
than we currently do in teacher education programs. This is the pipe-
line argument, so we can get folks who are willing to work hard, intellectually and pedagogically.

In terms of folks who are already in the system, I do not know.
Based on my experience as a teacher and now as a teacher educator, it
is clear that there are a lot of really great teachers out there, but there
are also a lot that are not that good. But these issues are endemic to
being a teacher in racist, capitalist North America; it is part and parcel
of the hegemony. The social studies, for example (an area that I work
in), is dominated by a lily-white racist perspective, and those of us who
are more radical within the discipline are seen as on the fringe. Things
just do not seem all that great right now in schools, especially under
No Child Left Behind (NCLB), which is neo-liberalism for schools.
That is, NCLB is designed to privatize education by setting up schools
to fail by implementing racist and classist standardized tests and then
under funding schools' efforts to prepare for them. After "failure,"
formerly public schools and their budgets are handed over to private
for-profit mismanaging companies.

Curry: The world exists as it does because we, the vast majority of
humanity, allow it through our consent—we reproduce it. Schooling is
central here from the boss's perspective, because it serves part of the
function of manufacturing this consent. In the business press, on issues of education, the focus is therefore not so much can those who
are to be workers do the work, but rather, are we willing? That is, willing to sell our labor power for a wage far less than the value it produces. This is absolutely fundamental in terms of the perpetuation of
capitalism because without our consent, the system would fall. The
same analysis can be made of the illegal occupation of the Americas.
It is the people, the settlers and the settled, who perpetuate the occupation. Without our active consent, there would be no occupation.
That is, it is the labor power of wage earners who do the work of occupation as soldiers, police, factory workers, oil drillers, et cetera.

Marc: I like the terms and the notion of "occupied lands" and "settler-
community" because they are helpful because they are provocative.
For me they can serve a very useful function in teacher education and

other locations of discursive struggle for thinking about *what is*, and pushing students to delve into and break apart hegemony and see other possible counter-hegemonies. At the same time, for me, the notion of occupation conjures up the notion of ownership. I support the analysis because anything along those counter-hegemonic lines is needed and good. I therefore support the advancement of a nation called Aztlán, a nation for Palestinians, and a nation for the historically oppressed Jewish community, for example. In other words, I support the right of oppressed people to come together and resist their oppression even if it means supporting things that I am disgusted with such as borders (nations).

At the same time we support one another, we must be willing to critique things that have been carried over from the dominant society such as notions of ownership and control. Even though I think nation states such as the United States and international federations such as the United Nations are illegitimate sources of coercive power, they can be held to their own laws in useful ways. That is, they can be used in positive or negative ways. For example, supporting Native land rights is a good first step is countering the hegemony of U.S. state capitalism, but in the long run we need to move beyond the notion and practice of nationhood. At the same time it is not the place of white radical scholars to be telling Native people who the "good" and "bad" tribal leaders are, and what they should be doing to move beyond capitalism and beyond the notions of property and nationalism. That is not to say that white radicals should not have an analysis. We should. We just need to learn to not think we are always right. Whites need to learn how to listen and therefore how to be in solidarity with other people, Natives and non-Natives alike. It is not the place of whites to tell people of color not to worry about issues of race and ethnicity because it is all about social class. That is inappropriate and not helpful. I think it is a numerical minority of white radicals who act paternalistically, and they are the ones who give other white radicals a bad name and reputation among non-whites.

Chapter 9

Conclusion: Indigenous Philosophy as Twenty-first Century Lifeboat: The Critical Pedagogy of the Zapatistas

While much of the Western world was celebrating New Year's Eve December 31, 1993, the administration of U.S. President Bill Clinton was busy pushing the North American Free Trade Agreement (NAFTA) through Congress, submitting it for review at roughly three in the morning, and therefore as quietly as possible. However, not everyone in North America (such as much of the Left and the Indigenous of Mexico) was oblivious to the emergence of this "agreement," as *the bosses* called it, even though technically, NAFTA is a treaty because it is a "formal agreement between sovereigns," which need "two-thirds vote in the Senate to pass," which it did not receive, and should therefore legally be revoked, failing to have met even the most superficial semblances of democracy (Forbes, 1995, p. 186). However, as we have seen throughout this book, such illegality is not an aberration for the settler-states of North America. As NAFTA was being fraudulently signed into existence, a large segment of central Mexico's Mayan Indigenous population declared war against the Mexican government, demanding land, bread, education, justice, and peace, for example.

However, for many of Mexico's Mayan-based communities (the Tzetazal, Tzotzil, Chole, Mam, Zoque, and Tojolabal in particular, see McLaren, 2000), their struggle was much bigger than NAFTA. The Zapatista uprising was a response to five hundred years of predation (Benjamin, 1995; Chomsky, 1995; McLaren, 2000; Ross, 2000). NAFTA and its neo-liberal foundation represent just the most recent manifestation of Columbian pedagogy that continues to insist that the "Indios" are brass metal people occupying the crude realm of the body, that feared and hated barbaric wilderness of sensuality, and thus devoid of valuable knowledge, that is, devoid of meaningful epistemology, and are therefore "natural" slaves and susceptible to the whims of their "natural" masters, the gold metal people, the primarily, if not exclusively, non-Indigenous ruling elite landowners and government. Paving the way for NAFTA, the Mexican government altered *Article 27* of their Constitution and thus the *ejido* system revoking the state's protection of Native communities traditional communal lands, under which lies vast quantities of untapped "natural resources," such as one of the hemisphere's largest reserves of crude oil (discussed below). How did this pave the way for NAFTA?

Under NAFTA capital is more mobile. That is, it can cross borders with few regulations or taxation. With Native lands unprotected and therefore open for foreign purchase and the Mexico/U.S. border open for the free movement of capital (while simultaneously restricting the movement of people by militarizing the border with not only more physical Border Patrol officers but with more aggressive and armed enforcement tactics), many Mayan people felt the increasing tenuousness of their ancient ways and began mobilizing a resistance movement. Confirming the Mayans' suspicions, Mexico had begun negotiating with U.S. agribusiness to import grains, which would displace the Mayan economy—an economy largely based on the production of corn—thereby forcing the people off their lands and into urban centers in search of work, thereby removing the human barrier to the Lacandón nature preserve, the center of Zapatista insurgency. The small, impoverished Mayan farmers, whose farming equipment consists of sticks alone with no oxen, do not even begin to have the technological and financial means to compete with imported grains produced by U.S. corporate farming giants. With NAFTA many of the Mayan people knew that their own displacement would inevitably follow unless they took a stand. Many of these Native Americans decided to *just say no* to NAFTA and giving up their land and that which defines and enables them to be who they are—land-based *people of the corn*.

* * *

In this final chapter we briefly explore how the Indigenous knowledge of the Mayan people of Chiapas, Mexico, has shaped international politics, influencing the new, *new* Left. We also consider how these insights might be understood as constituting the critical pedagogy of the Zapatistas. In this discussion we are challenged to consider the implications for our own philosophies and future and/or current practice as educators. Finally, we conclude this book by reconsidering and therefore reengaging the idea of being called to action as outlined in the Preface.

***

Those who call themselves Zapatistas, as mentioned above, are Indigenous Mayans from the state of Chiapas in central Mexico, many from the Lacandón Jungle. By naming themselves *Zapatistas*, they invoke the memory of the famed, martyred, rebel-leader of the Mexican Revolution (1910–1917), Emiliano Zapata, himself a Zapoteca "Indio." Zapata led a group of Indigenous Mexicans in a struggle for land and the right to be land-based people. What this discussion and analysis point to are the invaluable insights traditional people offer those of us who are the most fully indoctrinated into the world's settler-state and imperial societies about solidarity and therefore democratic practice. It is argued (remember Chapter Four) that the democratic insights of Indigenous knowledge combined with critical theory offers humanity the philosophical tools we need to save ourselves from ourselves, and, unified, can therefore be described as a lifeboat. While critical theory offers invaluable insights for our struggle *against neo-liberalism and for humanity*, to paraphrase the Zapatistas, the following discussion focuses exclusively on Indigenous knowledge because of the extent to which colonialist interests have subjugated it.

In other words, in the following chapter, we examine, once again, the knowledge predator has been so bent on exterminating for the past five hundred years—if it was not so powerful and potentially insurgent, it probably would not have been targeted for extermination as it has (see Chapter Four). The intended message in this final chapter is that an Indigenous-informed social order is not merely an interesting utopian possibility to consider, but the very existence of life just might be dependent on the success of its implementation (Benjamin, 1995; Bergstrom, Cleary & Peacock, 2003; McLaren, 2000; Ross, 2000). For example, in *The Seventh Generation* (discussed in Chapter Four) Bergstrom, Cleary and Peacock (2003) make the case for the importance of approaching not only Native education, but everything we participate in, clearly and coherently, by drawing on the urgency within Indigenous prophecies that tell us,

> Either we begin to live in concert with the earth and get others to do so as well, or the consequences will change life as we know it. If we don't repair our actions towards the earth, its living things, and ourselves, and if we don't return to the role of the protector of the earth, there will be a terrible result. (p. 2)

With this sense of urgency fueling our passion to know, our "epistemological curiosity" (Freire, 2005), let us now turn to our first discussion and examine the impact the Mayan of central Mexico, through the Zapatistas, have had on segments of the Western Left focusing on the transformation of the "white" man, who would become known as Subcomandante Marcos. Embedded within the discussion that follows is qualitative evidence that suggests that the Zapatistas stand as yet another example of hope that humanity will "return to the role of the protector of the earth"—*one more* because there are other examples of people returning "to the role of the protector" such as the work being done in the Northwest regions of the United States by tribal governments in collaboration with scientists from settler-state universities restoring wild salmon runs (as discussed in Chapter Three).

* * *

That the people of the world would come together was inevitable, from an indigenous perspective, but what is not inevitable, from this way of understanding, are the relationships people forge with each other and with the rest of the natural world. That the settler-state Left would be attracted to Indigenous movements is not surprising. That the settler-Left would approach Native peoples as missionaries is also not surprising, especially given the insights provided throughout this volume. What *is* surprising for those who are *not* Indigenous is that when such settler missionaries approach Native peoples and are truly dedicated and committed to democratic movement against oppression and exploitation, they find themselves undergoing pivotal ideological transformations as their exposure to the Indigene challenges them to rethink how they see themselves in the world in relation to others and the world in general. In *The War Against Oblivion: The Zapatista Chronicles* (2000), John Ross argues such was the case with the famed non-Native sub-commander of the Zapatistas, "Marcos." Outlining Subcomandante Marcos' transformation, Ross (2000) notes:

> The Tzeltales and Tojolabales of the Cañadas soon relieved the new-comer of his pre-packaged ideological baggage. ...The resiliency and deeply spiritual mindset of the

communities that told their authorities what to do and not the other way around, changed the young intellectual who now operates under the name of Subcomandante Marcos. He was not the first missionary so transformed. (p. 7)

Supporting Ross's observation in an interview with Nettie Wild (1998) in her award winning documentary, *A Place Called Chiapas*, Marcos asks Wild how long she has been in Chiapas with the Indigenous. Responding to Wild's calculation of a few months, Marcos tells her that she has much to learn because he had been there for twelve years (now roughly twenty two) and was only beginning to "understand." What is it that Marcos alluded to that is so difficult to understand? The object of difficulty can only be the practice of creating and living democratic community with not only people, but with all animate and inanimate objects—all that is. That is, to transform oneself from one who sees *himself* as a savior, to one who is a participant, and therefore a student of how to be a democratic participant in the context of a communal form of community, and therefore a student of the Indigene in general and the Indigenous Comandantes of the Zapatista Army of National Liberation in particular is the challenge heeded by Marcos. Churchill's (1995) following description of the Indigene offers considerable insight into the depth of complexity embedded within Indigenous philosophy, which Marcos seems to hold in such high esteem, especially in the context of challenging neo-liberal capitalism and creating a new social order. According to Churchill (1995):

> By my estimation, the collectivism of traditional indigenous societies, the spiritual relationality (dialectics) of their worldviews, their accompanying ecologism and political egalitarianism are essential signposts necessary for the establishment of a new, just, and humane world order. I see indigenous nations, as discrete and ongoing entities, having a crucial role to play in informing the construction of revolutionary non-indigenous societies. (p. 351)

Churchill's description of Indigeneity and its transformative potential in the context of settler-state hegemony helps philosophical Westerners, which could be *anybody*, understand that the process of gaining control of land and human labor power, in the long term, has required an attack on Indigenous knowledge and ways of understanding and humanizing the world. It could therefore not be otherwise that the Zapatistas' campaign has been an affirmation of self in the context of a global ruling class that has denied their existence and relevance for the last five hundred long years. In their first international gathering hosted in La Realidad (Reality), Chiapas, which they referred to as

"An Encounter" against neo-liberalism and for humanity, Marcos, serving as the spokesperson for the predominantly non-Spanish-speaking Indigenous Comandantes, addressed the international gathering summarizing their efforts to be heard. Because of its relevance, a sizable excerpt is reproduced below:

> We are the Zapatista National Liberation Army... In the cities and plantations, we did not exist. Our lives were worth less than those of machines or animals... We were silenced. We were faceless. We were nameless. We had no future. We did not exist... We did not count. We did not produce, we did not buy, we did not sell... Then we went to the mountains to find ourselves... Our dead, who live in the mountains, know many things. They speak to us of their death, and we hear them...Stories that come from yesterday and point toward tomorrow... The mountains told us to take up arms so we would have a voice. It told us to cover our faces so we would have a face. It told us to forget our names so we could be named. It told us to protect our past so we would have a future. (The Zapatistas, 1998, pp. 20–22)

What the EZLN (Zapatista Army of National Liberation) does particularly well through their public speech, as demonstrated by Marcos, is non-romantically draw on their indigeneity to inform their struggle against the most current manifestation of Columbian pedagogy/predator, that is, the encroachment of capitalism. That is, they do not advocate for a return to the past, but rather draw on their Indigenous cultural and philosophical strengths to create a movement for a less oppressive future. I would attribute the *naturalness* of their success at articulating their purpose, in part at least, to the fact that the Mayan of central Mexico were never subjected to the cultural genocide of the boarding school experience as their relatives north of "the border" were. As a result, the Mayan of the Zapatistas think and act like Mayan not *something else*. For example, the EZLN is not led by a charismatic figure that strategically plans the movement on behalf of the people, as tends to be the tradition in the West for both hegemonic and counter-hegemonic mobilizations, with anarchists serving as the most obvious exception. Rather, the decisions governing Zapatista activity are made by committees (see below) and not by *a* leader. Such an organizational structure makes it nearly impossible to identify a single leader that, if assassinated, would significantly destabilize the organization. While figures such as Subcomandante Marcos have emerged as leaders, the messages they have fought to be heard have consistently come from the community, from the Indigenous Comandantes, as demonstrated in the excerpt provided above from the first Encounter.

As we have witnessed over the past thirteen years since their uprising, the seemingly simple act of being heard has had transformative implications due to the power of what the Zapatistas have had to say, which has consistently been informed by their Indigenous philosophy. As suggested above, the Zapatistas have been teaching not only Marcos, but the West in general, about what the West has called democracy. Central to democratic practice is dialogue. It is therefore not surprising that the EZLN have commented that they picked up arms not to seize control of state power, but to create a space for dialogue where all perspectives are welcome. It is precisely this commitment to dialogue that has earned them the respect of the international community—that and the fact that they have not engaged in armed resistance since their initial uprising January 1, 1994 (McLaren, 2000).

This example highlights the democratic impulse of the EZLN, and, as a result, contextualizes Marcos's famous phrase regarding the Zapatistas' strategic vision, "a world where many worlds fit." The Zapatistas' organizational framework with an emphasis on local control and decision making has come to be known in the Western world as the model for the *new social movements*. The emphasis on collective, widespread leadership has spread throughout the world and can be witnessed, especially in anarchist circles, wherever there is movement against the further globalization of capitalism. While central Mexico's Indigenous Mayan population, including those not associated with the Zapatistas, differ from their northern Native American brothers and sisters in the United States and Canada in the extent to which they have been victimized by cultural genocide, they share significant similarities such as surviving physical genocide and extreme poverty, and as a result, their susceptibility to outside manipulation and coercion.

For example, Native Americans in both the United States and in Mexico constitute the most impoverished human groups in those societies while residing on some of the most mineral and thus "resource rich" land (from a capitalist perspective that does not acknowledge the sacredness of place) in the Western Hemisphere. Churchill (2002) reflects on this paradox noting that in the United States the Navajo Nation "...possesses a land base...[with]...an estimated 150 billion tons of low sulfur coal, about forty percent of 'U.S.' uranium reserves and significant deposits of oil, natural gas, gold, silver, copper and gypsum, among other minerals" (p. 21), which overwhelmingly tend to be "developed" by non-Native outsiders, who then in turn profit while the local Indigenous community is left with the often deadly environmental bill and no form of economic livelihood. Other Native peoples in the United States possess similarly endowed reservation lands, such as the Lakota and their neighbors and traditional rivals the Crow. Because of the wealth extracted from their lands, Native Americans should be the wealthiest people in the United States, but instead, they are the poorest and most oppressed according to every imaginable social indicator (Churchill, 2003a). Again, the situation of Mexico's Mayan communities is astonishingly similar to that of their northern neighbors. Summarizing this Mayan material reality, McLaren (2000) notes:

> Chiapas produces vast quantities of petroleum, electricity, coffee, wood, and cattle. It also harbors major petroleum reserves that are second only to those of Venezuela in the Western Hemisphere.... Despite this abundance, most houses are without electricity; over 50 percent of the work force earns less than U.S. $3.32 a day; and approximately 80 percent of the children suffer from malnutrition. (p. 54)

It should therefore come as no surprise that the Mexican federal government has taken advantage of this vulnerability (i.e., the people are hungry) in their attempts to divide Mayan communities and weaken the Zapatista insurgency. Through such tactics as routinely distributing food in northern Mayan communities (reminiscent of the U.S. Army using food to lure tired and hungry Lakota to the soldier forts in the mid-to late 1800s as outlined in Chapter Two of this volume), the Mexican army has managed to facilitate the development of Mayan paramilitary death squads emblazoned with contradictory names such as *Peace and Justice*, which have been enthusiastically supported by the United States because the EZLN has managed to sour the environment for investment opportunities in Chiapas. For example, sometime between 1997 and 1998 Peace and Justice received a grant for half a million U.S. dollars from the Mexican government while U.S. military aid to Mexico also increased substantially during this same period (McLaren, 2000). These terrorist paramilitary groups, such as Peace and Justice, have also been well armed with weapons such as AK 47 assault riffles. Peace and Justice and other similar groups have been terrorizing the three hundred villages and municipalities in Chiapas participating in the Zapatista rebellion resulting in a number of massacres where women, children, and even infants and unborn babies were slaughtered (McLaren, 2000; Ross, 2000). The relatively successful objective of these actions by the Federal Mexican Army has been to foster inter-Indigenous conflict and warfare. These ancient tactics of divide and rule form the foundation of the emergence of what Malcolm X referred to as the House Slave and the Field Slave, which are dialectically interrelated terms of particular relevance to our present discussion. My somewhat symbolic use of the terms "house slave" and "field slave," it should be noted, is not intended, in any way, to belittle the brutality and genocide of the African slave trade. The decision to employ these terms, rather, is designed to highlight their contemporary relevance signifying a level of continuity between chattel slavery and wage slavery that most of us do not want to admit, for to admit our current state of enslavement demands radical action, and our tendency toward a fear of freedom (Freire 2005) poses a significant barrier to our own emancipation. This is the challenge of critical pedagogy and therefore the relevance of Malcolm X as a critical pedagogue.

Malcolm X (2002), while not a critical theorist or Native American, offers valuable insights into both understanding the concrete conditions of the world and possible paths of dissent in the context of Zapatista philosophy helping us better understand the project of liberating not only the land but the mind as well from a forced and thus unjust occupation. Malcolm X's description of the house slave and field slave in particular are concepts of invaluable use here. The house slave is someone who is conditioned to see their own interests as one and the same with the oppressors'. The Zapatistas talk about how the government sends liars and tricksters to their communities intoxicating the people with much needed food and then fooling them into becoming house slaves, that is, supporters and active participants of their own oppression by oppressing their brothers and sisters. In the larger context of capitalism, whiteness was similarly created to serve this function, that is, to turn all people of European descent, working class or otherwise, into house slaves. The house slave, to paraphrase Malcolm X (2002), is the one who cries when the masters' house is burning down. The house slave is the one who talks about "our" company, "our" military, or "our" schools, while those relegated to the status of worker, in reality, have none of these things. That is, the economy, the school, and the military are under the control of the bosses and are therefore designed to serve *his* interests, which are antagonistically related to the interests of the vast majority of humanity, whom Marx interchangeably referred to as the "working class" and the "proletariat." House slaves, therefore, support the bosses, and as a result, spite themselves. In other words, and as alluded to above, the primary task of the house slave is to control the field slave by confusing the people about what is sane and what is insane. The house slave argues that it is insane to resist the system, when in reality fighting the bosses is the only sane thing to do. Put another way, the house slave is completely and utterly insane, engaged in reactionary suicide. The field slave, on the other hand, is quite sane, and engaged in revolutionary suicide by executing the internal house slave, which is the equivalent of becoming critically conscious and empowered to take action.

Field slaves, to reiterate and expand our analysis, are the ones who are critically conscious of their position and lot in life, and therefore cheer when the masters' company goes bankrupt, or is otherwise in a state of crisis. The Zapatistas are proud field slaves, that is, they are critically conscious, actively engaged participants—actively engaged against the system that limits our participation and manifestation of self-sufficiency that is natural to the human condition, which capitalism is inherently set against because it demands people forfeit control of their creative capacities to be put to work producing commodities for others to consume. The field slave knows that we have no military because the military is nothing more than the heavy hand of capital needed for its insatiable appetite for raw materials and markets—primitive accumulation (as discussed in Chapter Three). If we the people/labor/the oppressed need protection, if we need military protection, then we have to train ourselves to be soldiers, which, democratically conceived, requires proficiency in not only physical combat, but ideological and pedagogical warfare as well. The Zapatistas created the Zapatista Army of National Liberation, which, as a body politic, demonstrates its propensity for pedagogical democracy by creating the conditions for dialogue and the free exchange of ideas *for humanity and against neo-liberalism—where neo-liberalism is conceived as a contemporary manifestation of the Columbian spirit of predation*. To be a democratic soldier—a true soldier of the people—requires becoming proficient in ideas, which schools can be used to help develop among large groups of people through revolutionary curriculum and pedagogy.

The field slave knows that we have no schools, that the vast majority of current institutions of education throughout the world are not "our" schools, but rather represent "they schools" as hip-hop group Dead Prez so aptly named them. We also therefore know that the project of humanization can be furthered along by either creating new liberation schools, or by taking over the ones that exist to serve the interests of self-rule and democracy rather than the hegemonic maintenance of the ruling class. Ultimately, a true revolutionary army of the people is thus the people properly educated to think for self with the capacity to detect hegemonic trickery and indoctrination. Towards these ends, the Zapatistas have created their own liberation schools within the municipalities they control (Ross, 2000). The EZLN's active engagement with the world represents not just the consciousness of a field slave, but the consciousness of an *empowered* field slave who has reclaimed control of her labor power and put it to work in the service of self-determination, and therefore not a slave at all. Such a consciousness—the consciousness of an empowered subject—not only leads to the denouncement of the world that exists, but to the announcement of a more just future, and therefore demands informed action towards the materialization of that undetermined future. As we learned in Chapter Four, this is critical pedagogy—to denounce, announce, and then take action (and repeat until utopia, and then repeat again just to make sure). Based on this analysis the empowered field slave/revolutionary is an abolitionist/critical pedagogue engaging her sisters and brothers in transformative praxis against slavery/capitalism. For the Zapatistas this has been a pedagogy for a world where many worlds fit, which represents an epistemology that views knowledge as equally distributed rejecting the myth of the metals. Zapatista practice and discourse actively lives the knowledge that all people are capable of self-rule, thereby fulfilling what is an essentially human ontological need for hope (Freire, 1999). Let us now further consider the implications this perspective could potentially have on our future and/or current practice as critical educators.

Critical Pedagogy and the EZLN

Again, the EZLN offers something critical educators need more than anything else—hope. Without hope, an ontological human need, as Freire (1999) reminds us, we are immobilized, hopeless, and cynical. If the Mayan of central Mexico, who constitute some of the most oppressed people in the Western Hemisphere, can find the strength and empowerment to stand up against their deadly oppressors (supported by the might of the United States government) and collectively say "no," "ya basta," then there is hope for those less oppressed, yet still dehumanized, to chime in the chant and practice of saying "NO." For example, there is hope that the 90% white teaching force of Canada and the United States can become critically conscious and join the struggle against neo-liberalism and for humanity, not as a favor to those less fortunate, but as an act of self-preservation and self-defense against a system that understands nothing but profit regardless of the human and environmental costs. What has made this hope I speak of so powerful and instructive, embodied in the fact that the Zapatistas have been uncompromisingly saying NO since 1994, has been the *way* they have said it, the way they have lived it.

Their call and action has clearly been that of the Indigenous. The strength of the Zapatistas' praxis is therefore firmly rooted in Native American philosophy of the Mayan persuasion.

In order to understand this Mayan philosophy and how it might inform our own practice against neo-liberalism (i.e., capitalism) and for humanity as current and/or future educators, we need to consider a bit closer Zapatista pedagogy in the context of how they organize their communities. The relatively small Zapatista communities of around one hundred families regularly assemble once a week where every decision that affects the community is debated and voted on. In these community assemblies everyone has the right to speak, and everyone has a vote. Sub-assemblies have also been created to work on particular projects such as sewing and cattle cooperatives. The primary assembly also elects delegates to organize work. Each community also appoints delegates to represent them at regional meetings. Delegates are also sent to the council that is responsible for organizing the rebellion, the Clandestine Revolutionary Indigenous Committee (CCRI). It is these councils of delegates that lead the Zapatistas, not the rebel army. Every council decision, every delegate, every Comandante, every Subcomandante are always susceptible to being recalled if they are perceived as not respecting the people or doing their jobs. This is the basic framework of the Zapatista system of self-government, that is, their internal democratic pedagogy. These decisions and framework operate in the context of refusing to acknowledge the legitimacy of the laws of the federal or local Mexican government. In other words, EZLN-liberated communities take as their place of departure the practice of saying "NO," providing contemporary substance to Karl Marx's (1867/1967) observation that "...revolutions are not made by laws" (p. 751). Similarly, many in the West who are empowered democratic teachers are engaged in the process of figuring out how to transform schools into liberated zones that refuse to acknowledge the legitimacy of top-down federally mandated pre-packaged curriculum that is *for* neo-liberalism and therefore *against* humanity.

The clarity and coherence needed to put these ideas into practice—to make them a reality—reveals the objective fact that the struggle against capitalism and the education that supports it is the only sane thing to be a part of because supporting a system that is fundamentally *against* humanity can be nothing other than insane. Put another way, coddling is not the correct action to take against bullying—dialogue and real consequences have proven to be far more effective. At this point it is important to restate that the philosophical underpinnings informing this analysis, which the EZLN draws on in their engagement with the concrete context of government is specifically Indigenous even though to "Westerners" it may seem "Western." In other words, the representative style of government of the Zapatistas might seem to resemble "Western" forms of governing such as the United States government. It is important to note, however, that the United States government was modeled, in part, after Native American confederations such as the Iroquois, the Creek, the Choctaw, the Huron, and the Cherokee (Grinde Jr. & Johansen, 2001). In "Perceptions of America's Native Democracies" Donald Grinde Jr. and Bruce E. Johansen (2001) contextualize the formation of the United States, noting that

> The colonists forming the United States were charged with...molding their own emerging nation, so it should not be surprising that early government in the United States (especially under the Articles of Confederation) greatly resembled native systems in many ways. This is not to say that the founders copied Indian societies—if they had, we would have evolved precincts along family lines, and our senators and representatives would be nominated solely by women—but to say that the native systems of governance, along with European precedents, were factored into a new ideological equation. (p. 85)

Women, in Mayan communities, like the traditional societies of their northern Native American relatives, also hold a significant amount of political power, which is one of the ways that distinguishes their organizational structure from the settler-state system they reject and refuse to recognize as legitimate. The EZLN internal structure is therefore not Western, but rather specifically Indigenous. We might name this approach an *Indigenous dialectics*.

Revisiting a Call to Action

Before I conclude this book, and before we conclude our discussions, I would like to, once again, *call you to action*. This call to action is a desperate plea for us to wake up and realize what we are doing to ourselves—we are killing each other—we are participating in a system set on self-destruction (as noted throughout this book). Along these same lines, Marx described capitalism as embodying the contradictions that would give way to a new social order. That is, capitalism violently creates poverty by expropriating the wealth created by the labor power of the vast majority of humanity, and those in poverty and who are therefore suffering under the capitalist system, are the future grave diggers of capital. In other words, capitalism creates the conditions for its own demise. Summarizing this point, Marx (1867/1967) argues that "force is the midwife of every old society pregnant with a new one" (p. 751). Aware of this very real potential of the masses, critically empowered as field slaves, rising up and slaying their oppressors, the bosses have devised an elaborate system of indoctrination as a preventative measure designed to create a nation of house slaves. The *Indian* Boarding School Project outlined in Chapter Four can be understood as part of this conspiracy to transform Native Americans into house slaves. These efforts to keep humanity in our place have only ever been, and can only ever be, partially successful because, while our humanity can be limited, it can never be fully destroyed, to paraphrase Paulo Freire. It is therefore not surprising that there exists a culture of resistance that has spread throughout society. It has been the objective of this book to support and advance this tendency toward resistance against what we might coin the "house-slavification" of the world's peoples.

The future is in your hands, and so informed, I invite you to become a critical educator, an agent of change, part of the solution, and no longer part of the problem, that is, no longer a coddler of the aggressor/a house slave. This final invitation and challenge is presented in the spirit of solidarity and support realizing that for those of us socialized to support the system, saying "no" to the bosses is one of the hardest things we could do, but the most necessary. We therefore end the book with a warm embrace and an outstretched hand of unconditional solidarity. As you close this book, consider one last time what it means to be an educator in Native North America. In so doing, consider the following questions:

o   What have the insights and arguments presented throughout this book offered you in terms of creating your philosophy of education?
o   What barriers might you face in becoming the kind of teacher you envision yourself becoming?
o   What might you do to overcome those obstacles?
o   What have these insights suggested about the value of creating collective approaches to education?
o   What is your own belief about what constitutes knowledge and how it is produced?
o   Is everyone capable of producing knowledge, or just an elite few? Explain.
o   How has this book challenged you to consider what it means to educate for democracy?

o   What does it mean to be partly responsible for educating/socializing the next generation of the settler-community?

o   According to your own identity, what is your role supposed to be in the maintenance of the settler-state?

o   Why might you wish to subvert your institutionalized role as both a citizen and as a teacher?

o   What might you do to make yourself more critically conscious?

o   What new questions has this reading fostered within you, and where might you find answers?

o   Where might you go from here; with whom might you travel; and how might you get there (and why)?

References

Abu-Jamal, M. (1997). *Death Blossoms: Reflections from a Prisoner of Conscious.* Farmington, PA: Plough Publishing House.

Abukhattala, I. (2004). "The New Bogeyman Under the Bed: Image Formation of Islam in the Western School Curriculum and Media." In Joe Kincheloe and Shirley Steinberg (Eds.). *The Miseducation of the West: How Schools and the Media Distort Our Understanding of the Islamic World.* London: Praeger.

Acuña, R. (1988). *Occupied America: A History of Chicanos.* New York: HarperCollins.

Adams, D. (1995). *Education for Extinction: American Indians and the Boarding School Experience 1875-1928.* Lawrence, Kansas: University Press of Kansas.

Anderson, S. E. (1995). *The Black Holocaust for Beginners.* New York: Writers and Readers.

Associated Press. (1999). "Niagara Mohawk Plants Among New York's Top Polluters," *Fluoride Action Network.* [Online] Available at: http://www.fluoridealert.org/pollution/1267.html.

Bakan, J. (2004). *The Corporation: The Pathological Pursuit of Profit and Power.* New York: Free Press.

Banks, J. (2003). *Teaching Strategies for Ethnic Studies: Seventh Edition.* New York: Allyn and Bacon.

Beckham, S. (2006). *Oregon Indians: Voices from Two Centuries.* Corvallis, Oregon: Oregon State University Press.

Benjamin, M. (1995). "Interview: Subcomandante Marcos." In Elaine Katzenberger (Ed.). *First World, Ha Ha Ha! The Zapatista Challenge.* San Francisco: City Lights.

Bergstrom, A., Cleary, L., & Peacock, T. (2003). *The Seventh Generation: Native Students Speak About Finding the Good Path.* Charleston, West Virginia: Clearinghouse on Rural Education and Small Schools.

Bernal, M. (1987). *Black Athena: The Afroasiatic Roots of Classical Civilization: Volume 1: The Fabrication of Ancient Greece 1785-1985.* New Brunswick, New Jersey: Rutgers University Press.

—— (2001). *Black Athena Writes Back: Martin Bernal Responds to His Critics.* London: Duke University Press.

Bey, H. (2003). *T.A.Z.: The Temporary Autonomous Zone, Ontological Anarchy, Poetic Terrorism.* Brooklyn, NY: Autonomedia.

Bigelow, B. (1998a). "Discovering Columbus: Re-reading the Past." In Bill Bigelow and Bob Peterson (Eds.). *Rethinking Columbus: The Next 500 Years.* Milwaukee, WI: Rethinking Schools.

—— (1998b). "Once Upon a Genocide: Columbus in Children's Literature." In Bill Bigelow and Bob Peterson (Eds.). *Rethinking Columbus: The Next 500 Years.* Milwaukee, WI: Rethinking Schools.

—— (2001). "On the Road to Cultural Bias: A Critique of 'The Oregon Trail' CD-ROM." In Bill Bigelow, Brenda Harvey, Stan Karp, and Larry Miller (Eds.). *Rethinking Our Classrooms: Teaching for Equity and Justice: Volume 2.* Williston, VT: Rethinking Schools.

Bigelow, B., Harvey, B., Karp, S. & Miller, L. (2001). "Introduction." In Bill Bigelow, Brenda Harvey, Stan Karp, and Larry Miller (Eds.). *Rethinking Our Classrooms: Teaching for Equity and Justice: Volume 2.* Williston, VT: Rethinking Schools.

Bigelow, B., & Peterson, B. (1998). *Rethinking Columbus: The Next 500 Years.* Milwaukee, WI: Rethinking Schools.

Black Elk, F. (1992). "Observations on Marxism and Lakota Tradition." In Ward Churchill (Ed.). *Marxism and Native Americans.* Boston: South End Press.

Blue Scholars. (2006). *Blue Scholars.* Seattle, WA: Blue Scholars.

Blum, W. (1995). *Killing Hope: U.S. Military and CIA Interventions Since World War II.* Monroe, Maine: Common Courage Press.

Blumm, M. & Bodi, L. (1999). "What the Treaties Promised the Indians." In Joseph Cone and Sandy Ridlington (Eds.). *The Northwest Salmon Crisis: A Documentary History.* Corvallis, Oregon: Oregon State University Press.

—— (1994). *A Radical, Democratic Critique of Capitalist Education.* New York: Peter Lang.

Brosio, R. (2000). *Philosophical Scaffolding for the Construction of Critical Democratic Education.* New York: Peter Lang.

Buchal, J. (2006). "The Philosophical Problem in Salmon Recovery." In Robert T. Lackey, Denise H. Lach, and Sally L. Duncan (Eds.). *Salmon 2100: The Future of Wild Pacific Salmon.* Bethesda, Maryland: American Fisheries Society.

Buffalo Water Authority & American Water. (2007). "Annual Drinking Water Quality Report for 2006–2007." Buffalo, NY: *City of Buffalo – Division of Water.*

Chomsky, N. (1995). "Time Bomb." In Elaine Katzenberger (Ed.). *First World, Ha Ha Ha! The Zapatista Challenge.* San Francisco: City Lights.

—— (2001). *The Common Good: Interviewed by David Barsamian.* Chicago, IL: Odonian Press.

Churchill, W. (1995). *Since Predator Came: Notes from the Struggle for American Indian Liberation.* Littleton, Colorado: Aigis Publications.

—— (1997). *A Little Matter of Genocide: Holocaust and Denial in the Americas, 1492 to the Present.* San Francisco: City Lights.

—— (1998). *Fantasies of the Master Race: Literature, Cinema and the Colonization of American Indians.* San Francisco: City Lights.

—— (2002). *Struggle for the Land: Native North American Resistance to Genocide, Ecocide and Colonization.* San Francisco, California: City Lights.

—— (2003a). *Life in Occupied America.* Oakland, California: AK Press.

—— (2003b). *Perversions of Justice: Indigenous Peoples and Angloamerican Law.* San Francisco, California: City Lights.

—— (2003c). *On the Justice of Roosting Chickens: Reflections on the Consequences of U.S. Imperial Arrogance and Criminality.* Oakland, California: AK Press.

—— (2004). *Kill the Indian, Save the Man: The Genocidal Impact of American Indian Residential Schools.* San Francisco, California: City Lights.

Churchill, W. & Vanderwall, J. (1990). *Agents of Repression: The FBI's Secret Wars Against the Black Panther Party and the American Indian Movement.* New York: Seven Stories Press.

Cleary, L. & Peacock, T. (1998). *Collected Wisdom: American Indian Education.* London: Allyn and Bacon.

Cone, J. & Ridlington, S. (1999). *The Northwest Salmon Crisis: A Documentary History.* Corvallis, Oregon: Oregon State University Press.

Crawford, J. (1995). "Cheikh Anta Diop, the 'Stolen Legacy,' and Afrocentrism." In Albert Mosley (Ed.). *African Philosophy: Selected Readings.* Upper Saddle River, NJ: Prentice Hall.

Dei, G., Hall, B., & Rosenberg, D. (Eds.). (2002). *Indigenous Knowledges in Global Contexts: Multiple Readings of Our World.* Toronto: OISE/UT.

Deloria, V. (1985). *Behind the Trail of Broken Treaties: An Indian Declaration of Independence.* Austin: University Of Texas Press.

—— (1992). "Circling the Same Old Rock." In Ward Churchill (Ed.). *Marxism and Native Americans.* Boston: South End Press.

—— (1994). *God Is Red: A Native View of Religion.* Golden, Colorado: Fulcrum.

—— (2001). "American Indian Metaphysics." In Vine Deloria Jr. and Daniel R. Wildcat (Authors). *Power and Place: Indian Education in America.* Golden, Colorado: Fulcrum Resources.

—— (2006). *The World We Used to Live In: Remembering the Powers of the Medicine Men.* Golden, Colorado: Fulcrum.

Deloria, V. & Lytle, C. (1984). *The Nations Within: The Past and Future of American Indian Sovereignty.* Austin: University of Texas Press.

—— (1987). *American Indians, American Justice.* Austin: University of Texas Press.

Deloria, V. & Wildcat, D. (2001). *Power and Place: Indian Education in America.* Golden, Colorado: Fulcrum Resources.

Desai, G. & Nair, S. (2005). *Postcolonialisms: An Anthology of Cultural Theory and Criticism.* New Brunswick, New Jersey: Rutgers University Press.

Eagleton, T. (1991). *Ideology: An Introduction.* New York: Verso.

Edmondson, B. (2000). "Environmental Affairs in New York State: An Historical Overview." [Online] Available at: http://iarchives.nysed.gov/pf/print.jsp?page=http://www.archives.nysed.gov/a/researchroom.

Erdrich, L. (2003). *Original Fire: Selected and New Poems.* New York: Harper Collins.

Fanon, F. (1963). *The Wretched of the Earth.* New York: Grove Press.

Fischer, E. (1996). *How to Read Karl Marx.* New York: Monthly Review Press.

Fixico, D. (2001). "Foreword." In Susan Lobo and Kurt Peters (Eds.). *American Indians and the Urban Experience.* New York: Altamira Press.

Flogging Molly. (2006). *Whiskey on a Sunday.* LA: SIDE ONE DUMMY.

Forbes, J. (1993). *Africans and Native Americans: The Language of Race and the Evolution of Red-Black Peoples.* Chicago: University of Illinois Press.

—— (1995). "Native Intelligence: NAFTA Is Unconstitutional." In Elaine Katzenberger (Ed.). *First World, Ha Ha Ha! The Zapatista Challenge.* San Francisco: City Lights.

Foster, J. (1996). "Introduction." In Ernst Fischer (Author). *How to Read Karl Marx.* New York: Monthly Review Press.

Freire, P. (1970). *Pedagogy of the Oppressed.* New York: Continuum.

—— (1998). *Pedagogy of the Oppressed.* New York: Continuum.

—— (1999). *Pedagogy of Hope: Reliving Pedagogy of the Oppressed.* New York: Continuum.

—— (2004). *Pedagogy of Indignation.* London: Paradigm Publishers.

—— (2005). *Teachers as Cultural Workers: Letters to Those Who Dare Teach.* Boulder, CO: Westview Press.

Gonzalez, R. (1992). *Without Discovery: A Native Response to Columbus.* Seattle, Washington: Broken Moon Press.

Grande, S. (2004). *Red Pedagogy: Native American Social and Political Thought.* New York: Roman & Littlefield.

Grinde, D., Jr. & Johansen, B. (2001). "Perceptions of America's Native Democracies: The Societies Colonial Americas Observed." In Susan Lobo and Steve Talbot (Eds.). *Native American Voices: A Reader: Second Edition.* Upper Saddle River, New Jersey: Prentice Hall.

Hill, D., McLaren, P., Cole, M. & Rikowski, G. (2002). *Marxism Against Postmodernism in Educational Theory.* Lanham, MD: Lexington Books.

Israel, J. (2002). *Radical Enlightenment: Philosophy and the Making of Modernity 1650–1750.* Oxford: Oxford University Press.

—— (2006). *Enlightenment Contested: Philosophy, Modernity, and the Emancipation of Man 1650–1752.* Oxford: Oxford University Press.

James, D. (1995). "'The Instruction of Any' and Moral Philosophy." In Albert Mosley (Ed.). *African Philosophy: Selected Readings.* Upper Saddle River, NJ: Prentice Hall.

James, G. (1954/2005). *Stolen Legacy: Greek Philosophy Is Stolen Egyptian Philosophy.* Deweyville, Virginia: Khalifah's Booksellers & Associates.

Katz, W. (1986). *Black Indians: A Hidden Heritage.* New York: Simon & Schuster.

Kincheloe, J. (2001). *Getting Beyond the Facts: Teaching Social Studies/Social Sciences in the Twenty-first Century.* New York: Peter Lang.

—— (2004). *Critical Pedagogy Primer.* New York: Peter Lang.

Kincheloe, J., Slattery, P. & Steinberg, S. (2000). *Contextualizing Teaching: Introduction to Education and Educational Foundations.* New York: Longman.

Kharem, H. (2004). "The Great European Denial: The Misrepresentation of the Moors in Western Education." In Joe Kincheloe and Shirley Steinberg (Eds.). *The Miseducation of the West: How Schools and the Media Distort Our Understanding of the Islamic World.* London: Praeger.

—— (2006). *A Curriculum of Repression: A Pedagogy of Racial History in the United States.* New York: Peter Lang.

Lackey, R., Lach, D., & Duncan, S. (2006a). "Introduction: The Challenge of Restoring Wild Salmon." In Robert T. Lackey, Denise H. Lach and Sally L. Duncan (Eds.). *Salmon 2100: The Future of Wild Pacific Salmon.* Bethesda, Maryland: American Fisheries Society.

—— (2006b). "Wild Salmon in Western North America: The Historical and Policy Context." In Robert T. Lackey, Denise H. Lach and Sally L. Duncan (Eds.). *Salmon 2100: The Future of Wild Pacific Salmon.* Bethesda, Maryland: American Fisheries Society.

LaDuke, W. (1992). "Preface: Natural to Synthetic and Back Again." In Ward Churchill (Ed.). *Marxism and Native Americans.* Boston, MA: South End Press.

—— (2005). *Recovering the Sacred: The Power of Naming and Claiming.* Cambridge, MA: South End Press.

Lemkin, R. (1944). *Axis Rule in Occupied Europe: Laws of Occupation, Analysis of Government, Proposals for Redress.* Washington, D.C.: Carnegie Endowment for International Peace.

Loewen, J. (1995). *Lies My Teacher Told Me: Everything Your American History Textbook Got Wrong.* New York: Touchstone.

Lyons, S. (2005). "The Termination and Removal of Ward Churchill." Indian Country. http://www.kersplebedeb.com/mystuff/s11/churchill_lyons.html

Malcolm X. (2002). *By Any Means Necessary.* New York: Pathfinder.

Malott, C. (2006). "Schooling in an Era of Corporate Dominance: Marxism Against Burning Tires." *Journal for Critical Educational Policy Studies.* 4(1). [online] Available at: http://www.jceps.com/?pageID=article&articleID=58.

—— (2007). "Cuban Education in Neo-Liberal Times: Socialist Revolutionaries and State Capitalism." *Journal for Critical Education Policy Studies.* 5(1). [Online] Available at: http://www.jceps.com/?pageID=article&articleID=90.

Malott, C. & Peña, M. (2004). *Punk Rockers' Revolution: A Pedagogy of Race, Class, and Gender.* New York: Peter Lang.

Marshall, J., III. (2001). *The Lakota Way: Stories and Lessons for Living.* New York: Penguin Compass.

—— (2004). *The Journey of Crazy Horse: A Lakota History.* New York: Penguin Books.

Marx, K. (1843/1978). "Contribution to the Critique of Hegel's *Philosophy of Right.*" In Robert Tucker (Ed.). *The Marx-Engels Reader: Second Edition.* New York: W.W. Norton.

—— (1844/1978). "Contribution to the Critique of Hegel's *Philosophy of Right.* Introduction." In Robert Tucker (Ed.). *The Marx-Engels Reader: Second Edition.* New York: W.W. Norton.

—— (1867/1967). *Capital: A Critique of Political Economy: Volume 1: The Process of Capitalist Production.* New York: International Publishers.

Marx, K. & Engels, F. (1932/1996). *The German Ideology.* New York: International Publishers.

McLaren, P. (2000). *Che Guevara, Paulo Freire, and the Pedagogy of Revolution.* New York: Roman & Littlefield.

—— (2002). "Marxist Revolutionary Praxis: A Curriculum of Transgression." *Journal of Critical Inquiry into Curriculum and Instruction,* 3(3), 36–41.

McLaren, P. & Farahmandpur, R. (2005). *Teaching Against Global Capitalism and the New Imperialism: A Critical Pedagogy.* New York: Roman & Littlefield.

McNally, D. (2001). *Bodies of Meaning: Studies on Language, Labor, and Liberation.* Albany, NY: State University of New York Press.

Memmi, A. (1965). *The Colonizer and the Colonized.* Boston: Beacon Press.

Mohawk, J. (2000). *Utopian Legacies: A History of Conquest and Oppression in the Western World.* Santa Fe, New Mexico: Clear Light.

Mokhiber, R. & Weissman, R. (1999). *Corporate Predators: The Hunt for Mega-Profits and the Attack on Democracy.* Monroe, Maine: Common Courage Press.

—— (2005). "The 10 Worst Corporations of 2005." *Multinational Monitor.* 26(11), 1–30.

Neihardt, J. (1932/2004). *Black Elk Speaks: Being the Life Story of a Holy Man of the Oglala Sioux.* London: University of Nebraska Press.

Newton, H. (1973). *Revolutionary Suicide.* London: Wildwood House.

Perlman, F. (1985). *The Continuing Appeal of Nationalism.* Detroit: Black & Red.

Podur, J. (2006). "Six Nations Does Not Stand Alone." [Online] Available at: http://www.zmag.org/content/showarticle.cfm?SectionID=30&ItemID=10152.

Porfilio, B. & Hall, J. (2005). "'Power City' Politics & the Building of a Corporate School," 3(1). [Online] Available at: http://www.jceps.com/?pageID=article&articleID=38.

Porter, K. (1996). *The Black Seminoles: History of a Freedom-Seeking People.* Miami: University Press of Florida.

Rediker, M. & Linebaugh, P. (1993). "The Many-Headed Hydra: Sailors, Slaves and the Atlantic Working Class in the Eighteenth Century." In Ron Sakolsky and James Koehnline (Eds.). *Gone to Croatan: Origins of North American Dropout Culture.* Brooklyn, NY: Autonomedia.

Rikowski, G. (2004). "Labour's Fuel: Lifelong Learning Policy as Labour Power Production." In Dennis Hayes (ed.). *The RoutledgeFalmer Guide to Key Debates in Education.* London: RoutledgeFalmer.

Robbins, W. (1999), "The World of Columbia River Salmon: Nature, Culture and the Great River of the West." In Joseph Cone and Sandy Ridlington (Eds.). *The Northwest Salmon Crisis: A Documentary History.* Corvallis, Oregon: Oregon State University Press.

Ross, J. (2000). *The War Against Oblivion: The Zapatista Chronicles.* Philadelphia, Pennsylvania: Common Courage Press.

Ryan, R. (2006). *Clandestines: The Pirate Journals of an Irish Exile.* Oakland: AK Press.

Sakolsky, R. & Koehnline, J. (1993). *Gone to Croatan: Origins of North American Dropout Culture.* Brooklyn, NY: Autonomedia.

Sarton, G. (1952). *Ancient Science Through the Golden Age of Greece.* New York: Dover Publications.

Semali, L. & Kincheloe, J. (Ed.). (1999a). *What Is Indigenous Knowledge? : Voices from the Academy.* New York: Falmer Press.

—— (1999b). "Introduction: What Is Indigenous Knowledge and Why Should We Study It?" In Ladislaus M. Semali and Joe L. Kincheloe (Eds.). *What Is Indigenous Knowledge? : Voices from the Academy.* New York: Falmer Press.

Shah, A. (2007). "Global Issues." [Online] Available at: www.globalissues.org.

Skinner, L. (1999). "Teaching Through Traditions: Incorporating Languages and Culture into Curricula." In Karen Gayton Swisher and John W. Tippeconnic III (Eds.). *Next Steps:*

Research and Practice to Advance Indian Education. Charleston, West Virginia: Clearing-house on Rural Education and Small Schools.

Smith, A. (2005). *Conquest: Sexual Violence and American Indian Genocide.* Cambridge, MA: South End Press.

Smith, T. (2005). *Decolonizing Methodologies: Research and Indigenous Peoples.* New York: Zed Books.

Stannard, D. (1992). *American Holocaust: Columbus and the Conquest of the New World.* New York: Oxford University Press.

Steinberg, S. (2004). "Desert Minstrels: Hollywood's Curriculum of Arabs and Muslims." In Joe Kincheloe and Shirley Steinberg (Eds.). *The Miseducation of the West: How Schools and the Media Distort Our Understanding of the Islamic World.* London: Praeger.

—— (2007). "Hollywood's Curriculum of Arabs and Muslims in Two Acts." In Donaldo Macedo and Shirley Steinberg (Eds.). *Media Literacy: A Reader.* New York: Peter Lang.

Straus, T. & Valentino, D. (2001). "Retribalization in Urban Indian Communities." In Susan Lobo and Kurt Peters (Eds.). *American Indians and the Urban Experience.* New York: Altamira Press.

Taggert, WM. (1896). "History of the United Trades and Labor Council." *Official Programme and Journal of the United Trades and Labor Council of Erie County and Vicinity.* Buffalo, New York: United Trades and Labor Council.

Talbot, A. & Galbreath, P. (2006). "Salmon Restoration—A Native American Perspective from the Columbia River. In Robert T. Lackey, Denise H. Lach and Sally L. Duncan (Eds.). *Salmon 2100: The Future of Wild Pacific Salmon.* Bethesda, Maryland: American Fisheries Society.

Tatum, B. (1997). *"Why Are All the Black Kids Sitting Together in the Cafeteria?" and other conversations about race.* New York: Basic Books.

Thornton, R. (1987). *American Indian Holocaust and Survival: A Population History Since 1492.* London: The University of Okalahoma Press.

Thorpe, D. (2001). "The Spirit of the People Has Awakened and Is Enjoying Creation Through Us: An Interview with Jeanette Armstrong, Okanagan." In Susan Lobo and José Barreíro (Eds.). *Native American Voices: A Reader.* Upper Saddle River, New Jersey: Prentice Hall.

Tippeconnic, J., III. (1999). "Tribal Control of American Indian Education: Observations Since the 1960s with Implications for the Future." In Karen Gayton Swisher and John W. Tippeconnic III (Eds.). *Next Steps: Research and Practice to Advance Indian Education.* Charleston, West Virginia: Clearinghouse on Rural Education and Small Schools.

Torres, C. (1998). *Democracy, Education, and Multiculturalism: Dilemmas of Citizenship in a Global World.* New York: Roman & Littlefield.

Trudell, J. (1995). "John Trudell Interview & 'Johny Damas' film by Toe Knee Stanger." [Online] Available at: http://www.youtube.com/watch?v=WpBHz-NgJ84.

Vizenor, G. (1990). *Crossbloods: Bone Courts, Bingo, and other Reports.* Minneapolis: University of Minnesota Press.

Wild, N. (1998). *A Place Called Chiapas.* New York: New Yorkers Video.

Wildcat, D. (2001a). "Indigenizing Education: Playing to Our Strengths." In Vine Deloria and Daniel R. Wildcat (Authors). *Power and Place: Indian Education in America.* Golden, Colorado: Fulcrum Resources.

—— (2001b). "The Schizophrenic Nature of Western Metaphysics." In Vine Deloria and Daniel R. Wildcat (Authors). *Power and Place: Indian Education in America.* Golden, Colorado: Fulcrum Resources.

Wilkinson, C. (2005). *Blood Struggle: The Rise of Modern Indian Nations.* New York: Norton.

Williams, A. (1932). *A Child's Story of the Niagara Frontier.* Buffalo, NY: Privately Published.

Wilner, M. (1931). *Niagara Frontier: A Narrative and Documentary History.* Chicago: S.J. Clarke Publishing.

Wilson, P.L. (1993). "Caliban's Masque: Spiritual Anarchy & The Wild Man in Colonial America." In Peter Lamborn Wilson (Ed.). *Pirate Utopias: Moorish Corsairs & European Renegadoes.* Brooklyn, NY: Autonomedia.

Yazzie, T. (1999). "Culturally Appropriate Curriculum: A Research-Based Rationale." In Karen Gayton Swisher and John W. Tippeconnic III (Eds.). *Next Steps: Research and Practice to Advance Indian Education.* Charleston, West Virginia: Clearinghouse on Rural Education and Small Schools.

Zapatistas, The. (1998). "Remarks at the Opening Ceremony of the Encuentro." In Greg Ruggiero and Stuart Sahulka (Eds.). *Zapatista Encuentro: Documents from the 1996 Encounter for Humanity and Against Neoliberalism/The Zapatistas.* New York: Seven Stories.

Zinn, H. (1995). *A People's History of the United States: 1492–Present.* New York: Perennial.

Studies in the Postmodern Theory of Education

General Editors
Joe L. Kincheloe & Shirley R. Steinberg

Counterpoints publishes the most compelling and imaginative books being written in education today. Grounded on the theoretical advances in criticalism, feminism, and postmodernism in the last two decades of the twentieth century, Counterpoints engages the meaning of these innovations in various forms of educational expression. Committed to the proposition that theoretical literature should be accessible to a variety of audiences, the series insists that its authors avoid esoteric and jargonistic languages that transform educational scholarship into an elite discourse for the initiated. Scholarly work matters only to the degree it affects consciousness and practice at multiple sites. Counterpoints' editorial policy is based on these principles and the ability of scholars to break new ground, to open new conversations, to go where educators have never gone before.

For additional information about this series or for the submission of manuscripts, please contact:

> Joe L. Kincheloe & Shirley R. Steinberg
> c/o Peter Lang Publishing, Inc.
> 29 Broadway, 18th floor
> New York, New York 10006

To order other books in this series, please contact our Customer Service Department:

> (800) 770-LANG (within the U.S.)
> (212) 647-7706 (outside the U.S.)
> (212) 647-7707 FAX

Or browse online by series:
> www.peterlang.com